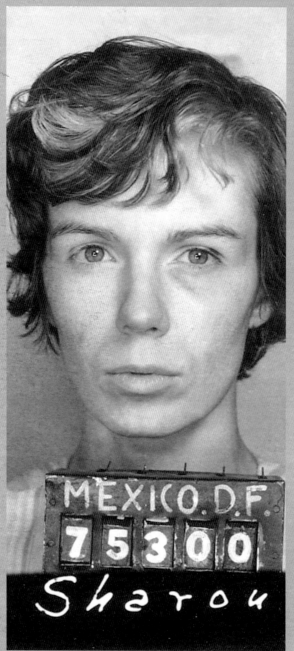

KANSAS CITY Crime Central

150 years of outlaws, kidnappers, mobsters and their victims

Monroe Dodd

KANSAS CITY STAR BOOKS

Published by Kansas City Star Books

1729 Grand Boulevard

Kansas City, MO 64108

All rights reserved

Copyright © 2010 Kansas City Star Books

No part of this book may be reproduced, stored in a retrieval system or transmitted in any form or by any means, electronic, mechanical, photocopying, recording or otherwise, without the prior consent of the publisher.

First Edition

Edited: Monroe Dodd/PortLight

Design: Jean Donaldson Dodd/PortLight

ISBN 978-1-61169-001-9

Library of Congress Control Number: 2010913600

Printed in the United States of America
by Walsworth Publishing Co. Inc.
Marceline, Mo.

Introductory illustrations

P. 1. Charles Binaggio, leader of the Kansas City mob in the 1940s, after he was shot to death in 1950.

P. 2. From left: Robert Berdella, midtown Kansas City torture-murderer of the 1980s; Sharon Kinne, implicated in the 1960s in two shooting deaths in the Kansas City area and one in Mexico, where she fled while awaiting trial in Jackson County, Missouri; Richard Eugene Hickock, born and reared in Kansas City and Edgerton, Kansas, who in 1959 devised a scheme to rob the Clutter family farm in southwest Kansas and was hanged in four murders.

Pp. 4-5. Background: Aftermath of an explosion in the River Quay entertainment district in 1977.

P. 6. Sueanne Hobson, convicted of arranging for her son and a friend to kill her stepson in 1980.

CONTENTS

Foreword 7

Murdered at Midnight	Rev. Thomas Johnson	8
The Most Extraordinary Criminal	Jesse James	14
Mob Violence	Levi Harrington	24
Wicked Stepmother	Belle Carr	30
Armed for "The Lord"	Adam God	36
Bad Medicine	Thomas Swope	42
Successful and Vulnerable	Michael Katz	50
Taking Nelly Don	Nell Donnelly	54
Swept Away	Mary McElroy	60
The Massacre	Union Station Massacre	66
"All Hell Broke Loose"	Bonnie and Clyde	74
On the Spot	Ferris Anthon	80
Ghosts & Gore	Election Day Murders	88
Gangland Style	John Lazia	94
Unsolved	Leila Welsh	100
Getting Behind Schedule	Charles Binaggio	108
Where is My Son?	Bobby Greenlease	114
Remorseless	Lowell Lee Andrews	122
Cold Blood	Dick Hickock	126
La Pistolera	Sharon Kinne	134
To the Rescue	Primitivo Garcia	142
Left for Dead	Jo Ellen Weigel	146
Ambushed	Leon Jordan	150
Mob Rule	The River Quay	154
Family Dysfunction	Sueanne Hobson	166
Notorious	Bob Berdella	172
Gone in an Instant	Kansas City Firefighters	178
Senseless Death	Aaron Frazier	184
Gone Missing	Richard Grissom	190
A Family Affair	Debora Green	196
Persuasion	John E. Robinson Sr.	202
Who is She?	Precious Doe	208
Diluted	Robert Courtney	212
Out of the Blue	Ali Kemp	218

Bibliography/Suggested Readings 226
Acknowledgments 228
Illustration credits 229
Index 230

FOREWORD

Kansas City boasts a richly endowed pantheon of crimes and criminals. From Jesse James, our homegrown antihero, to Bonnie and Clyde, who simply passed through our area but did so rather noisily, Kansas City's list of the bold and the bad covers a wide range of wrongdoing. The Kansas City area has spawned internationally famous killers such as Richard Eugene Hickock and the aforementioned Mr. James. In these pages you'll also find murderous night riders and Hollywood-style hitmen. You'll find their victims, too, some innocent as the snow and some as ruthless as their assailants.

This book contains kidnappers, con men and child-killers along with mobsters and mutilators and questionable practitioners of the healing arts. One of those practitioners was suspected of giving typhoid to an entire family, not to mention nursing several people to their graves. Another diluted prescriptions for life-saving drugs, making a bundle as patients wasted away.

A crime became eligible for this volume if it was shocking or saddening, as in the kidnapping and murder of little Bobby Greenlease, or if it happened to someone prominent, as in the kidnapping of garment mogul Nell Donnelly. Other crimes drew great attention at the time they were committed and still do, such as the Union Station massacre. Still others led to a baffling or revealing string of later events, such as the gangland hit on Ferris Anthon, the aftermath of which displayed the corruption among Pendergast-era police and prosecutors as they strove to protect a mob gunslinger. Finally, intrigue always attaches to unsolved crimes such as the curious slaying of Leila Welsh. Most of the crimes and criminals included in this book won their spot by fulfilling several of these requirements.

Many of these stories remain at least a bit memorable to anyone with a passing interest in Kansas City's past. Nevertheless, as a person who is smitten with our city's history, I confess to having spent a lifetime unaware of at least a couple. All the crimes here had some ramification or the other that had eluded me. Many readers, I suspect, will feel the same way.

Constraints of time and space prevented including some of Kansas City's crimes and criminals who met the criteria. In fact, except for the obvious megacrimes that Kansas Citians still talk about, the contents of this volume were chosen subjectively, it being impossible to calculate mathematically the importance of a crime.

Several of these crimes and criminals already have spawned their own full-length books. A few — Bobby Greenlease and also the crimes of the 1930s "wide-open city" — have inspired more than one author over the years. Jesse James has inspired a bookcaseful of works.

This book is a survey of our criminal history. It does not try to solve any of the crimes. Included is a list of sources and suggested readings. For some topics, the material is scanty; they cry out for further investigation by someone: an author, a scholar, a crime fan.

Kansas City is, indeed, rich in crime history, but why? Kansas City has endured a couple of rounds in its history that promoted criminal behavior. Our position on the frontier in and after the Civil War led to a batch of guerrilla misdeeds and outlawry afterward. Certainly, our renowned dance with machine rule in the 1930s led to things being as wide open for criminals as they were for Kansas City jazz and for the governmental sins of the era. Perhaps that experience extended into the mob violence of the 1970s. Otherwise, it's anyone's guess why we were afflicted with such a range of criminals and crime.

Most of the criminals described here came to sorry ends — their own murders or their executions, or their long years in prison. Indeed, many of them led rather sorry lives. With the possible exceptions of Jesse James and John Lazia, none of these criminals has earned even a rogue's respect. Most of the stories in this book end in anything but an inspiration to pursue life on the wrong side of the law.

So many lawbreakers compressed in one book may cause a touch of melancholy about the human condition. Occasionally they did that to me. Relief came quickly, however, upon recalling that criminals compose a tiny minority of humankind. Bad actors like these become noteworthy precisely because they and their crimes are rare and usually repulsive.

— *Monroe Dodd*

Murdered at midnight

A mysterious band of horsemen guns down the wealthy missionary and namesake of Johnson County.

THE CRIME

» **When:** 1865

» **What:** Thomas Johnson, founder of the Shawnee Indian Mission and property owner on both sides of the border, was shot to death.

» **Where:** Rural Jackson County, Missouri

» **Status:** Unsolved

New Year's night 1865 was bitterly cold, and snow lay on the ground in the countryside of Jackson County, Missouri. Inside the home of the Rev. Thomas Johnson, all the fires were out, all the lamps were doused and all the family was asleep. Only the head of the household lay awake.

Now 62 years old, Thomas Johnson had made quite a name for himself along the border. Long before there was a state of Kansas or even a Kansas Territory, Johnson founded a Methodist mission to the Shawnee Indians in the wilds west of Missouri. He operated the mission for two decades and more. It became not only a training ground for Shawnee youth but also a prosperous farming enterprise for the minister and his family. He also kept business interests in Westport, the nearest town, and in Kansas City. When the Kansas Territory was formed in the 1850s, Johnson was among its leaders. When counties were drawn, the territorial council named one after him.

Thomas and Sarah Johnson, missionaries and businesspeople.

In the late 1850s, Johnson left the mission and his namesake Johnson County and moved to Missouri with his family. They set up housekeeping in a two-story house in what was then rural Jackson County, a little more than two miles northeast of the town of Westport and about the same distance southeast of Kansas City. Johnson's two-story mansion was the centerpiece of a 600-acre farm. Here he could have spent his days as a

Guerrillas roamed the countryside of western Missouri, some fighting for a cause in the Civil War and some simply for plunder.

gentleman farmer, except for the fact that the Civil War was on, and life in these parts was a constant peril.

Perhaps that was why Johnson lay awake on the first full night of the new year. Only an hour or so before, a militia patrol had visited the house, receiving its orders. Because of his prominence on both sides of the state line, Union authorities in Kansas City had named Johnson a corporal of the guard, which made him the director of the militia in his neighborhood. The militia's duty was to patrol the otherwise unpoliced countryside.

Gangs of bandits roamed this sparsely settled western country, some proclaiming allegiance to the Union, others to the Confederacy, and many bearing little real allegiance to anything other than their own enrichment. Their tactics were simple: Ride up to a house, shoot anyone they had to, take what they wanted and ride away.

Farms such as the Johnsons' were vulnerable. Unless the militia patrols happened to be near, the only defense for a home in these parts would have to be mounted by its occupants. Now, as midnight passed and the second day of 1865 began, Johnson's militia patrol probably was far from his home.

Sometime after midnight, Thomas Johnson heard the sound of horses' hooves. It was a peculiar time for peaceful folk to be out, particularly in cold weather.

The riders, whoever they were, began shouting, calling to the house.

Johnson arose and went to the front door. With him came his wife, Sarah Johnson. She had been by his side for 40 years, had accompanied him when the Methodist church assigned him to the Indian Territory 35 years before and had helped run the Indian mission.

The Johnsons' front door was a heavy hardwood affair with glass panels on either side. Thomas Johnson opened it, but only a few inches. Looking out into the moonlit night, he heard the visitors ask for directions, either to Westport or to Kansas City. He told them. Then they asked for a drink of water. He pointed to the well, which had a dipper hanging next to it, and told them to

The farm home where Thomas Johnson died. Kansas City eventually incorporated the area, originally in rural Jackson County.

help themselves.

Sarah Johnson could see men dismounting. She counted at least eight. They were armed with pistols.

Some entered the gate and headed for the well, just as they had said. Ominously, some walked straight for the front door, where Johnson stood.

Close it, she begged her husband.

Just as he did, the intruders raised their pistols and fired. One slug blasted through a panel of the door and struck Johnson in his midsection. Struggling, he leaned against the door and locked it. Then he slid down to the floor. More bullets cracked through windows on either side of the door. The house was under assault.

Sarah Johnson retrieved a shotgun and a small pistol and carried them upstairs to the Johnsons' 25-year-old son, William Johnson, who had been awakened by the shooting. He went to the porch balcony and aimed at the gunmen, but the shotgun misfired. He then grabbed a shotgun from a hired man who lived with the Johnsons and began firing it. One of the attackers was hit and screamed.

Meanwhile, some of the gang set fire to the house. Heedless of the danger, Sarah Johnson took a bucket of water to the back porch and extinguished the flames.

Either because of the sudden knowledge of William Johnson's presence in the house, or because Sarah Johnson shouted that her husband had been killed, the riders retreated to their horses and rode into the night.

Then, with dawn approaching, Mrs. Johnson rang a bell on the back porch, one used to call workers to meals and also to spread an alarm. By 7 a.m. a hundred or so people from the area had gathered at the farm and more came later from Kansas City and Westport.

The raiders took no money, no horses, no property, nothing except the life of one of the best-known and wealthiest men of the region. Johnson's murder — his assassination? — was done on purpose, but almost a century and a half later, no one knows why.

If it was for political revenge, Johnson's busy career had given partisans on either side a reason to dislike him.

Johnson was born in Virginia in 1802. His parents later moved the family to Missouri. After studying to become a Methodist minister, he was posted in the 1820s to a pastorate in Arkansas, and afterward to churches in Missouri. Having spent his formative years in slaveholding states, Johnson sided with the slavery adherents in the great debate that consumed the country in the early 19th century.

In 1830 Shawnee Indians from the east were moved to a reservation west of the Missouri border and south of the Kansas River in the newly formed Indian Territory, Johnson's church assigned him to start a mission among them. He constructed a log school and residence in a bend of the Kansas River about 10 miles upstream from its mouth at the Missouri River. The mission, which about 40 Shawnee attended, was surrounded by a little less than 40 acres of farmland.

In 1839, the mission was moved south and east, to an area only a couple of miles from the Missouri line and much closer to Westport, Missouri. The new mission, intended to serve the children of the Shawnee, Delaware and several other tribes in the area, was built along the Westport Road, which delivered people and commerce to and from the western trails.

At the new site, Johnson and the Shawnee he recruited fenced off a plot for apple trees and corn, and built brick structures for a school, a dormitory and administration. At both mission sites, the idea was to train Indian youth in the white man's occupations and religion. Boys learned farming or various trades, and girls learned to sew and garden. While there, the young Shawnee and others tended the farm, which proved fruitful indeed and built the wealth of its founder. Eventually, the mission grounds covered more than 2,000 acres. Attendance peaked at about 200 Indian children.

In the middle 1840s, the Methodist church split over the issue of slavery and most Missouri Methodists joined the southern branch. Because the Shawnee mission was sponsored by Missouri Methodists, it fell under the southern branch, too.

That proved acceptable to Johnson, who not only sided with the South over slavery, but also owned slaves. By most accounts about a half-dozen helped work the mission farm.

In the middle 1850s, a new treaty with the Shawnee was created, dividing the Shawnee reservation between the Indians and the U.S. government, which would sell its part to white settlers. What had been Indian Territory was declared Kansas Territory.

As one of the leading citizens of the border area and one of the new territory's wealthiest residents, Johnson was elected to the territorial legislature that was supposed to guide Kansas toward statehood. Several of its sessions took place in his mission, one of the few places in the new territory capable of handling an assemblage of delegates. At least once, Johnson presided over the council, which tried but failed to bring Kansas into the union as a slave state. Later the territorial capital moved to Lecompton and still later to other spots in the eastern part of the territory.

During these sessions, the territorial government began naming counties. The one in which they were sitting they named for Thomas Johnson. Eventually, it became Johnson County in the free state of Kansas.

In 1858, Johnson turned management of the school over to a son and moved about five miles east to the 600-acre farm in Jackson County. The mission closed four years later.

Despite his southern, pro-slavery leanings — and his adherence to the southern branch of the Methodist church when it split off — Johnson favored keeping the United States together. When the Southern states seceded and the Civil War broke out in 1861, he sided with the Union.

He took a spot on the board of a Kansas City bank alongside Robert Van Horn, publisher of the *Journal of Commerce* newspaper and a staunch Union man. Van Horn occasionally visited Johnson at his Jackson County farm.

Symbolizing the complexity of the brother-against-brother conflict, Johnson's eldest son joined the pro-Northern Kansas

From the Olathe (Kansas) Mirror, *January 1865.*

> The raiders took no money, no horses, no property, nothing except the life of one of the best-known and wealthiest men of the region.

militia and another joined the Confederate army.

For the few thousand residents of Kansas City, Westport and Independence during the Civil War, life was edgy despite the presence of Union troops. Outside the organized towns, things were downright dangerous.

In August 1863, the Union commander for the district issued an order — known as Order No. 11 — that attempted to deny Confederate bushwhackers shelter by removing residents of several Missouri border counties from their homes.

Thomas Johnson, with his reputation for support of the Union, was authorized to house many of the refugees at his Jackson County farm, and 15 to 20 families stayed there. When the Union commander ordered some Missourians to sign a loyalty oath, Johnson was appointed to vouch for them.

According to one version of the cause of Johnson's murder, that practice led to his death. As the story goes, a woman came to Johnson, asking him to support her statement that she was loyal to the Union. If he agreed, she could remain in Jackson County. Knowing her to be not only a Confederate sympathizer but also a spy, Johnson refused. She was forced to move out of the area, angering her and her associates enough to lead to an avenging raid on Johnson's home.

Other accounts hold that bushwhackers had developed a general antipathy for Johnson's pro-Union activities.

In reporting Johnson's slaying in its January 3 edition, the pro-Union Robert Van Horn's *Journal of Commerce* in Kansas City blamed it on bushwhackers. The Confederate sympathizers, the newspaper said, were spending the winter near Hickman's Mill several miles south of the Johnson farm. In the obituary the newspaper complained that the Union district commander was aware of their presence but had made "no effort to drive them out."

In the next day's paper, Van Horn continued the criticism:

"We should like to know who is the commander of the District of Central Missouri, and whether he intends to allow that little gang of bushwhackers about Hickman's Mill to stay there all winter and rob and murder with impunity? — Since last October this portion of the District has been literally abandoned by the District commander and its citizens have been at the mercy of the deeds of the brash."

Civil War passions raged long after the war's end, and by the end of the 19th century, pro-Southern historians were spreading the word that Johnson was slain not by Confederate sympathizers, but by Kansas Redlegs, Unionists who abhorred Johnson's slaveholding background.

Later yet, local historians began blaming not politics but greed. According to the story, said to be based on the words of William Johnson, the minister's son, Thomas Johnson had made a practice of lending money to neighbors.

One loan of $1,000 was coming due in the final days of 1864, the story went, and Johnson wanted it repaid promptly so he could lend it to someone else. Under pressure from Johnson, the borrower scraped together the money and repaid him, then spread word among his neighbors Johnson would have $1,000 in cash at his house. This borrower, one story said, was the brother of a prominent bushwhacker.

What the first borrower and the people he told did not know was that Johnson lent the $1,000 to someone else right away.

If the story was true, it would lend credence to the idea that robbery was the motive. One account of events of the night has a raider shouting to his fellow riders that they should forget about getting the money — evidently a reference to the $1,000. As the story continued, Johnson's son the next day organized a posse of Union soldiers and rode to the home area of the man to whom his father lent the money. There they found information that led them to the killers, and the Johnson party killed all except one.

There is at least one other reason given over the years: A clique of land-hungry speculators wanted to kill Johnson and grab the three square miles of land that he had acquired in Johnson County, Kansas.

Whatever the cause of his death, a multitude of people — the largest ever gathered in the area, according to one report of the day — assembled on January 4 for his burial, in a plot at the old Shawnee Indian mission.

Like the surviving buildings of the Shawnee Indian Mission, the cemetery now belongs to the state of Kansas and is administered by the Kansas State Historical Society. It lies next to Shawnee Mission Parkway in Fairway.

Thomas Johnson's home in Jackson County, Missouri, survived until 1917, when it was razed. The site has become part of incorporated Kansas City, and is at 35th and Agnes streets.

As for the county named for the missionary and businessman, its half-million-plus population makes Johnson County the largest in Kansas.

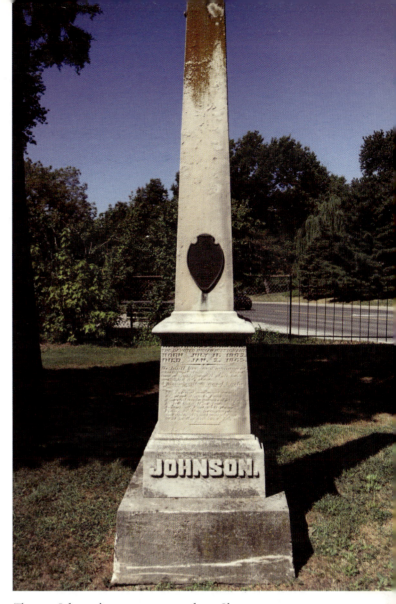

Thomas Johnson's gravestone near busy Shawnee Mission Parkway in Fairway, Kansas.

The weathered text on the gravestone reads:

He built his own monument
which shall stand in peerless beauty
long after this marble shall have
crumbled into dust.
A monument of good works

The voice at midnight came
He started up to hear
A marked arrow pointed at his frane
He fell but felt no fear
Servant of God well done
Praise be him in his employ
And while eternal ages pass
Rest in thy Savior's Joy

The most extraordinary criminal

A sympathetic populace, still stinging from the Civil War, often looked the other way at the James gang.

THE CRIMES

- **When:** 1866-1882
- **What:** Brothers Jesse and Frank James became legendary robbers.
- **Where:** Throughout the Midwest. Clay County was home.
- **Status:** Jesse was never captured before he was shot and killed by Bob Ford in 1882. Charges against Frank were dropped, and he lived a peaceable life until his death in 1915.

With the end of the Civil War in spring 1865, the lawlessness and violence that had ruled the Missouri-Kansas border subsided, but it did not end. From the ranks of bushwhackers there survived a few who formed mounted outlaw gangs. In Missouri, some kept on as if the war had not finished, attacking Unionists and the radical Republicans who governed the state, and others turned from political revenge to pure outlawry. They robbed banks and businesses and occasionally even the general public. They also struck railroads, blocking the tracks, holding engineers at gunpoint, looting the express cars in which money was shipped and sometimes shooting and killing clerks and conductors.

The greatest of the postwar hoodlums — certainly in the popular imagination — was Jesse James. He combined bravado with success in breaking the law, and his exploits heartened unrepentant Southern sympathizers in western Missouri. James was born and grew up about a dozen miles northeast of Kansas City, on his parents' farm near Kearney in Clay County. As a teenager Jesse James spent time in the band of William Clark Quantrill; as an adult he recruited former bushwhackers and other gunslingers from his own neighborhood and from rural Jackson County. The James gang — Jesse and a changing lineup of partners in crime, often including his brother, Frank James — ranged from Kentucky and West Virginia on the east to Minnesota on the north, and often retreated as far south as Texas. All the while, the James family kept a home in Missouri, and time and again Jesse James returned to targets along the railroad lines that radiated from Kansas City. Jesse James and his accomplices won a reputation for boldness and the full attention of the public.

In the decade after the Civil War, victims, witnesses and law enforcement officers began naming Jesse James as perpetrator of crimes far and wide. Eventually, dropping his name stamped the crime as important and intriguing — not to mention potentially

Jesse James as a guerrilla in the Civil War, when he learned his trade.

Newspaper accounts of Jesse James' purported exploits: From left, the Kansas City Fair, Blue Cut robbery and Glendale robbery.

unsolvable. Reports of Jesse James' involvement often were based on abundant speculation and scant evidence. Once, he was named as a participant in a train robbery in Kansas on one day and a bank robbery 500 miles away in Mississippi on the next. Newspapers attributed crime after crime to him, creating the image of a ubiquitous and unstoppable villain.

Some publications cloaked Jesse James in the mantle of the Lost Cause, a hero to Southern sympathizers in the postwar years when the North stood triumphant both politically and economically. *The Kansas City Times*, owned and edited by former Southerners, was Jesse James' most active publicity machine early in the outlaw's career. The pro-Southerners and others also made Jesse James

The James farm near Kearney in Clay County, Missouri.

out to be a Robin Hood who concentrated his efforts on banks and railroads — two businesses detested by large segments of rural Americans.

Combined with the outlaw's alliterative name, the legends created around Jesse James resonated easily amid the political tides running in America.

The facts alone were stunning. The robberies that can be attributed to him were, indeed, boldly handled. In every event, Jesse James inevitably went unpunished. Time after time, he escaped trouble because of his guile, his energy and his luck, and the authorities never caught up with him while he was alive. He was never charged, never put on trial and never made to answer the accusations against him in court.

Groundwork for the James legend-making began soon after the Civil War with a spate of bank robberies in western Missouri, all in an arc 35 to 60 miles from Kansas City. In February 1866, only 10 months into peacetime, perhaps a dozen armed men rode into Liberty, the seat of Clay County, and up to the Clay County Savings Bank. Most kept watch outside while two entered the bank, pulled a revolver on the tellers, vaulted the counter and began stuffing thousands of dollars worth of gold and silver coin, currency and bonds into sacks. As they departed with almost $60,000 of loot, one bandit fired at a passerby he suspected of trying to shout an alarm. The bullet struck and killed a William Jewell College student. The holdup gained renown as the first daylight bank robbery done in peacetime.

The authorities and the public immediately suspected former bushwhackers, some of whom had served with Quantrill and some of whom were friends of Jesse and Frank James. Were the James brothers on the scene? There was not much evidence either way; today, historians doubt either was there. More bank robberies followed in western Missouri: Lexington in October 1866, Savannah in March 1867, and Richmond in May 1867. Sometimes, bankers were killed in the holdups. In some of them, it was rumored that Jesse James had taken part. At that point, he was far from notorious. But as his name cropped up in later robberies, speculation grew that he had participated in the earlier robberies, too.

In spring 1868, Jesse James, supposedly with Cole Younger and other bandits, was said to have robbed a bank in Russellville, Kentucky, of more than $10,000.

Then came the event that would firmly begin the James legend. In December 1869, two men walked into a bank in Gallatin in northwest Missouri, shot the cashier in the head and chest and another man in the arm. They grabbed what turned out to be mostly worthless paper and fled. Townspeople rallied into the street, firing at the bandits. One of the bandits was thrown from his horse, the other turned back for him, and the two rode away on the other man's horse. The animal left behind was

> Time after time, he escaped trouble because of his guile, his energy and his luck, and the authorities never caught up with him while he was alive.

Thomas Hart Benton's memorable portrayal of the James gang at work, from his mural in the House Lounge of the Capitol in Jefferson City, Missouri.

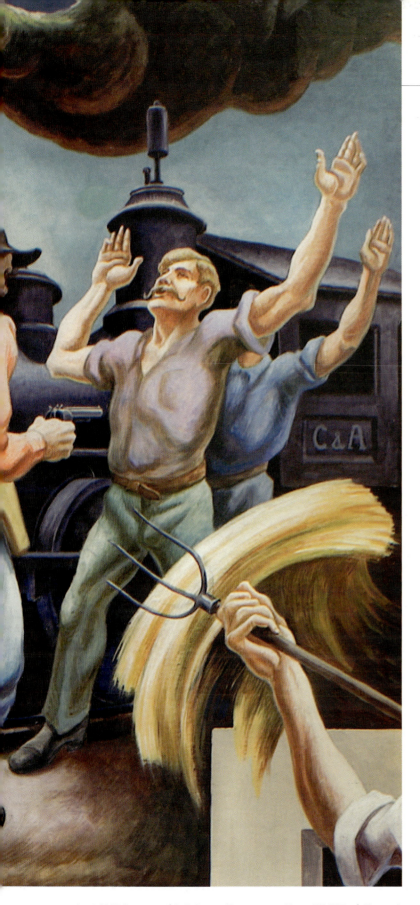

Art © T. H. Benton and R. P. Benton Testamentary Trusts/UMB Bank Trustee/Licensed by VAGA, New York, NY

identified as belonging to Jesse James. Infuriated Gallatin residents, seeking revenge, rode the 60-odd miles south to Liberty. Joined by a Clay County sheriff's deputy, they headed for the James' parents' farm near Kearney. When they arrived, the stable door swung open and Frank and Jesse James rode swiftly away. Pursuit failed.

Eventually, a letter over the signature of Jesse James appeared in *The Kansas City Times*, denying involvement in the Gallatin heist but also saying he would not surrender for trial. Any trial in these parts, the writer claimed, would be unfair. Also appearing were affidavits from solid citizens of Clay County saying the James boys were known to be honorable and giving alibis for Jesse in the Gallatin matter.

Nevertheless, the reputation of the James gang was formed and its elusiveness was established. From then on, the name of Jesse James was typically dropped when holdups occurred and — as William A. Settle Jr. pointed out in his *Jesse James Was His Name* — from that time on the James boys were outlaws, "with a price on their heads."

In June 1871, four men robbed a bank in Corydon, Iowa, just north of the Missouri border, and made off with $6,000. Pursuers followed them south into Missouri, toward the home of the Jameses, and then lost track. A year later, in April 1872, the James brothers and three other men were identified by authorities as having robbed a bank in Columbia, Kentucky, killing one clerk and wounding another but departing with little cash.

The James' notoriety got a further boost in 1872. On September 26, the Kansas City Industrial Exposition, a grandiose form of county fair, was in full swing, drawing an estimated 10,000 visitors from several states. Three masked men on horseback arrived at the gate, and one of them walked up to a cashier at the ticket booth. He demanded the cash box and reportedly produced a revolver to help make his case. According to one account, he identified himself as Jesse James.

As the holdup man seized the cash box, the cashier grappled with the robber. Just then, one of the outlaws fired his weapon. The cashier let go of the robber and the three dashed away on horseback. Their haul was $978, and no one was hurt except a little girl who was either shot or stepped on by a horse; she recovered.

The robbery inspired a writer at *The Kansas City Times*, John Edwards. An unreconstructed Confederate who was a Southern general's aide in the Civil War, Edwards offered a mild slap at the robbers — "What they did we condemn" — and promptly praised their daring — "The way they did it we cannot help admiring." He praised the existence of certain survivors of the Border Wars who still lusted for adventure and probably concocted letters to the editor that purportedly were signed by three legendary bandits of old Europe, claiming "We only kill in self-defense" and "We rob the rich and give to the poor." Within a month, a letter bearing the name of Jesse James appeared in *The Times*, denying involvement in the fair and meanwhile claiming that he could never expect a fair trial, anyway. The reading public, meanwhile, promptly connected James to the robbery at the fair.

At *The Times* and in later jobs at other Missouri newspapers, Edwards glorified the acts attributed by others to Jesse James, denied that the James brothers could have been involved, and then argued that if the brothers *were* guilty of the deeds they would have had good reason because of the way ex-Confederates had been treated by Unionists during and after the Civil War.

Convoluted as his arguments were, Edwards launched and nurtured the legend that would grow around Jesse James. The James gang, meanwhile, was nurturing a new victim: the railroads and particularly the express companies that carried money.

In January 1874, the first train robbery in Missouri occurred near Gads Hill in the southeastern part of the state. Passengers and the express safe were robbed and the mail bags rifled. The James brothers immediately fell under suspicion and circumstantial evidence was strong: the outlaws left behind a press release in the form of a telegram to the St. Louis paper where John Edwards now worked. The message described the robbery in glowing terms.

In 1874, Muncie, Kansas, was a small flag stop along the Kansas Pacific railroad. The site lay in the bottomland of the Kansas river in what was then rural Wyandotte County, only a dozen or so miles by rail from the West Bottoms of Kansas City, Missouri. At midafternoon on December 8 of that year, Muncie became part of Jesse James lore when five men on horseback rode up to a grocery and post office that served as a railroad station.

Above: Jesse James in the middle 1870s. Below: John Edwards, writer at several Missouri newspapers and James' chief exponent.

They asked the agent when the train was due from the west. Learning that it would arrive in about 20 minutes, they pulled a gun and began rifling the drawers. They forced railroad employees to block the track with crossties. When the train steamed up, the agent flagged it to a halt and the gunmen ordered the engineer to pull the express car up the track a short distance. Two of the bandits entered and forced the Wells, Fargo and Company employee inside to open the safe. With a haul estimated at $30,000, the outlaws rode away.

Hours later, near the Kansas River, the gang divided the proceeds of the robbery. They departed, leaving behind small bills and empty envelopes, some bearing Wells, Fargo express seals. The James gang was blamed by some, but only one of the perpetrators was caught — by a policeman in Kansas City. The captured outlaw had more than $1,000 and jewelry identified as having been shipped on the Kansas Pacific train from a jeweler in Lawrence, Kansas.

The robbery at Muncie was bad business for the railroads and the express companies who hauled valuables aboard the trains. Each depended on the trust of its customers. They hired the Pinkerton detective agency to investigate earlier robberies and set them wholeheartedly on the trail of Jesse James and his gang. In the process the Pinkertons lost three agents. They also tried in vain to raid the James family farm in Clay County. There, one night in late January 1875, they succeeded only in wounding Jesse James' mother, Zerelda, and killing a youthful half-brother of Jesse when an incendiary device they tossed into the home exploded.

Jesse James and his wife, Zee, whom he had married in Kansas City, then moved to a small town near Nashville, Tennessee, and took the names John Davis and Josie Howard. By 1876, the outlaw was back in Missouri and back to old business.

In July 1876, the pattern recurred in Missouri, this time near Otterville, a hamlet in Cooper County about 100 miles east of Kansas City. Horsemen appeared out of the woods, stopped a passing train, and held guns on the passengers while others took more than $15,000 from the safes of two freight companies in the express car. One of the robbers was captured and claimed that the James brothers had taken part in the theft.

Two months later, eight men tried to rob a bank in Northfield, Minnesota. When a clerk refused to open the safe, they slashed his throat and then shot him dead. They wounded a clerk, who ran out and sounded the alarm, and suddenly the outlaws found themselves under fire from townspeople. Two of the band were killed and another member badly hurt. Hastily formed posses captured three of the fleeing bandits and killed another. Two of the bandits who split away from the other survivors escaped, and they were thought to have been Jesse and Frank James. Both were struck by bullets during or after the fight.

Three years passed, and despite much speculation and rumor, nothing solid was known about the James brothers' whereabouts.

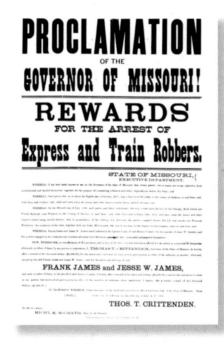

Then came October 8, 1879. That night, in the tiny community of Glendale south of Independence and about 17 miles east of Kansas City in Jackson County, several men carrying firearms rode up to a store, took eight to 10 men hostage and marched them to the railroad station, where they ordered the agent to signal halt to an eastbound Chicago & Alton train. The bandits disabled the telegraph, robbed a railroad auditor who happened to be there and piled rocks on the track. As the train rolled to a halt, they fired pistols as a warning to passengers who were watching, knocked out the express agent and grabbed a bag containing about $6,000 in cash and the rest in checks and other financial paper. After releasing the prisoners, the gang rode off. One member who was later arrested and put on trial told authorities that Jesse James had been involved.

From then until early 1881, Jesse James spent his time moving from place to place in the Nashville area and pulling holdups in Kentucky, Tennessee and Alabama.

By May 1881, Jesse James, his wife and two children were living unmolested and evidently unnoticed in Kansas City under the name of J.T. Jackson.

Two months later, in July 1881, a gang of men boarded a Chicago, Rock Island and Pacific train at Cameron, Missouri, about 50 miles northwest of Kansas City. As the train steamed north it came to the tiny town of Winston, where more bandits came aboard. A few miles beyond Winston, as the conductor was collecting fares, a man in a linen duster stood, drew a revolver, told the conductor to raise his hands and promptly fired several times, striking and killing the conductor. Another bandit fired, and a passenger was hit and killed. Two of the outlaws entered the express car, knocked down the clerk and with his key emptied the safe. Other gang members forced the engineer to stop the train. Then all of the outlaws disappeared into the night.

Suspicions were strong that the James brothers were involved. Among other things, the slain conductor was found to have been aboard the train that took the Pinkerton agents to the James farm in Clay County the night of their raid in 1875. Jesse, Frank and various other James gang members had been spotted from Olathe, Kansas, to Winston in the days before the event.

Republican-leaning newspapers charged that Missouri Democrats, among whom were numerous James sympathizers, were responsible and scolded the state government for not rounding up the criminals.

On July 28, the governor of Missouri, Thomas Crittenden, offered a $5,000 reward for the arrest of Jesse and Frank James and $5,000 more on the conviction of one or both. The offer cited the Glendale robbery of two years before and the Winston heist.

On September 7 of that year, a group of men piled rocks and logs on the Chicago & Alton tracks at a place called Blue Cut not far from the Glendale stop in Jackson County. As at Glendale, they fired their weapons to intimidate passengers, made the engineer stop the train, forced open the express car and demanded that the clerk open the safe inside. It contained little of value. The express clerk was beaten and the nearly 100 passengers aboard the train were searched and robbed.

The next day, replying to questions from newspaper reporters, the engineer said the leader of the group had shaken hands with him, called him a brave man and given him "$2 for you to drink the health of Jesse James."

If the robber was Jesse James, Blue Cut was the last train robbery he or his gang would pull.

In November 1881, he moved his family to St. Joseph, Missouri, where he lived under the name Thomas Howard.

Living with the family the next spring was a newly recruited gang member, Robert Ford, who covertly had his eye on the governor's reward money. The morning of April 3, 1882, when Jesse James had placed his firearms aside to help straighten a picture on the wall, Ford shot him in the back of the head. He and his brother, Charley Ford, fled, and then promptly telegraphed the governor of Missouri and announced they had killed their man. They expected to get the reward, but it was never revealed whether they did.

The Kansas City Times gave over its entire first and second pages to accounts of the slaying and of the history of Jesse James. The two-year-old *Kansas City Star* quickly sold out all its copies.

The next day, *The Star* had this to say about the outlaw:

"For many years past, he has been at the head of a gang of outlaws and bandits whose bold and daring outrages have filled the country with wonder, and the fame of whose exploits has even crossed the seas.... All things considered, Jesse James was undoubtedly the most extraordinary criminal of recent times."

Gratified though the newspaper was that James "is no more," it acknowledged admiration for "his remarkable nerve, his wonderful daring…his unfailing coolness and

From The Kansas City Star: *Most extraordinary*

The killing of JESSE JAMES is one of the most important events that has ever happened in the state of Missouri. For many years past he has been at the head of a gang of outlaws and bandits whose bold and daring outrages have filled the country with wonder, and the fame of whose exploits has even crossed the seas, and penetrated the capitals of the old world. All things considered, JESSE JAMES was undoubtedly the most extraordinary criminal of recent times. He planned his operations with consummate skill and carried them out with phenomenal audacity and boldness. During all these years he has managed, with truly wonderful skill and cunning, to elude the pursuit of vigilant officers, and to evade the keenest detectives in the land. Heavy rewards have been offered for him for years past, and yet, while there was a price upon his head, he coolly walked the streets of Kansas City and St. Joseph, and ever and anon, in the haunts which have been familiar to him since childhood, appeared and committed some crime even more daring and startling than its predecessor. JESSE JAMES and his comrades have done more harm to the state of Missouri—have done more to injure its good name abroad,

Above: The Kansas City Times *gave over its entire front page to the death of Jesse James and a recounting of his deeds. Below, his grave marker in Clay County, already vandalized by souvenir hunters, in 1926.*

his undaunted pluck." Had those qualities been turned to improving the good of mankind, *The Star* said, "Jesse James might have been a benefactor instead of a curse to the human race."

Jesse James was buried a few days later at the family farm near Kearney. Hundreds of acquaintances and curious neighbors looked on. Later, his body was moved to the Mount Olivet cemetery in Kearney.

In the years that followed, and well into the 20th century, romantic legend clung to Jesse James, through books and magazine articles, through motion pictures and a 1960s television series. That he was brought down through a betrayal, and shot in the back while unarmed, helped bring sympathy to the famous bandit.

In autumn 1882, Frank James negotiated terms for his own surrender, and he turned himself in at the governor's office in Jefferson City on October 4. He was charged with the Gallatin bank robbery, and with train robberies at Winston, Blue Cut and Cooper counties. He was eventually taken to Muscle Shoals, Alabama, to answer for a robbery there. Throughout, a combination of friendly juries and skillful legal maneuvering kept Frank James a free man. From then until his death in 1915 he lived a peaceful life, and he was buried in Independence, Missouri.

Mob violence

A white Kansas City policeman is shot to death, a black man is accused, and a crowd takes matters into its hands.

THE CRIME

- » **When:** 1882
- » **What:** A Kansas City policeman was shot dead and an innocent man blamed and lynched.
- » **Where:** West Bottoms, Kansas City, Missouri
- » **Status:** The policeman's real killer was sentenced to two years in prison in 1884.

As dinnertime neared on an early spring evening in 1882, Kansas City policeman Patrick Jones headed home. For Jones, home lay on St. Louis Avenue in the West Bottoms, where wooden, working-class residences still outnumbered warehouses and saloons seemed to outnumber every other business. Jones was one of thousands of Irish-Americans who had migrated to Kansas City for jobs on the railroads, in construction, in the slaughterhouses, in the stockyards and in various services — including the Kansas City police force. The roster of the force was generously populated with Irish surnames.

The part of town where Jones lived, although inside Missouri, was known as West Kansas, a holdover from the days when it lay just beyond the westernmost limit of Kansas City. Homes of working-class first-generation and immigrant Irish dotted the lowland and the sides of the West Bluffs. Patrolman Jones, his wife, Mary, and five children lived across the street from the American House, a two-story saloon and hostelry owned by James Pendergast. In a few years, Pendergast would begin developing a political powerhouse centered on that very neighborhood.

Black people lived and worked in the bottoms, too, some of them Exodusters and others who had left the rural South in the 1870s seeking a better life in northern cities. Among the black residents of the area was 23-year-old Levi Harrington, who made a living as a plasterer's helper and doing other manual labor. Harrington lived with his wife, Maria, and four children ranging in age from an infant to 8

Officer Patrick Jones, above. Right: the West Bottoms in a bird's-eye map looking southwest. Union Depot is at upper left. The bridge where Levi Harrington died is below it and next to the bluff.

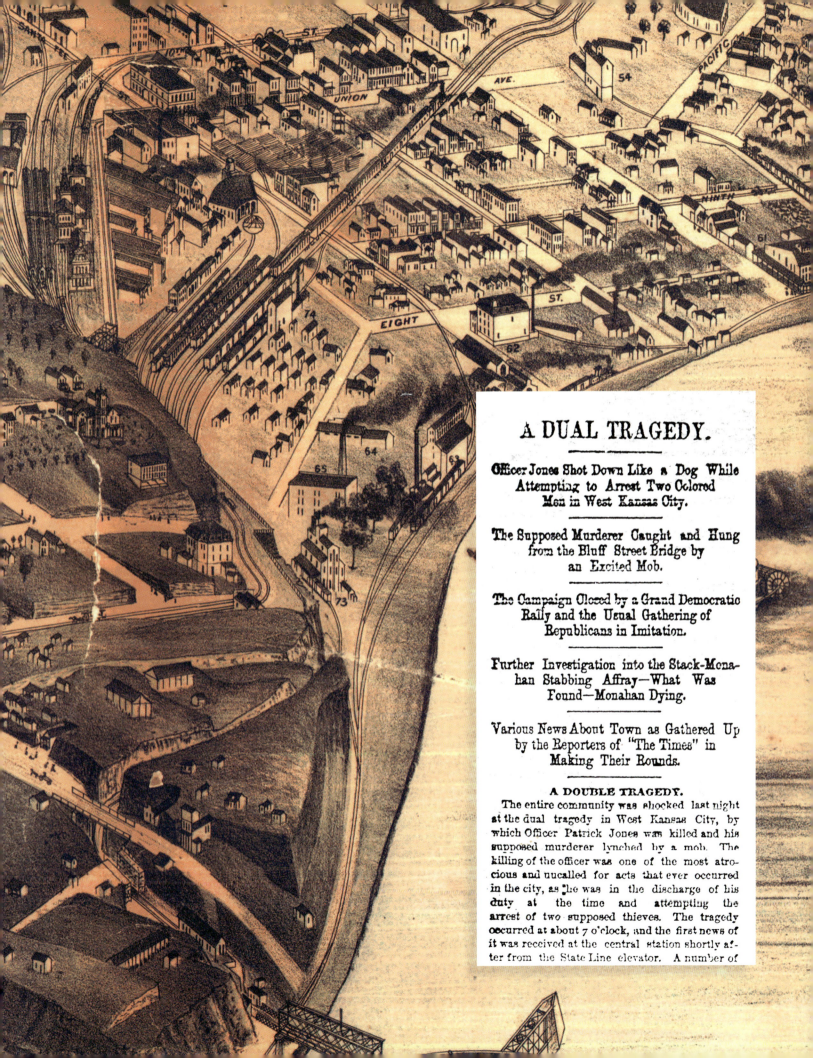

A DUAL TRAGEDY.

Officer Jones Shot Down Like a Dog While Attempting to Arrest Two Colored Men in West Kansas City.

The Supposed Murderer Caught and Hung from the Bluff Street Bridge by an Excited Mob.

The Campaign Closed by a Grand Democratic Rally and the Usual Gathering of Republicans in Imitation.

Further Investigation into the Stack-Monahan Stabbing Affray—What Was Found—Monahan Dying.

Various News About Town as Gathered Up by the Reporters of "The Times" in Making Their Rounds.

A DOUBLE TRAGEDY.

The entire community was shocked last night at the dual tragedy in West Kansas City, by which Officer Patrick Jones was killed and his supposed murderer lynched by a mob. The killing of the officer was one of the most atrocious and uncalled for acts that ever occurred in the city, as he was in the discharge of his duty at the time and attempting the arrest of two supposed thieves. The tragedy occurred at about 7 o'clock, and the first news of it was received at the central station shortly after from the State Line elevator. A number of

THE WEST KANSAS HORROR

years. Their home was a small house on Ninth Street, just east of the state line.

Darkness was approaching that night, April 3, and Mary Jones was about to call her family to supper. Her husband, his police beat finished for the day, had been detained on his way home by George Miller, who owned a grocery nearby. With a major city election coming the next day, Miller meant to talk a little politics with Jones.

About 7 p.m., two black men carrying large containers walked past Jones and Miller, still talking.

"Stolen goods," Miller, who was white, told Jones, who also was white.

Jones followed the two men a short way west along St. Louis Avenue. When they broke into a run, the patrolman did, too. He followed them into a vacant lot. One of the men being chased turned and fired twice at Jones, ran a little farther, turned and fired again. Jones staggered and fell. Miller heard the three shots, as did several others in the neighborhood. So did Mary Jones.

She raced down the street. There she found her husband, his billy club and pistol still tucked in his belt, face down on the ground, dying. Next to him lay two casks of butter, bearing an address that showed they were to have been shipped to a Kansas town south of Kansas City. The men Jones was chasing had raced off in opposite directions, one east along St. Louis Avenue and the other west, toward the Kansas line.

An employee at a nearby grain elevator, equipped with one of the then-new telephones, called Police Headquarters and soon 12 policemen — a sizable part of the small Kansas City force — appeared in the Bottoms. Passersby, meanwhile, carried Jones' body to his home. He was 39 when he died. As word spread through the neighborhood, a crowd gathered in the avenue, growing large enough to block it.

Just to the north, at Ninth and Hickory streets, a blacksmith named Matthew Jones was walking home for

> **Latest Developments Concerning the Double Tragedy of Monday Night—Grave Doubts as to the Guilt of the Victim of the Mob—Grant Arraigned for the Murder of Jones—He Pleads Not Guilty—His Past Record.**
>
> As the excitement attendant upon the election and the killing of Jesse James subsides, public attention is directed somewhat strongly to the lynching affair of Monday night. A good deal of doubt has been expressed as to the guilt of the man Harrington, who was lynched, and although the probabilities are that he was the man who shot Policeman Jones,
>
> **IT IS BY NO MEANS CERTAIN.**

the evening. Suddenly a crowd came into view, running toward him, pursuing a black man. "Stop him!" members of the crowd shouted, claiming the man had shot Patrick Jones. Matthew Jones, unrelated to the slain officer, seized him.

He was Levi Harrington, who stoutly protested that he had not fired the deadly shot. Nevertheless, Matthew Jones and some of the man's pursuers escorted the suspect to a beat patrolman, who took him to the tiny West Bottoms police outpost near Union Depot.

Word reached the gathering near the scene of the slaying that a suspect had been caught, and the crowd surged to the police substation. They demanded that police turn him over to them. The police refused.

For several reasons, they had doubts that Levi Harrington was in fact the gunman. George Miller, the man who encouraged patrolman Jones to arrest the two men in the first place, was taken inside the jail to see Harrington. Miller said that Harrington did not resemble

Union Avenue in the West Bottoms, where the mob followed the policemen escorting Levi Harrington.

either of the men he had seen.

Accounts varied on whether Miller told the same thing to the mob outside.

Whether he did or not, the crowd calmed for a while, yet one policeman overheard continued rabble-rousing against Harrington. The little police station wasn't safe for Harrington or them, he believed. Three men could force open the door and 50 could turn the whole structure over.

Firebrands in the crowd kept up a cry: "Hang him! Shoot him!"

Police Captain Dennis Malloy, second-in-command to the chief, worried that the mob would storm the tiny station. Overruling a couple of police who doubted the wisdom of his plan, he ordered two policemen to escort Harrington to the main city lockup on Second Street, on the bluffs near City Market. The guard grew to seven officers.

They left the station on the run. The mob, now numbering in the hundreds, frightened them. Already, some of its members were carrying ropes, clearly aiming to hold a lynching. Not long after they left the substation, the police detail retreated with Harrington into a restaurant on Union Avenue, opposite Union Depot, and descended to the cellar. They waited there for things to cool down.

Meanwhile, another black man was brought into the restaurant. At least some of the crowd had begun chasing him, too. Part of the police detail, hoping to decoy the mob away from the restaurant, escorted that man out the door. Some of the mob followed, but the police confiscated a wagon to rush him safely away. He was later released.

At the restaurant, meanwhile, the proprietor grew nervous because the fury of the mob outside continued unabated. Carrying a lantern, he descended to the cellar and demanded that the police remove Harrington from his business. They escorted him out the back door and through an alley. They were quickly spotted.

Fending off the mob, which by then had grown to more than 300, some of whom were throwing stones, they proceeded on a run with Harrington up Union Avenue. They got as far as a rickety bridge that carried traffic over the railroad tracks to Bluff Street. As they approached the bridge, someone in the crowd threw a rope around Harrington's neck. One policeman removed it.

Another policeman shouted, "Mob law won't go!" A man in the crowd replied, "By God, I saw this man shoot Jones and we are going to hang him."

At the bridge, the mob overpowered the policemen. Several of the police later testified that they had been struck by stones, pushed back and hauled away from their prisoner, Harrington. Although the officers were armed, they fired no shots.

The mob seized Harrington, wrapped a rope around his neck and hurled him over the side of the bridge. Almost instantly, someone shot the hanged man from above.

Then the rope was cut and Harrington dropped to the tracks below. He lay there dead, the victim of Kansas City's only recorded lynching.

Hours later, police in Kansas City, Kansas, just across the state line, arrested George Grant on suspicion that he had killed officer Jones. Like Levi Harrington, Grant was black. Fearing yet more mob violence, police kept the matter quiet and locked Grant up on the Kansas side. Grant, an ex-convict who had served a five-year term for burglary, had been arrested more than a dozen times in the decade or so that he had lived in the area.

Three days later, patrolman Jones was buried on East 18th Street. The police force led his cortege, followed by an honor guard from the Fire Department, where he had also served. He was the second member of the Kansas City police to die in the line of duty; the first had been

> **The mob seized Harrington, wrapped a rope around his neck and hurled him over the side. Almost instantly, someone shot the hanged man from above.**

killed only four months earlier.

Across the state line, meanwhile, residents collected money to benefit Harrington's widow and children. J. G. Cougher, a white man who had employed Harrington in late 1881, wrote a letter to *The Star*, contributing money and urging others to do the same. Harrington was buried in Westport.

At an inquest into the lynching, the police were unanimous in saying they would not have been able to stop it.

"If any shots had been fired," one testified, "we would all have been killed. The whole force could not have saved him."

None of the policemen said they could identify the ringleaders of the mob.

By that time, evidence was becoming overwhelming that Levi Harrington was not the man who killed officer Jones. Instead, he had been at a saloon, waiting for a political meeting to begin, when the shots were fired. According to an interview in *The Star*, a man who had been at the saloon with Harrington, along with Harrington's father-in-law and others, said the group heard the shots fired. Only then, he said, did Harrington and others go to see what happened.

The real killer of Patrick Jones, according to his own admission, was George Grant, captured the night of the slaying. In late 1884 Grant pleaded guilty to manslaughter in the shooting death of the policeman. It was his fourth trial in the crime; he had been convicted twice and the verdict overturned and a third time escaped punishment because of a hung jury. This time, the prosecutor was unable to call his primary witnesses and in a plea bargain Grant was sentenced to two years in prison.

Afterward, a reporter for *The Star* asked Grant's lawyer what role Levi Harrington had played the night of the slaying of Patrick Jones.

Harrington was not with him, the lawyer quoted Grant as saying. In fact, Grant had not even seen Harrington that evening.

In late May 1882, a grand jury indicted two men in the lynching — George Miller, the grocer who urged patrolman Jones to arrest the two black men walking by, and Matthew Jones, the blacksmith who handed Levi Harrington over to the police.

Both denied they had been at the bridge where the lynching took place. The case against Miller eventually was dropped, and in December 1883, after two trials and two hung juries, Jones was acquitted based on several witnesses' statements that he was not at the bridge.

Who, then, did lynch Levi Harrington? Not one of the policemen admitted to recognizing any of the perpetrators. The city was left only with speculation that the mob was led by yet another man named Jones, this one called "Buffalo Pat" Jones, perhaps a relative of the slain officer. That Jones quickly left town and later died somewhere in a western state.

> Relief for the Harrington Family.
> To the Editor of The Evening Star:
> I hand you herewith one dollar for the relief of the destitute family of Levi Harrington, the innocent colored man lynched by the mob. Harrington worked for me from June to December last, and I must say that I never had a more faithful or honest man in my service. He was sober and industrious, saved his money, and cared for his family as well as he could. His wife is also an industrious, faithful woman, and is doing all she can to take care of her five children, but is much in need of help. I think that while we contribute so freely to "Betty and the baby," and other similar objects, we should not forget the destitute families in our own city, especially when they are the victims of such terrible wrongs as the Harringtons have suffered.
> J. G. Cougher, Plasterer,
> 1912 Sixth st., Kansas City, Kas.
>
> An Evening Star reporter this morning called at the residence of Mrs. Levi Harrington, a little shanty, plainly but

Wicked stepmother

A 3-year-old is murdered and a Liberty man is hanged for the deed, which was aimed at pleasing his new wife.

THE CRIME

- **When:** 1897
- **What:** A 3-year old girl was pitched into the Missouri River, where she was found dead.
- **Where:** Clay and Jackson counties, Missouri
- **Status:** Her father was sentenced to death and hanged. The mother went free.

Two duck hunters were tramping along the south bank of the Missouri River one autumn morning in 1897 when something on a sandbank caught their eye. There, not far from the mouth of the Blue River, lay an object in a few inches of water, washed by the current. Coming closer, they found it was the body of a child — a girl. Her arms were bound together and a stone tied to her by ropes. She wore a heavy coat over a dress, and shoes and stockings.

The hunters notified the Jackson County coroner, who had the body moved to a Kansas City funeral home. That was Sunday, October 17. For the next eight days she remained unidentified. In that time, several people came forward with identification of the girl, and theories about her death, and even names of suspected murderers. All proved wrong. Then authorities began learning about a little girl who, neighbors said, had been very badly treated in her short life.

Those clues led police and sheriff's deputies north of the Missouri River, to a house on Gallatin Street six blocks from the heart of the town of Liberty. What they found opened a series of shocking revelations about a 3-year-old child who suffered horrific abuse, a stepmother who, by all accounts, fit the definition of "wicked," and a compliant father willing to murder his own daughter.

On October 25, a Kansas City policeman and a Clay County sheriff's deputy drove a buggy to a farm northwest of Liberty and arrested a laborer who was digging postholes for fenceposts. They told the man, William Carr, that he was under arrest in the death of his daughter, Belle Carr.

Carr — 39 years old, more than 6 feet tall, strikingly thin and also illiterate— sank to his knees. The authorities handcuffed him and drove him to the jail in Liberty. From there, he was taken south across the river to Kansas City in Jackson County, the jurisdiction in which the girl's body was found.

There the story unfolded. Belle was one of two children by William Carr's first marriage to a woman from northeast Kansas. The couple also had a 5-year-old daughter, Mae. In 1896, about year after his first wife died, Carr married Bettie Stephens of Liberty. The new wife had a child by a former marriage, a boy of 9.

The children of William Carr and the child of the former Bettie Stephens argued frequently. When punishment was dished out, Belle Carr suffered the most.

CARR, THE MURDERER.   BELLE CARR,   MRS. CARR.
The Murdered Child.

Neighbors said they often the sound of blows being struck, and of Belle screaming in the night and of Bettie Carr's angry voice. The night Belle disappeared, the neighbors said, the child was hurt "awfully." Bettie Carr told her husband that Belle had fallen from a shed roof. To the neighbors, she said Belle had fallen from a loom.

At first, William Carr denied having anything to do with the child's death. He told authorities that he had taken Belle for a walk on October 10, found a group of campers willing to take the little girl and left her with them.

Within 24 hours, however, Carr confessed to killing her himself. The confession came at Kansas City Police Headquarters, where he had undergone interrogation by the police chief, a detective and an assistant prosecutor.

According to his new story, Carr set out on foot with Belle the Sunday afternoon of October 10. They left Liberty, walking south. When the girl grew tired, he carried her. By dusk, father and daughter had covered about nine miles, and reached a bluff on the north side of the Missouri River near the hamlet of Randolph. Carr said he found a flat stone, tied a piece of rope around it and then tied the other end of the rope around Belle.

Lifting her with both arms, he hurled the girl into the river, where she landed with a splash and disappeared.

In Randolph, Carr boarded a train back to Liberty.

Why had he done it? Little Belle, he said, fought continually with the son of his new wife and also with

CARR CONFESSES.

THREW HIS OWN LITTLE GIRL INTO THE MISSOURI.

ADMITS THE ATROCIOUS CRIME.

SHOWS NOT A TINGE OF PITY OR OF REMORSE.

IT WAS THE ACT OF A FIEND.

HIS ONLY DESIRE SEEMS TO BE TO SHIELD HIS WIFE.

As He Saw Her Body Disappear He Says His Only Thought Was That She Was Out of the Way— Talks Freely in His Stupid Way.

William Carr, laborer; ignorant, unable to read or write; tall, loose-jointed, muscular; fiendishly cruel in his home life, blunted in conscience, dwarfed and warped in human feeling, has confessed that he murdered his little 3-year-old daughter, Belle, by binding a stone upon her breast and casting her, breathing and conscious, into the Missouri river. He admitted the crime to the police of this city yesterday afternoon, after having been locked up only twenty-four hours.

This awful confession of one of the most deliberate, atrocious and causeless murders was made without a trace of remorse, without a syllable of regret, without a

---

other children. Bettie Carr issued an ultimatum to him: Do something about the 3-year-old or she would leave him.

Neighbors, meanwhile, were threatening to take the Carrs before authorities for abusing the child.

To end all the strife, William Carr said, he simply wanted to be rid of the girl.

"I knew she was out of the way and that my wife would be happy," he said in his confession. "That's all I cared for."

Did he felt any remorse? a reporter asked.

"No, I can't say that I had any remorse," Carr replied. "I did feel a little heavy about the heart occasionally, though."

Word of Carr's confession spread quickly in Clay County, and late on the night of October 26 Kansas City police escorted Carr on foot from the city lockup at Fourth and Main streets to the better-secured Jackson County Jail a few blocks away. Four days later he was taken by train to Liberty. On November 4 he was indicted in Belle's murder. Bettie Carr was charged with injuring the child.

Talk continued about Bettie Carr's role in the child's death. Had she delivered the blows that caused the welts found on the girl's head by the coroner? Had those blows killed Belle even before her father took her away? Had Bettie Carr demanded that William Carr dispose of Belle's body? She was released on bond, her trial scheduled for early the next year.

By mid-November, William Carr's trial got under way — and quickly came to an end. Carr's attorneys decided to present no defense. For its part, the prosecution offered enough evidence to establish the crime. One of its witnesses, Jackson County Coroner T. D. Bedford, said wounds on the girl's body indicated that she died either of a blow or of strangulation before she was tossed into the river. The question was, How long before?

Steadfastly, William Carr maintained that he had done the killing. At least one witness had seen Carr carrying the girl that Sunday afternoon and recalled that the child's eyes were open.

With no defense presented, the jury quickly convicted Carr. In sentencing him, the judge expressed his disgust:

"Your flimsy excuse that the child was quarrelsome and disagreeable to your wife's 9-year-old son cannot be accepted by the court.

"Men and women commit many crimes and for many motives. You assign no motive that is worthy of consideration. If your confession and other statements are to be believed, you stand a singular instance in the annals of crime: a confessed and convicted murderer without a reasonable motive for your crime."

The judge sentenced Carr to hang on December 17 in Liberty.

As his execution neared, Carr was visited most days by his wife. The couple spoke to one another in hushed tones that jailhouse eavesdroppers failed to make out. Occasionally, the couple chuckled. One day, Bettie Carr asked a doctor about the deadliest poison she could acquire. Presuming any poison she bought would have been used to help William Carr commit suicide, the jailers kept Bettie Carr away from him for a while.

Five days before his hanging, Carr grabbed a medicine bottle from another prisoner, swallowed the contents, broke up the bottle, ground down the glass between his tin cup and the jail floor, and swallowed it. He survived the suicide attempt, but not before grabbing a chair and trying to strike a doctor who tried to give him an emetic.

Meanwhile, the Clay County sheriff and his deputies began preparations for the hanging. A gallows was constructed on the north side of the courthouse,

Bettie Carr, stepmother of the murdered 3-year-old child Belle. Below, the Carr family home in Liberty.

surrounded by a 24-foot fence.

Sheriff Jacob H. Hymer sent out 130 invitations to the event:

"You are hereby invited to witness the execution of William Carr, Friday, December 17, 1897, at 11 o'clock a.m., for the murder of his little daughter, Belle Carr."

The invitations were snapped up, and the sheriff turned down pleas to issue more.

On the eve of the hanging, Carr was visited by his wife and by his foster mother, her husband and a cousin of Carr's first wife. Bettie Carr monopolized his attention.

"He paid no attention to me," his foster mother said. "He only looked at that woman, his wife. She was all he thought of."

The cousin of the first Mrs. Carr was angry:

"That woman, his wife, sat next to him. She kept her eyes on him all the time. I watched her. I tell you it is mesmerism….She, she, that woman, Mrs. Carr, is the murderess….If it was his hands that did the deed it was her mind that provoked him to it. She watches him as a cat does a mouse. She has him in her power."

Observers — reporters, jail workers and other inmates — remarked how often William and Bettie Carr laughed in their conversation. They considered it a strange way for a condemned man to act.

After the family left, a minister and two divinity students from William Jewell College sat with Carr, offering him consolation.

About 2 a.m., Carr asked to see one of his guards, with whom he had grown familiar. He asked the guard to tell him what people thought. The guard replied that

A newspaper illustration of William Carr, as he stood to leave the courtroom during his murder trial.

people thought Carr was taking the fall for his wife's actions against Belle.

"She's innocent, I tell you," he said.

"Then what sort of a damned man are you to throw your own child in the river?" the guard asked. "You know, Bill, that your wife mistreated that child….You know that the very day before you threw her in the river your wife knocked her down with a poker three times and the third time she lay there and your wife yanked her up by the arm and dragged her into the house. Neighbors saw that."

To that, a sullen Carr replied, "It isn't true!"

Later, Carr fell asleep.

At 10:15 a.m., three-quarters of an hour before his scheduled hanging, the sheriff came to his cell, read the death warrant and then led him out the courthouse door and up the steps to the gallows.

"Don't delay it; go straight ahead," Carr said to a deputy. After quickly arranging the noose, Sheriff Hymer pushed the lever that opened the trap below Carr's feet. Within minutes, he was dead.

That was not the end of the day's excitement however. Only about 50 of the 130 invitees had made it inside the stockade before the execution, which had taken place well before the scheduled 11 a.m. A disappointed crowd, some with tickets and some not, was still clamoring to get in when the hanging took place. Someone cried, "He's hanged!" and the crowd surged against the fence, tore off some of the boards and scrambled through the opening to see the results of the hanging. Some swarmed up the gallows; children peered down through the trap door at Carr's body, dangling below.

> **"I knew she was out of the way and that my wife would be happy. That's all I cared for."**

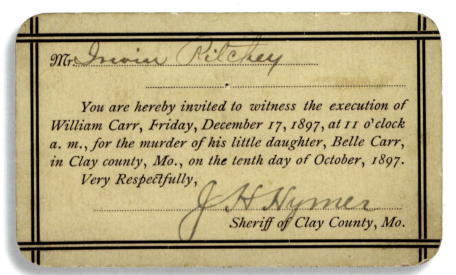

Invitation to William Carr's execution in Liberty, Missouri.

Eventually, the body was cut down, examined, prepared by an undertaker and taken to his widow's home on North Gallatin Street. A crowd followed the body every step of the way, not dispersing until Bettie Carr slammed the door of her house on them.

Then the case took another strange turn. As it happened, the curious would have a chance after all to see William Carr hang, thanks to the new technology of motion pictures. Producers had arranged with the sheriff to mount a kinetoscope, an early movie camera, just outside the stockade and inside a small enclosure so spectators would not notice it. They succeeded in filming the procession to the gallows and the moment of hanging.

The day after Christmas, Edison Phonograph Co. advertised that the film would be shown at a theater at 12th and McGee streets in Kansas City, admission 15 cents, 25 cents and 50 cents. Just as promptly, nearby business owners and *The Star* condemned the showing as a "barbarous exhibition."

Sheriff Hymer, meanwhile, cut up the rope used to hang Carr and distributed it to several people as a souvenir.

William Carr was buried in Randolph, not far from where he threw his daughter into the Missouri River. His other daughter, Mae, was put up for adoption.

As for Bettie Carr, her trial for maiming her stepdaughter went to court in mid-June 1898.

According to the coroner who examined the child's body, there was a sore over the left eye and wounds over the right temple and on the knee. He believed they had occurred before Belle Carr was pitched into the river.

According to a woman who had lived in the house with the Carrs, she often heard Bettie Carr whipping and mistreating Belle. Eight other neighbors told similar stories and one said Belle was singled out for abuse. In her appearance on the witness stand, Bettie Carr said the sores on the body were boils and bee stings.

A report in *The Kansas City Journal* reported her courtroom demeanor this way:

"She laughed and talked as if the case did not contain horrible facts, the remembrance of which would make the blood of the bravest chill."

Perhaps she knew something. The jury told the judge it could not reach a verdict. Her trial was re-scheduled in March 1899, but prosecutors dropped the charges for lack of evidence. Bettie Carr was set free.

Advertisement from The Kansas City Journal.

Armed for "The Lord"

Street preachers, adults and children, produce revolvers and open fire on police. In the end, five people die.

THE CRIME

- **When:** 1908
- **What:** Shooting death of two policeman and an innocent bystander by sidewalk evangelists, two of whom also died.
- **Where:** Near the City Market, Kansas City, Missouri
- **Status:** Believed insane at the time of the shootings, cult leader James "Adam God" Sharp was sentenced to 25 years in prison. He was released early, in 1924, and lived in Joplin until 1946.

A group of street evangelists — a woman, four girls and a boy — stood on the corner of Main and Fifth streets late on the afternoon of December 9, 1908, singing songs and collecting money in a hat placed on the pavement. Sidewalk preaching was not uncommon on the streets surrounding the City Market in those days, but the sight of children taking part was.

The little group had gathered $4 or $5 from passersby when a juvenile court officer, George M. Holt, approached. He quieted the singing.

The children, he told the woman, ought not to be out on the street, soliciting money. If they were living in Kansas City, they should be enrolled in school.

"What business is it of yours?" the woman asked.

Pressed by the officer, she told him her name was Melissa Sharp. She was a traveling evangelist who lived with her husband, another couple and several children on a houseboat tied up on the south bank of the Missouri River. When the group was not walking the streets, singing and taking donations, it held services at the Workingmen's Mission at 309 Main St.

The woman of God cursed as she shepherded the children north on Main toward the mission. Officer Holt followed. At the mission he received an even ruder greeting from the group's ultimate leader, a fiery, bearded 51-year-old man who wore his hair almost to his shoulder.

Melissa Sharp, above. Louis Pratt, below.

James and Della Pratt's four surviving children, who were taught to be gun-toting street evangelists. Most accounts say Mary was 11. Willie Engnell, unrelated to the others, had traveled with the group but did not participate in the battle.

He was Melissa's husband, James Sharp, but that wasn't the name he shouted at officer Holt. Sharp announced himself as "Adam God, the father of Jesus Christ."

Amid more curses, Sharp threatened to kill Holt and any police who got in the evangelists' way.

"Adam God" had one more loud message for Holt: "Get out!"

A fellow evangelist and the father of the five children, Louis Pratt, joined the group and he along with James and Melissa Sharp drew revolvers. James Sharp swung his at Holt, missing him once and then striking the officer on the head. The children began scratching and hitting Holt.

Holt, his head bleeding, retreated to Police Headquarters, which stood on Main Street not far from the mission. Sharp and his wife followed. So did Pratt. The children, who ranged in age from 4 to 14. came, too. Like the adults, the little evangelists carried firearms.

"We'll show these sheep thieves," Sharp shouted as his band marched along. "We'll sing in front of their police station! Let them dare to stop the father of Jesus Christ!"

At the southwest corner of Fourth and Main, across from the ornate City Hall and Police Headquarters, they formed a semicircle. There the group sang hymns — as James Sharp and Pratt openly gripped their revolvers. Sharp also carried a knife. Hundreds of curiosity seekers gathered around.

Holt, meanwhile, reported the incident to his captain, who dispatched a policeman, Albert O. Dalbow, to confront the group.

Fourth and Main streets, where the shootout began. Below: James Sharp after his arrest.

"The sergeant," Dalbow told Sharp, "would like to see you."

Did Dalbow come in peace? Yes, he said, and extended his hand to Sharp.

Just then a police lieutenant intervened. He walked up, stood behind Dalbow and pointed a revolver over Dalbow's shoulder at Sharp.

"Drop that knife," the lieutenant ordered. "Drop that gun."

At that, Sharp's associate Pratt raised his own weapon and fired. He struck Dalbow several times and grazed the lieutenant. Enraged, Sharp himself began firing. Dalbow staggered away and fell dead at the steps of a nearby emergency hospital.

Each of three adult evangelists and three of the girls raised their revolvers. The crowd scattered.

Police poured out of the headquarters, revolvers drawn. Shots rang out in every direction. One errant bullet killed a horse a block away, another went through the wagon driver's hat, and another broke the window of a saloon. Still another bullet struck and killed a 72-year-old retired farmer, A.J. Selsor, who had come to City Hall to pay a utility bill and happened upon the commotion.

Sharp began grappling with a police captain, slashing him with his knife.

Now, policeman Michael Mullane headed for Pratt, who fired at him but missed. He, Melissa Sharp and one of the Pratt girls went after Mullane, their revolvers drawn. Mullane fired at Pratt, wounding him in the leg but, following the chivalric code of the day, did not fire at the woman and child. As Mullane retreated behind a laundry wagon, however, the woman and child fired at him. Mullane walked to the police station, where he fell to his knees, saying, "Boys, I'm badly hurt." He died of his wounds shortly afterward.

Pratt crawled along the sidewalk, still firing at police. Some member of the Adam God group brought him a revolver. Kneeling, he fired away and struck a detective, Patrick Clark, twice. As Pratt prepared to fire at another policeman a police lieutenant inside City Hall shoved a rifle through the window glass and shot Pratt. He fell to the ground, mortally wounded.

Another shot knocked the revolver from James

Sharp's hand. As blood poured from the hand, Sharp bolted west on Fourth Street.

With Louis Pratt down and James Sharp fleeing, Melissa Sharp and the Pratt children ran west on Fourth Street and then turned north on Delaware. Melissa Sharp, her revolver drawn, was tackled by three policemen at Second and Delaware. She was arrested, as was 12-year-old Lena Pratt.

Her sisters Lulu, 13, and Mary, 11, reached the riverbank and boarded the houseboat where the evangelists lodged during their stay in Kansas City. There, they met their mother, Della Pratt.

A police inspector and captain arrived, demanding that Della Pratt surrender. She refused, and the occupants of the houseboat began singing. A crowd of onlookers gathered at the riverbank, along with about 20 policemen.

They watched as Della Pratt and daughters Lulu and Mary climbed into a skiff and untied it from the houseboat. Lulu tucked herself into the bottom of the boat, under a canvas cover. Della and Mary rowed out into the river, where chunks of ice floated past. The police captain ordered his men to fire at the boat's waterline, hoping to sink it. They fired.

Commandeering a ferry, the police approached the skiff. They found Della Pratt in the frigid water alongside, trying to escape the gunfire. Mary Pratt had gone overboard, too. Neither was injured.

One of the police shots, however, had struck Lulu Pratt in the back of her head. She had been lying in the bottom of the skiff, where the police were aiming. She died before she could be taken to shore, the last casualty of the bloody day.

That brought the death toll to five — patrolmen Dalbow and Mullane, evangelist Pratt, his daughter Lulu and the retired farmer.

It was the bloodiest moment of violence in the city's first six decades.

Aiming below the waterline, police fired as Della, Lulu and Mary Pratt escaped in a skiff. Lulu was struck and killed.

Who were these people, the "Adam God" cult? In recent years, they had wandered the great plains, as far south as Oklahoma and as far north as Canada, regaling anyone who would listen with an aggressive, unique and rather patchwork religious message. Gaining and losing adherents as they traveled, their band had numbered as many as 30 people. At the time of the Kansas City shootout, it had about a dozen devotees.

Most of the time, the group's guiding spirit was the messianic figure of James Sharp.

According to Melissa Sharp, who had grown up in southwest Missouri, she and James had lived a godless life until one night in 1903. At a farm they owned near Woodward, Oklahoma, James Sharp saw a meteor streak across the sky. The event affected Sharp deeply and the couple converted to the religious life. They wandered from place to place, preaching. For a while, their son accompanied them. Along the way, others joined.

In Oklahoma City, one vocal member of the group gave Sharp and his wife the names "Adam" and "Eve" and called their son "Abel." This member also persuaded the Sharps that they were sinless, like Adam and Eve in the Garden of Eden, and should walk naked through the streets of Oklahoma City. In 1905, walk naked they did — and were committed to an asylum for it.

To his followers, Sharp was a prophet, a second Jesus.

As for the name, "Adam God," Sharp at one point said that God was the father of Adam, the Bible's first man. That gave Sharp the family name, "God," and the first name, "Adam."

The phrase "Adam God" was first known to have

PATRICK CLARK JOHN COUGHLIN
ALBERT O. DALBOW MICHAEL MULLANE

"When a policeman tried to stop us, our religion teaches us that we have the right to shoot and kill. A policeman is a serpent and ought to be killed. The Constitution gives us that right."

been used in 1852 by Brigham Young when he was president of the Mormon church. In various speeches, Young offered the idea that Adam was not only the first man, but also the father of Jesus. The notion did not become a coherent doctrine, and it has been repudiated by the church and ignored by most of its members.

Whether Brigham Young's concept or his use of the phrase "Adam God" was even known to James Sharp is impossible to say.

The Sharps' wanderings took them to Kansas City in 1906 and then to Topeka, Denver and elsewhere in the west, often drawing crowds because of the presence of the children.

In North Dakota, they bought rifles, supposedly because their preaching put them in peril. They crossed into Canada, but were run back to the States by Mounties after Sharp threatened them with a rifle.

His son Lee left the group in Canada. Another son named Harry had not been heard from in years.

Along the way, authorities uncovered details about Sharp's undistinguished past. He had helped run a poker game in Oklahoma, and, according to some witnesses, engaged in bootlegging.

Back in North Dakota, the cult members further armed themselves with revolvers, traded their horses and wagons for a houseboat, and drifted down the Missouri River to Kansas City, arriving about the beginning of December 1908. They tied up at the foot of Wyandotte Street and promptly set out to sing and preach around the City Market.

Occasionally, they wandered south into more prosperous parts of town, serenading pedestrians at Petticoat Lane and Grand Avenue.

The Adam God cult resembled other groups of street preachers and singers who plied the sidewalks of Kansas City in those days. Some were legitimate believers. But others used religion as a cloak for theft, always excusing themselves by saying that God had ordained their actions. Many such groups asked for donations.

What set the Adam God and his followers apart was the children. Louis and Della Pratt and their five offspring joined the cult about 1906. In earlier visits to Kansas City the Pratts evidently had had run-ins with the law over their use of young ones. At least twice they appeared in court to answer for their children's truancy.

Although the children lacked formal education, they were well-schooled in the murky doctrine of Adam God. In the aftermath of the riot, Mary Pratt was questioned by police and city officials, and she proved a determined witness.

"When we stood on the street corners and sang for the people we felt repaid, for we knew we were doing the Lord's work," she said. "They didn't make us sing. We did it because we loved to do so.

"Those big guns we carried were for protection. Papa says this is a free country and we could carry firearms if we wanted to."

Even to the extent of firing on policemen?

A policeman, the child declared, "has no right to stop us when we are preaching and singing on the street."

"When a policeman tried to stop us," she continued, "our religion teaches us that we have the right to shoot and kill. A policeman is a serpent and ought to be killed. The Constitution gives us that right."

As the city tried to sort out the bloody results of what became known as the "Adam God Riot," there remained the question: Where was Adam God?

James Sharp had disappeared in the midst of the melee on Main Street, running west into a saloon and out the back door, and on to a barber shop in the West Bottoms. The barber — unaware of the turmoil downtown — trimmed his hair and beard. The entire time, James Sharp kept his hands in his pockets lest the barber see the bloody wounds inflicted on them during the violence.

Adam God — James Sharp — and his wife Melissa at their trial.

Authorities in surrounding towns and counties were notified and posses took up the hunt.

Two days after the riot, Sharp was found hiding in a haystack on a farm in the Monticello area in Johnson County. A farmer living west of Zarah, about six miles west of Shawnee, had telephoned a tip to the sheriff's office.

Fatigued from his flight and from loss of blood, Sharp surrendered without a fight and was taken to jail in Kansas City.

He gave interview after interview to the press, and spoke up often during his trial the next spring. His statements ranged wildly from defiant to defensive, sometimes hinting at regret but more often saying he was simply a vehicle for God's will.

On May 29, 1909, Sharp was found guilty of second-degree murder in the slaying of policeman Mullane, but instead of death or life in prison, the penalty was set at 25 years — a compromise among jurors. Some jurors believed Sharp was insane at the time of the crime and still was.

Five months later, Melissa Sharp was declared insane. Charges against her were dismissed, ending the trials in the case. For a while, she lived at the home of the matron of the Jackson County Jail.

James Sharp spent almost a decade and a half in prison before he was released early in 1924. First he returned to a houseboat on the Missouri, and then moved to Joplin, Missouri, where he operated as an evangelist.

He died in Joplin in 1946. By request of his wife, Melissa, the former Adam God was buried with no minister, no services and no ritual.

Bad medicine

Disease and death ravaged the Swope clan — all under the same roof. Was the culprit a covetous in-law?

THE CRIME

- **When:** 1909
- **What:** Mysterious deaths in a prominent family.
- **Where:** Independence, Missouri
- **Status:** Accused physician freed after his conviction was overturned.

In 1857, when Kansas was still a territory, a 30-year-old real estate speculator named Thomas Swope arrived in the Kansas City area, and without delay began buying land. He gained title to parcels in what would become downtown Wyandotte City — later Kansas City, Kansas. He acquired properties in the bottoms along the Kansas River where meatpacking plants would one day rise. He bought promising acreage east of the Missouri line in what would become downtown Kansas City, Missouri.

As the 19th century wore on, and the two Kansas Citys boomed, Swope sold his properties for far more than he had paid. His profits turned into a fortune and Swope turned into an occasional civic benefactor. He donated land for a hospital and supported other charitable endeavors. In 1896, he gave to Kansas City, Missouri, more than 1,300 acres of rural land just outside the city limits. It became Swope Park, the city's grandest.

One summer day in 1896, tens of thousands of people trekked out to the new park for its grand opening. Swope — as private as he was wealthy — refused to ride at the head of a parade into the grounds. Instead he walked across pastures to reach the site of the ceremony. As mayors and other dignitaries paid homage to him, Swope stayed off the stage and strolled through the crowd. *The Kansas City Star* of the day wrote that Swope, "probably the greatest property owner in Kansas City…moved about unknown and unheeded by the throng."

Few Kansas Citians even knew what Thomas Swope looked like, and he evidently wanted it that way. For years he operated out of an office in downtown Kansas City and lived mostly in hotels. He was childless, a lifelong bachelor. Late in life, he moved in with relatives in Independence. There, in a 26-room mansion on a 19-acre estate on Pleasant Street, Swope lived with Margaret "Maggie" Swope, the widow of his brother, Logan Swope. There, too, lived five of Maggie Swope's children and a couple of other relatives. They were the closest Thomas Swope could come to an immediate family.

As the years went by, Swope grew grumpy, and more private than ever. He had few

Thomas Swope, right.

The Swope Mansion in Independence

friends and there was little doubt why: he had grown to dislike small talk and what conversations he had were consumed by complaints about his health. Occasionally, he turned belligerent and launched into profane tirades easily audible outside his room. Of the people who lived in the house, he was close only to cousin James Moss Hunton, who was 63.

Swope divided his time between his office downtown, where he employed a single assistant, and his room at the mansion in Independence. As long as he was able, Swope insisted on riding the streetcar both ways. In September 1909, at age 82, he gave up going to the office.

He had a will, which because of his great wealth was an important document. His estate would be valued at $3.5 million, worth roughly $75 million in 21st-century money.

According to the will, the land and cash that composed the estate would be divided in specific bequests among his many relatives and certain charities. Money left over from the individual gifts — the residuary estate, which would amount to more than $1.4 million — would be divided equally among his nieces and nephews.

But Swope was having second thoughts, and by autumn 1909 he was considering revising his will to devote the residuary estate to the poor. Swope's idea was to enlarge the portion bound for charity, which would necessarily reduce the portion to be shared by his relatives. He discussed the change with Moss Hunton, the man designated as executor.

Suddenly, on the night of October 1, 1909, Moss Hunton was struck by a cerebral hemorrhage — known as "apoplexy" at the time. Unable to find the family doctor, nurses called another doctor, Bennett Clark Hyde. Hyde was the 38-year-old husband of one of Swope's nieces, Frances Swope Hyde. Doctor Hyde, according to the custom of the day, relieved pressure on Hunton's brain by draining blood.

To the nurse's horror, Hyde kept draining it beyond

the customary point until he had removed two quarts. That amounted to 40 percent of the blood in Hunton's body. Soon, the designated executor of Swope's will was dead.

The day after Hunton died, Swope hinted to his office assistant that he planned to name a new executor promptly and proceed with his plan to alter the will to give more money to charity.

The morning of October 3, while Hunton's coffin sat in one room of the mansion for viewing, Hyde left with Swope's nurse a capsule. He told her it contained a substance that would aid the old man's digestion. The nurse helped Swope take it.

In about 20 minutes, Swope began convulsing violently. His legs and eyes froze, his teeth clenched and his pulse raced. After a while, Hyde ordered the nurse to inject the patient with strychnine. Normally, the drug was used to stimulate heart activity, but Swope's heartbeat already was pounding quite rapidly. The nurse did as she was told. Swope's heart was still beating rapidly when Hyde ordered a second injection of strychnine. Then came a third and perhaps a fourth and fifth. Swope hung on until that evening.

At 7:15 p.m. he died — about 11 hours after taking the capsule that purportedly would help his digestion.

As he had with Hunton, Hyde listed the cause of Swope's death as apoplexy. A nurse noticed that the symptoms of the two men were nowhere near the same; Swope's convulsions were far more violent than Hunton's.

Thomas Swope's body lay at the Kansas City Public Library, where the public could view the coffin. An array of flowers stood nearby, labeled "Kansas City Mourns." From there, Swope's remains were taken to a church for funeral services.

The coincidence of Swope and his cousin, two decades apart in age, dying in the same house of supposedly the same ailment within days of each other — and treated at the end by the same doctor — had not been forgotten when Thanksgiving rolled around. A few days later, at the end of November, more sickness plagued the mansion.

One by one, at least nine persons — ranging from family members to a houseguest to the servants — came

Dining room of the Swope mansion. Was typhoid transmitted here?

down with typhoid. The youngest was 14. All except one of the victims recovered.

The lone fatality was 31-year-old Chrisman Swope, whose condition appeared to be improving when Hyde gave him a capsule. Just as the family patriarch had done two months earlier, Chrisman went into convulsions about 20 minutes after taking the pill. He legs became rigid and his eyes froze. Hyde, as he had with the elder Swope, ordered the nurse to give Chrisman in injection of strychnine. More injections followed. On December 6, Chrisman Swope died. This time, Hyde listed the cause as meningitis.

In late December, Chrisman's sister Margaret, 20, also apparently recovering from the typhoid attack, took a capsule at Hyde's direction. She, too, went into violent convulsions like her brother and uncle. Like them, her reaction began about 20 minutes after having taken the capsule. By chance, the family doctor, George Twyman, was in the mansion at the time and treated her. She survived.

As 1910 began, the toll stood at four Swope relatives treated by Hyde, three of whom died, three of whom had gone into convulsions after taking a capsule prescribed by him — and a houseful of people unaccountably stricken with typhoid.

The family hired a squad of nurses to care for the victims, and they grew suspicious of Hyde and his methods. The nurses took their views to Dr. Twyman.

Reluctantly — Hyde was, after all, a member of the family — Twyman began to agree that something was wrong. He spoke with the family lawyer and soon afterward with Hyde himself.

Hyde was told to leave the mansion and to stop caring for people there.

Hyde's mother-in-law, Maggie Swope, needed little convincing. The matriarch of the Swope mansion had never liked Hyde and never wanted her daughter to marry him. She had learned that Hyde had at times in the past played the part of a gigolo, carrying on with divorcees while he borrowed money from them. Despite Maggie Swope's disapproval, Frances Swope and Bennett Hyde were determined to be married, and in 1905 they eloped. Eventually, the family accepted their union. Thomas Swope had bought the couple a house at 3516 Forest Avenue in Kansas City.

Now, Maggie Swope's old worries about Hyde returned. Frances was in line to receive money from her uncle's estate; if fewer Swope relatives existed to share the inheritance, Frances — and her husband, Hyde — would receive a greater portion.

Clues were coming to light that appeared to confirm the suspicions of the nurses, Dr. Twyman and Maggie Swope. In early November, a month after Thomas Swope's death, Hyde had asked a Kansas City doctor and bacteriologist to provide him cultures of typhoid, diphtheria and other bacteria. Ostensibly they were for experiments in a laboratory Hyde maintained at his office. After the nurses went to Twyman with their suspicions, the bacteriologist talked his way into Hyde's laboratory and found that the tubes of typhoid cultures had been disturbed, as if typhoid bacteria had been removed from them.

Chrisman Hyde

Frances Swope Hyde

Family remembers recalled that the Hydes dined at the mansion on the Sunday before Thanksgiving 1909. The Hydes had brought bottled water, which they drank exclusively. Suspicion arose that Hyde had planted typhoid in the family water, which came from a cistern that was otherwise clean, or in the family's food. Typhoid typically took at least seven days to show symptoms, and the first symptoms began to appear seven days after that Sunday.

No autopsies had been performed on Thomas or Chrisman Swope when they died. Now, as a result of the growing distrust of Hyde, authorities decided the time had arrived. Because the ground was frozen in December when he died, Chrisman's coffin had been kept in a holding vault at Mount Washington cemetery. It was removed and opened for testing of the body by a specialist from Chicago. The specialist found no evidence of meningitis — the reason Hyde gave for Chrisman's death — but he did find traces of strychnine in the man's liver.

Thomas Swope's body, frozen solid by the winter chill, was retrieved in early January from Forest Hill Cemetery, where it was waiting for the completion of

Bennett Clark Hyde, in a portait and on the witness stand.

his eventual resting place, a memorial at Swope Park. The immediate results of an autopsy showed that Swope had died neither of disease nor of old age. His organs were transported to Chicago, where on January 31 it was announced that tests determined he had died of poisoning.

It was also learned that on at least three occasions from middle September through December, Hyde had bought cyanide of potassium from Brecklein's Pharmacy at Ninth Street and Grand Avenue. The store was only a block east of Hyde's office in the Keith & Perry Building at Ninth and Walnut. The purchase was curious because the substance typically was used only by jewelers and dentists as a solvent for gold. Also curious was how Hyde wanted the cyanide prepared — in capsules. On one occasion he told the curious pharmacist he wanted to kill some dogs that were giving him trouble.

As the accusations against Hyde mounted, Frances Swope Hyde vigorously defended her husband. The couple denied nearly every accusation.

Frances' mother remained undaunted. She hired as special prosecutor James A. Reed, a former mayor, and a future U.S. Senator and candidate for the Democratic presidential nomination. Reed was a skilled, tenacious and eloquent lawyer.

A coroner's jury began work on February 7 and shortly delivered its verdict: Swope had died of strychnine poisoning, and Hyde had administered strychnine. On February 10, 1910, Hyde was arrested and charged with the murder of Thomas Swope.

Next came a grand jury, which heard evidence for three weeks. On March 5, it indicted Hyde on 11 counts ranging from murder in the cases of Thomas and Chrisman Swope to manslaughter in the bleeding of Moss Hunton, to poisoning Chrisman's sister Margaret and seven others — family members, a friend, and servants.

His trial was scheduled to begin April 11.

Prosecutors would target Hyde for only one of the counts — the murder of the senior Swope. If they could convict him on that count, they believed, Hyde would be either hanged or imprisoned for life and no further prosecutions would be needed. They introduced a theory that Hyde had caused Swope's death by administering a combination of strychnine and cyanide. The two substances, they claimed, would cancel out the evidence of one another.

When the trial began, it riveted the attention of not only Kansas Citians but also newspaper readers across the country.

With a packed courtroom, scads of reporters, the defendant and the Swope family looking on, Reed and his fellow prosecutors called a series of witnesses to the stand, from the concerned nurses to the Chicago forensic experts. The prosecution cited the purchases from Brecklein's Pharmacy and the tubes of typhoid culture kept in Hyde's office. It also called to the stand a nurse who said that, after Moss Hunton's death, Hyde asked her to help persuade Swope to make Hyde his new executor.

Hyde's lawyer, Frank Walsh, pecked away at each prosecution witness, and then called his own set of experts to try to raise the possibility that Chrisman Swope could have died of meningitis. Walsh called the Swope autopsy faulty and said the poison it found was not cyanide but strychnine, which Swope had taken in tiny doses until a few weeks before his death.

Frances Swope contradicted almost everything the prosecution witnesses said — including the statements of her own mother — about dates and places and actions by her husband. Finally Hyde himself testified, confident at first and later showing worry as prosecutors bore down on his acquisition of bacteria and poisons.

In his closing argument, Reed showed off his oratorical arts. Referring to Hyde, he said:

"The typhoid followed that man like sharks follow a ship laden with dead."

After three days and two nights, the jury arrived at a verdict. On May 16, 1910, it found Hyde guilty of murder and sentenced him to life in prison. The Swopes and prosecution had won.

But the case did not end there.

The lawyers: Frank Walsh, above; James A. Reed, below.

In spring 1911, the Missouri Supreme Court overturned the verdict against Hyde, saying that despite much circumstantial evidence the prosecution had not proven that any of the Swope family members had been murdered. Without murder, there could be no murderer. Also, it criticized the trial judge for allowing prosecutors to present evidence about the other deaths and poisonings in the mansion; Hyde had been on trial only for Swope's murder. As of April 27, Hyde was a free man again, but only temporarily.

Again, he was tried for Swope's murder. In the middle of the proceedings a sequestered juror lost his wits — or seemed to — and fled the hotel. The judge declared a mistrial.

Once more the case was taken to trial. This time, the jury could not come to a unanimous verdict. Jurors reported that they had stood nine to three in favor of acquitting Hyde.

Along the way, the public and the press paid close attention to the sometimes outlandish doings in the courtroom.

"Witnesses have been carried fainting or hysterical from the stand," *The Star* said in summing up the contentious series of trials. "Spectators wedged themselves and stood breathless for hours to hear testimony.

"Jurors have argued themselves hoarse; one even went temporarily insane."

Between the state and the defense, a quarter of a million dollars was spent on the trials and appeals.

In 1914, five years after the deaths, the charges against Hyde were dismissed.

After his freedom was ensured, Hyde took up his practice again, but it dwindled as the 1910s wore on. He and Frances had two children.

In 1920, citing abuse of herself and their two children by her husband, she won a divorce, no doubt

Hyde's guilty verdict from 1910, which was later overturned by the Missouri Supreme Court. After several more trials, the charges against Hyde were dropped.

confirming her mother's earliest misgivings about Hyde. Even as the couple broke up, however, she continued to proclaim Hyde's innocence in the sicknesses and death at the Swope mansion in 1909.

Hyde moved back to his native Lafayette County, Missouri, where he practiced medicine until he died in August 1934, at the age of 62. In 1923, Maggie Swope sold the mansion to The Reorganized Church of Jesus Christ of Latter Day Saints. She outlived Hyde, dying in 1942 at age 87. She left only a few thousand dollars to be divided among her children.

As for Swope, his casket and remains in 1918 were transferred to a hill in Swope Park, which today is Kansas City's most-visited recreational area. Swope's memorial overlooks a ground that contains the city zoo, municipal golf courses, soccer fields, basketball courts and Starlight Theatre.

Despite much attention in newspaper and magazine articles at the time and on anniversaries of the deaths since, no book about the events in the Swope mansion was produced until 2009. That year, a longtime *Star* newspaperman and later journalism professor, Giles Fowler, published *Deaths on Pleasant Street: The Ghastly Enigma of Colonel Swope and Doctor Hyde*.

In his book, Fowler detailed the deaths and the accusations in the Swope case, and finished by putting the matter before an expert on poisoning. The expert, Edward M. Bottei, director of the Iowa Statewide Poison Control Center, pointed to the amount of strychnine found in Thomas Swope's body and estimated that it was sufficient to do away with him. Strychnine, administered several times in less-than-lethal doses, could have led to the convulsions and other symptoms observed in Swope the day he died, and then to his demise.

Cyanide, Bottei said, was an unlikely cause; it would have killed Swope promptly. Why then, did Bennett Clark Hyde purchase all those capsules of cyanide at Brecklein's Pharmacy in downtown Kansas City? Like other important events in this extensively documented case, it remains an unending mystery.

Successful and vulnerable

A drugstore magnate on his way to work falls prey to kidnappers. Their price is $100,000. They get it.

THE CRIME

- **When:** 1930
- **What:** Drug company founder Michael Katz was kidnapped and held for ransom.
- **Where:** On Ward Parkway near his home, Kansas City, Missouri and other places in the area.
- **Status:** The ransom paid, Katz was returned safely. The kidnappers were never caught.

By 1930, everyone in Kansas City knew the name Katz. Brothers Michael and Isaac Katz had transformed a cigar shop and confectionery at Eighth Street and Grand Avenue into a thriving set of downtown drugstores that had recently expanded to Kansas City, Kansas, St. Joseph, Missouri, and St. Paul, Minnesota. More were on the drawing board.

Katz advertising — featuring a ubiquitous black cat — dominated the newspapers, and the Katz outlets dominated the drugstore business by selling lots of items at low prices. In a freewheeling era of gangs and crime, the city marveled when it learned that Michael Katz, president of the Katz Drug Company, had been kidnapped for ransom.

The crime began unfolding about 9:30 a.m. on March 18, 1930, when Katz turned his Packard sports coupe on to Ward Parkway and headed north toward work. Out of the blue, two men in a Chrysler roadster forced his car to the curb.

One of them climbed on the running board, struck Katz in the head, forced him to the floor and grabbed the steering wheel. The couple sped away, accompanied by the rogues in the roadster.

Two hours later, a sometime bootlegger and gambler named Bennie Portman, who was an acquaintance of Michael Katz, received a telephone call. The person on the other end of the line instructed him to

The image of a black cat represented the Katz drugstore chain.

Above: Bennie Portman, a go-between; Right: Michael Katz.

Ward Parkway site of Michael Katz's abduction. Below left, Michael Katz's home on the same street.

The Sexton Hotel on crowded 12th Street in Kansas City.

go to a political party office near 12th and Central streets. Portman believed he ought to obey. As Portman pulled up to the curb at the appointed place, a stranger handed Portman an envelope. It was addressed to Louis Rose, one of the owners of the Sexton Hotel a couple of blocks east on 12th between Baltimore Avenue and Main Street. By mid-afternoon, Rose had read the letter. It appointed him as another go-between to arrange the ransom for Michael Katz. The prospect worried and angered Rose, but he complied. Like Portman, he was an acquaintance of Katz. As it turned out, Mike Katz had suggested their names to his captors.

Enclosed in the letter to Rose was another envelope addressed to Katz's brother, Isaac. About 4 p.m., Rose called the Katz drugstore offices. An anxious Isaac Katz and a business associate soon arrived at the Sexton hotel.

Inside the envelope, in his brother's handwriting, was the kidnappers' demand for Mike Katz's freedom: $100,000 in cash. Isaac Katz went home, leaving things in the hands of Rose, Portman and his business associate. On the morning of March 19, the group was sitting in a fourth-floor room at the Sexton when an unidentified caller telephoned. The ransom demand, he said, was not negotiable.

Unable to bargain and with their backs against the wall, the Katz group ordered the $100,000, in $100 and $500 bills, withdrawn from the Commerce Trust Company. It was delivered to the Sexton and wrapped in newspaper for transfer to the kidnappers.

Isaac Katz, Michael's brother

As instructed by the caller, Rose and Portman carried the package to the Coates House. There, a bellboy paged Rose to take a call in a telephone booth. The caller told Rose to carry the money to Reservoir Hill on Cliff Drive in the Northeast section of Kansas City.

Following instructions, the Katz intermediaries parked their car at the hill with the money inside and, keeping their eyes forward, walked away. They heard another car approach, pause and drive away. When they returned to their car, the bundle of money was gone.

With the ransom delivered, Rose and Portman headed back to the Sexton Hotel, where with two Katz representatives they waited. After three hours and several calls telling of a delay, at 7:15 p.m. the final call came.

Go to the Concourse — a park in the northeast section — the caller said.

"Your man is waiting for you there now," he added.

At the Concourse, under a colonnade, Rose, Portman and three Katz associates found Michael Katz, safe and carrying a hood that he had worn through most of the 30-hour ordeal. Katz, unable to see during his captivity, knew only that he had been kept a prisoner in two different houses.

Only after the kidnapping had ended did anyone call the Kansas City Police.

Before the ransom was paid, the bills were marked. Some turned up at a car dealer in Kansas City, where

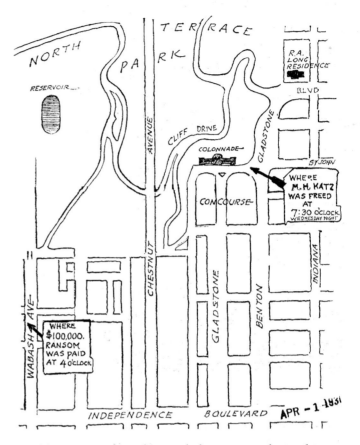

Final locations in the Mike Katz kidnapping, as depicted in The Kansas City Star.

someone had used them to buy a Buick coupe; the car was found wrecked on a highway and its occupants were arrested. They had an alibi, however, and Michael Katz could not identify them because he was never allowed to see them while in captivity.

More of the bills, totaling about $9,500, were found to have been deposited at Merchants Bank at Fifth and Walnut Streets. At the time Merchants was known to be used by bootleggers and gamblers.

The case was never solved. Michael Katz began riding to work in chauffeured automobiles with bullet-proof glass and other protection.

The drugstore empire headed by him and his brother continued to grow in his lifetime. He died at 74 in 1962.

Taking Nelly Don

A dress manufacturer and her chauffeur are kidnapped, but a close friend knows all the right people.

THE CRIME

» **When:** 1931

» **What:** Nell Donnelly and her chauffeur were captured and held for ransom.

» **Where:** At the Donnelly residence on Oak Street in south Kansas City and in Johnson and Wyandotte counties, Kansas.

» **Status:** Donnelly and Blair were released without ransom being paid, with the intervention of a close friend — and the mob.

A year and a half passed after Kansas City's first high-profile kidnapping before another took place. This time the victim was the wealthy Nell Donnelly, a nationally known figure in the making of women's wear.

Nell Donnelly laid the groundwork for her fortune in the early 20th century, when she moved to Kansas City from her native Parsons, Kansas. A skilled seamstress, she came up with designs for housedresses boasting ruffles and other frills. Those extras distanced her products from the plain cotton dresses of the day, and her concept of stylishness in inexpensive garments caught on. Her company prospered, and by 1930 Donnelly Garment Company was selling "Nelly Don" clothing nationwide and on its way to employing 1,000 people.

Her husband, Paul Donnelly, had provided the financial backing for the company when it began. He handled the money while Nell Donnelly handled the design and manufacture of dresses.

Successful as the Donnellys were, their marriage grew uneasy. Paul drank heavily, saw other women and one night at dinner threw an ashtray at his wife. Nell saw at least one other man. In September 1931, she announced that she and Paul had adopted a son; in reality she had given birth to the child herself at a hospital in Chicago. Paul Donnelly was not the father. That year, she turned 42 years old.

Paul Donnelly

Despite the strains, the Donnellys continued to live together at their home, 5235 Oak St. That address was her destination at 6 p.m. on December 16, 1931, when the Donnelly chauffeur, 28-year-old George Blair, picked Nell Donnelly up at her office at 19th and Walnut. He steered the Donnellys' 1928 Lincoln convertible sedan south, and as the car passed 52nd Street and began to pull into the driveway of the home, Blair found another automobile blocking the entrance. A group of men stood around it, as if discussing a

The Donnelly home at 5235 Oak Street.

mechanical problem.

It was a ruse they quickly dropped when the Lincoln arrived. One of them pointed a pistol at the Donnelly car and with two accomplices rushed Blair, overpowering him and then Nell. The men held the 28-year-old chauffeur at gunpoint while they bound him hand and foot. They struggled with Nell Donnelly in the back seat, finally subduing her as they drove the Lincoln west.

Across the state line in Johnson County, Kansas, the kidnappers transferred their two captives to another car. Then they drove 20 miles or so west to a 20-acre farm and creamery about 2½ miles northeast

The farmhouse near Bonner Springs, Kansas, where Nell Donnelly and George Blair were held for ransom. Left: The cot on which Blair was confined.

of Bonner Springs, Kansas, in Wyandotte County. There they escorted their victims into a four-room house. At gunpoint, Donnelly was forced to sit on a bed. Next to her Blair, still bound, was placed on a cot.

The next morning, December 17, the kidnappers delivered to James Taylor, a Donnelly family lawyer, a note in Nell Donnelly's handwriting and addressed to her husband. It gave the kidnappers' demand for $75,000 in exchange for Nell Donnelly's and George Blair's freedom. Failing payment, the note said, Nell Donnelly would be blinded and the chauffeur slain.

Taylor decided to get in touch with his close associate, James A. Reed, a redoubtable lawyer who had been mayor of Kansas City, three-term U.S. senator from Missouri and the prosecutor of Bennett Clark Hyde in the murder of Thomas Swope. The 70-year-old Reed was a neighbor of the Donnellys; the backyard of his home at 5236 Cherry adjoined the Donnellys' backyard. Reed was a friend of the family and, as it turned out, an extremely close friend of Nell Donnelly.

When word of the kidnapping reached Reed, he was in a trial in Jefferson City. Excusing himself, he strode out of the courtroom and drove west to Kansas City. His sudden departure piqued the interest of reporters. Soon word of Nell Donnelly's kidnapping leaked out.

Once he was home in Kansas City, Reed promptly took charge of matters. He began by declaring publicly that if Nell Donnelly were harmed in the slightest he would spend the rest of his life running her assailant to ground.

Then, as in the kidnapping of Michael Katz, the Kansas City underworld entered the picture. But where Katz's intermediaries were lesser figures in Kansas City's criminal circles, the people who would direct the rescue of Nell Donnelly came from the top ranks of the local mob.

The powerful and well-connected Reed was an ally of Thomas J. Pendergast, whose political machine was, in effect, running the city. Reed got in touch with John Lazia, the widely known leader of the Kansas City mob, who also was in league with Pendergast. Lazia put his associates on the case. They spread out across the city, searching for clues.

James A. Reed

Soon they found a restaurateur who knew the kidnappers' plans. From him, they learned the site of the farmhouse were Donnelly and Blair were being held.

Afterward, the restaurateur somehow got word to the kidnappers that their scheme was in trouble. The leaders of the kidnapping fled the farmhouse, leaving the captives in charge of two lesser figures in the matter. Those two eventually untied Blair — Nell Donnelly had not been tied — and suggested that both might go free soon.

In the wee hours of December 18, a Friday, the Lazia men forced their way into the farm home, brushing aside the two kidnappers who remained. One of the rescuers put his arm around Nell Donnelly's shoulders and said:

"Mrs. Donnelly, there has been a mistake. These men are from out of town. You have a lot of friends. We have come to rescue you."

They drove Donnelly and Blair to a spot on Kansas Avenue west of the Kansas River bridge. As the rescue vehicle roared away, Donnelly and Blair looked around. They decided to walk east along Kansas Avenue. A mile and a half away, near 12th Street in the Armourdale district of Kansas City, Kansas, they came upon an all-night café and confectionery, where they stopped.

At 4:10 a.m. — 34 hours after the kidnapping — Kansas City, Missouri, police received an anonymous call telling where the two could be found. Within an hour the police found Nell Donnelly and George Blair, safe.

No ransom was paid.

The kidnappers, as it turned out, were not from "out of town." To mob insiders, though, they were outsiders. The leading figure was Martin Depew, a local steam-shovel operator in his late 30s who had gathered information about the Donnellys from his wife, a nurse. In the week after Christmas 1930, his wife had spent three days at the Donnelly home caring for Paul Donnelly. After the thwarted kidnapping, Depew fled to South Africa, but was captured, returned to the United States, tried and sentenced to life in prison.

Walter Werner — a 15-year resident of the Kansas City area and a recently laid-off auto worker — drove the car that blocked the Donnelly driveway, and then drove the Donnelly car with the captives inside. When Nell Donnelly and Blair were moved to another car, Werner returned the Donnellys' Lincoln to a spot on the Country Club Plaza and then rejoined the kidnappers. Unlike Depew, Werner remained in Kansas City, where he was arrested. He, too, received life imprisonment.

Charles Mele, a Kansas City hotel clerk and a small-time area racketeer, helped guard Donnelly and Blair. He was an associate of the restaurant owner who told the Lazia associates where the two were held. Mele got 35 years.

Paul Scheidt, who worked at a milk plant in Bonner Springs and who leased the farmhouse where Blair and Donnelly were held, was acquitted. William Lacy Browning, a farmer from Holliday, Kansas, who recommended Scheidt's place as a lair, served a short sentence.

The kidnappers, from left: Martin Depew, the leading figure in the scheme; Paul Scheidt, who provided the farmhouse where Donnelly and Blair were held, and Charles Mele, who helped guard the prisoners. Depew fled but was eventually captured and sentenced to life in prison. Scheidt was acquitted; Mele received 35 years for his part in the crime.

In November 1932, Nell Donnelly divorced her husband of 26 years and took over the clothing company. In December 1933, she married James A. Reed. Reed, it turned out, was the biological father of the boy she claimed to have adopted. He legally adopted the child.

Donnelly Manufacturing continued to grow. In 1935, *Fortune* magazine named Nell Donnelly Reed as perhaps the most successful businesswoman in the United States. By the 1940s her company was described as the biggest of its kind in the world.

James A. Reed died in 1944. Nell Donnelly Reed survived him by more than four decades. In the middle 1950s, she sold her company and devoted her time to a position on the Kansas City school board and to political campaigns. Later, she served on the boards of the Midwest Research Institute, the Kansas City Art Institute and the Starlight Theatre Association. She donated the first acreage for what became the James A. Reed Wildlife Area in southern Jackson County.

An avid outdoorswoman, she was recorded as having shot the first buck of the hunting season in Michigan in 1980, when she was 91. Nell Donnelly Reed died in 1991 at the age of 102.

Nell Donnelly and James A. Reed were married in 1933. Reed legally adopted what turned out to be his biological son.

Swept away

The daughter of the city manager says her abuctors weren't so bad. In fact, only they understood her.

THE CRIME

» **When:** 1932

» **What:** City Manager's daughter Mary McElroy was kidnapped.

» **Where:** At her home at 21 W. 57th St., Kansas City, Missouri.

» **Status:** All kidnappers were caught and sentenced to prison terms. McElroy, who developed a fondness for her captors, committed suicide in 1940.

Kansas City's third celebrity kidnapping of the 1930s occurred in the most outrageous year in the city's criminal history. The abduction of Mary McElroy — followed in short order by the Union Station massacre, a shootout with the Clyde Barrow gang and a Hollywood-style mob hit on Armour Boulevard — made it clear that in 1933 Kansas City had earned the name "wide-open town."

By then, Kansas City was more than a place where folks partied in clubs and gambled until all hours with jazz as background music. In the city and its environs, criminals of all stripes and all alliances, local or out of town, operated freely. Too often, police were at best ineffective and at worst in league with crooks. As for the legal system, courts and prosecutors sometimes seemed to exist only to impede prosecution of criminals.

The kidnapping of Mary McElroy showed just how wide-open things were. Her captors struck at the puppetmaster of the Pendergast political machine, seemingly thumbing their noses at the alliance between the machine and the city's mob.

The victim was the child of Thomas J. Pendergast's handpicked city manager and right-hand man, Henry F. McElroy. No one associated with the Kansas City mob would have considered kidnapping his next of kin. The political machine made it possible for the mob to operate without restriction; the alliance was too tight.

On the morning of May 27, 1933, a Saturday, not long after McElroy had left for City Hall, two hoodlums posing as deliverymen arrived at the McElroy home near 57th and Main streets, just south of St. Teresa's school for girls. One of the men rang the bell, persuaded the family maid to open the door, and drew a revolver on her. The other man left the car, came to the door and showed a weapon. They forced the frightened housekeeper to take them to Mary. The city manager's daughter, then 25 years old, was upstairs in the bath.

When the gunmen announced their presence, Mary McElroy screamed. Soon she composed herself.

Despite the ominous circumstances, Mary McElroy assumed an air of boundless, buoyant self-confidence. She told her abductors to wait while she dressed. She put on a

The McElroy home near 57th and Main streets.

dress, made herself up, reached for her purse and gloves and pronounced herself ready to go.

The original plan of the two kidnappers, Walter McGee and Clarence Stevens, had been to kidnap Mary's brother, Henry, who was 23 years old. However, they were unable to find him. Possibly they were surprised that Mary was a grown woman and not a little girl; certainly they were surprised by her show of spirit. In that regard she resembled her father.

As city manager, Henry McElroy ran the affairs of Kansas City with an iron fist and in a manner that first and foremost benefited the political operation of his boss, Thomas J. Pendergast. McElroy presided over one of the biggest public building booms in the city's history; the Municipal Auditorium was his pet project in an era that also saw construction of a new City Hall, a new county courthouse and the paving of Brush Creek at the Country Club Plaza. He also oversaw patronage hiring, payments to machine allies for substandard or even no work, and the use of Pendergast concrete in various projects.

Except for her college years in Illinois, Mary McElroy had never moved away from home, and was the main support for her widowed father. She went with him to meetings of the City Council and stood by his side at ceremonies and on occasions of public business. Routinely she defended him and the Pendergast organization. Her

Mary's father, Henry F. McElroy, Thomas Pendergast's city manager and right-hand man.

father often dismissed his critics; Mary now dismissed the danger inherent in a kidnapping.

Her two abductors, McGee and Stevens, bundled her into their car, made her lie on the floor and covered her with a quilt. They drove west from the Country Club District across the state line to the then-rural road in Kansas that divided Johnson County from Wyandotte County. At a frame dwelling on the Wyandotte or north side of the road, on a farm about two miles north of the middle of Shawnee, they stopped. They took their prize victim to the basement.

At the house Mary met two more conspirators, Walter McGee's brother, George McGee, and Clarence Click, who owned the house.

Her left wrist was shackled and chained to a basement wall and there she remained. Her captors set her to work writing a ransom letter. During her captivity, her

The Wyandotte County, Kansas, house where Mary McElroy was held captive. Below: Clarence Stevens, left and Walter McGee.

kidnappers kept the area clean and lighted, and otherwise made their victim comfortable, even providing her a radio and a fan.

Over time, as they chatted, she and the kidnappers began to get along.

Meanwhile, on learning from the housekeeper about the kidnapping, Mary's father hurried from City Hall to his home, where he waited with his son for some word. Newspaper reporters allowed into the house saw Henry McElroy looking distressed, the first time they could recall seeing such an emotion in the previously indomitable city manager.

That evening, word arrived from the kidnappers. It came to the McElroy house in the form of a special-delivery letter carrying the ransom note in Mary's handwriting. In the letter, she said her captors wanted $60,000, which amount would increase if the press reported the matter or the police were called. Later that night, another special-delivery letter gave more details and told McElroy to wait at home the next morning. He dispatched police investigators, but Kansas City detectives were stumped. Even among local outlaws, the kidnappers were unknown. The usual underworld informants proved useless.

At 8:30 a.m. Sunday, May 28, the call came. The kidnappers again asked for $60,000 in ransom. The city manager began negotiating for his daughter, and by the end of a second call at 10:30 a.m., he had bargained them down to $30,000.

With the ransom agreed upon, it was arranged for the 67-year-old McElroy and his son to deliver the money to a spot on a bluff overlooking the Kansas River in Wyandotte County. There two men wearing masks and carrying

George McGee at the police station. Moments later he would throw the ink bottle in foreground at the photographer.

firearms met them and took the money.

That afternoon, Mary McElroy was released at the Milburn Golf and Country Club in Johnson County about four miles west of the state line. She was carrying a bouquet of roses provided by her kidnappers. She removed the bandana the kidnappers had used to blindfold her and waved as they drove away. The kidnappers waved back.

Her father and brother retrieved her from the clubhouse.

Afterward, she told The Associated Press about the hours of her kidnapping:

"At no time," she said, "did I expect to be returned alive. It appeared the best thing to hope for was a quick death."

Nevertheless, she decided to take a lighthearted course with her keepers. It worked.

"Considering the tenseness of the situation, we got along very well otherwise," she continued. "I learned to know them rather well, to conclude they were more desperate than bad and more cowardly than vicious."

Eventually, police tracked down three of the four perpetrators. The ringleader, Walter McGee, a 37-year-old truck driver and onetime convict from Oregon, was arrested in Texas. In his possession were bills with serial numbers matching those handed over for the ransom. He told the whole story. Police then tracked down his 21-year-old brother, George McGee, and Clarence Click, who was 27. The fourth member of the group, Clarence Stevens, got away.

Walter McGee was sentenced to death. It was believed to have been a first in the United States for the crime of kidnapping. George McGee was sentenced to life in prison. Clarence Click got eight years.

In their trials, the kidnappers revealed that they had concocted the idea for the kidnapping in a bar and spent a month planning it. Their only interest had been to make some easy money.

Unlike the kidnappings of Michael Katz and Nell Donnelly, the city's underworld could not help bring things to a conclusion. However, mob leader John Lazia was thought to have come up with the $30,000 in ransom money. The day after Mary was recovered, McElroy withdrew $30,000 from his own bank account. Was it to repay Lazia for providing the cash the day before?

Later, two mysterious deposits were made into McElroy's account, one in June 1933 for $16,000 and one in September 1934 for $14,000. Whatever their origin, the ransom payment wound up costing Henry McElroy nothing.

The matter did not end with Mary's release. The twenty-nine hours of her captivity had gone surprisingly well, and she had come to like — or at least feel sorry for — the outlaws.

Despite helping with her testimony to convict the men, and despite maintaining that their trials had been just, she felt bad about the outcome.

"I have nightmares about those men and the fates they brought on themselves," she told reporters. "I cannot forget them…. I cannot let them go."

She visited her kidnappers in prison and campaigned against the death penalty for Walter McGee. In that, she succeeded. With the help of her father, the governor of Missouri commuted the death sentence to life.

Even so the events consumed her. She became highly nervous, whether it was because the family received crank letters and calls, as her father said, or because the plight of the kidnappers weighed on her, as Mary said. Twice she was hospitalized for stress.

On February 10, 1935 — apparently overwhelmed by worry — she ran away from home. She boarded a bus headed for Chicago. She made it as far as Normal, Illinois, where the police chief and mayor intercepted the bus on behalf of her father. He sent a plane that brought her back to Kansas City.

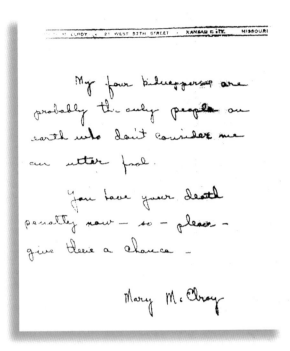

Mary McElroy's suicide note.

"I don't know why I fled from Kansas City," she told a reporter on the way back, "unless last night for a time I was completely haywire. Haywire from brooding."

In 1939, the Pendergast machine toppled. In April of that year, her father stepped down in disgrace.

That summer, Henry McElroy had a cataract removed from his eye. His health began to decline. In September he died of a heart attack. The entire time, Mary McElroy watched over him.

In late January 1940, she shot herself to death.
She left this note:
"My four kidnappers are probably the only people on earth who don't consider me an utter fool. You have your death penalty now — so — please give them a chance.
" — Mary McElroy."

An editorial in *The Kansas City Star* was sympathetic, calling her death "the pitiful end of a chain of events that began with the shock of the kidnapping, seven years ago.

"Her plight was one for infinite compassion. Poor Mary McElroy!"

The massacre

A failed attempt to spring a convict leaves five dead. The fog of battle muddles the facts, but leads to the modern FBI.

THE CRIME

- » **When:** June 1933
- » **What:** Four law enforcement officers and their prisoner were shot to death at Union Station.
- » **Where:** Kansas City, Missouri.
- » **Status:** One hoodlum, Adam Richetti, was executed. Other suspects were gunned down, yet the mystery persists about who did what to whom.

The bloody morning that brought Kansas City national infamy — June 17, 1933 — was caused by a team of hoodlums who tried to free a fellow gangster of only middling importance. The gangster was Frank Nash, a robber of trains and banks who had been serving time in Leavenworth Penitentiary but who escaped in 1930 and spent three years on the run. The law found him in Hot Springs, Arkansas, arrested him and started taking him back to the prison.

Nash, however, had underworld pals who wanted to set him loose.

Early on that warm Saturday in 1933, the men escorting Nash back to prison and the men who wanted to pry him away met and clashed in the parking lot in front of Kansas City's Union Station. As officers loaded Nash into a car for a ride back to prison, men carrying machine guns approached. In a riot of gunfire, four law-enforcement officers were shot to death. Despite all that bloodshed among Nash's guards, the rescuers failed. Nash, too, was killed, his brains blown away.

For Kansas City, the event marked yet another violent moment — this one acted out in front of the city's best-known building — in a train of local doings that kept appearing on the front page of U.S. newspapers.

For J. Edgar Hoover and his then-small federal agency, the Bureau of Investigation, the event proved a chance at fame and power.

The event earned enormous notoriety and started an intense investigation. It was labeled a "massacre." Yet almost eight decades later, important facts remained in dispute.

Frank Nash

The grisly aftermath of the Union Station shoot-out, right.

Otto Reed, chief of police of McAlester, Oklahoma

Joe Lackey, federal agent from Oklahoma City

Reed Vetterli, head of the Kansas City Bureau of Investigation office

Ray Caffrey, federal agent from Kansas City

Here are the facts that are not in dispute.

Nash, after a criminal career in Oklahoma that included convictions for murder and burglary with explosives, was sentenced to Leavenworth in 1924 for robbing a mail train in Oklahoma. In October 1930, as a prisoner who had earned the warden's trust, Nash was sent on an errand outside the prison. He used the occasion to slip away.

Three years later, the Bureau of Investigation traced Nash to Hot Springs, Arkansas, a notorious hangout for criminals on the run. Two agents from the Bureau's Oklahoma City office, Joe Lackey and Frank Smith, headed to Hot Springs to take Nash into custody. They took along the police chief of McAlester, Oklahoma, Otto Reed. Reed knew Nash and had pursued him for years. He would be helpful in the arrest.

Kansas City police detectives William J. "Red" Grooms, left, and Frank Hermanson.

On June 16, 1933, the three came upon Nash in a downtown Hot Springs cigar store. Lackey, Smith and Reed hustled Nash away at gunpoint, packed him into a car and drove him to the northwest Arkansas town of Fort Smith. That evening, they boarded a Missouri Pacific train headed north to Kansas City. The train was scheduled to arrive at 7 a.m. at Union Station, and it was arranged for the head of the Kansas City Bureau office to meet them.

Although Nash and his captors could have continued by train to Leavenworth, the connection would have required a layover of an hour or more at Union Station — too long for agents already worried about the security of their prisoner and themselves. Instead, they decided to escort Nash to the parking lot in front of the station. An agent from the Kansas City office of the Bureau, using his own car, would drive them the 35 miles to Leavenworth.

Nash's cronies, meanwhile, had learned of his capture. In a series of telephone calls across the Midwest, they hatched a plan to set Nash free. It fell into place overnight as the train carrying Nash crossed into Missouri.

The rescue effort would be led by Verne Miller, who had pulled off jobs with Frank Nash and counted him a friend. At the time Miller, who ran with various Midwestern gangs and occasionally was hired as a gunman by gangsters in the East, was living under an alias in a quiet, middle-class neighborhood in south Kansas City.

With help from other gunmen, Miller would get the drop on the law enforcement officers and force them to release Nash. If all went well, no one — neither lawmen nor gangsters — would be hurt.

As part of his preparation, Miller went to Union Station. He wanted to survey the scene and to meet with a kingpin of the Kansas City mob, John Lazia. Lazia's alliance with political boss Thomas J. Pendergast gave him control of much of the local rackets and of the Kansas City Police Department. Throughout the Kansas City underworld it was understood that Lazia expected to be apprised of big criminal enterprises. In a meeting at the Fred Harvey restaurant inside the station, Miller did just that — and may have asked for Lazia's help in the attempt.

Once everything was in place, the only thing left for the criminals or for the law was to wait for the arrival of the train carrying Nash.

It pulled into the station at 7:15 the next morning, 15 minutes late.

Miller and his crew arrived in the parking lot outside.

Waiting on the platform one level below was the

Verne Miller, friend of Nash

head of the Bureau's Kansas City office, Reed Vetterli. Accompanying him was Ray Caffrey, a new addition to the local office, who would drive Nash and his escort to Leavenworth. Alongside the agents were two Kansas City police detectives, William J. "Red" Grooms and Frank Hermanson.

Agent Lackey left the train to meet them. Having surveyed the platform to determine that things were safe, he went back aboard to help remove the prisoner.

Once off the train, Nash had seven guardians — the two Bureau agents and the police chief who captured him, the two Kansas City agents who met the train, and the two Kansas City policemen. All were armed.

Forming a "V", the seven marched the handcuffed Nash along the platform, up the stairs to the station's street level, down the wide corridor used by arriving passengers, through the cavernous lobby and out into the sunlight of that June morning.

Agent Caffrey's Chevrolet was parked outside Union Station's eastern doors, facing south along with other cars lining the curb. On the right or western side of the vehicle was a Plymouth.

Agent-in-charge Vetterli, who was unarmed, and the two Kansas City policemen, who carried .38-caliber handguns, walked to the front of the Chevrolet to keep watch. The vehicle was a two-door sedan, and entering the back seat required pushing the back of the front seat forward. One after another, agent Lackey and Chief Reed, each carrying a shotgun, got in through the passenger side. Nash began to sit between them, the customary place for prisoners, but Lackey told him to sit in front so the officers could watch him. Nash did so, sliding across the front seat behind the steering wheel to allow the passenger-side seat to be pushed forward so agent Smith could joint agent Lackey and Chief Reed in back. Smith carried a .38-caliber handgun and a .45 automatic. Now, with Nash's three captors in back and the prisoner still sitting behind the wheel, agent Caffrey, who carried a .38, shut the passenger door. He began walking around the front of the car to enter the driver's side.

At that instant, Verne Miller and his team appeared. Miller carried a machine gun lent to him hours before. At least one of his accomplices also had a machine gun.

Raising a weapon, one of the hoodlums shouted: "Put 'em up! Up, up!"

Shotguns, .38s, .45s and machine guns blazed away. Thirty seconds later, five people were dead.

First to die was the prisoner himself, a part of the back of his head blown away. Agent Caffrey, rounding the car, was struck and mortally wounded. Grooms and Hermanson, the Kansas City policemen standing in front of the car, dropped to the ground, dead. Chief Reed, sitting in the back seat, was struck and killed, too.

Agents Lackey and Smith, sitting next to Reed, ducked in time to avoid being killed. Agent Vetterli, outside the car, hit the ground, then jumped to his feet and raced toward the station doors amid the gunfire.

With Nash and the four officers dead in the parking lot and their mission botched, Miller and his colleagues entered their car and raced away.

After a couple of days at his home on Edgevale, Miller left town and began a life on the run. He was not only the object of a nationwide manhunt by the Bureau, but also the anger of his fellow gangsters for bringing so much attention and heat on the underworld.

The event earned enormous notoriety and started an intense investigation. It was labeled a "massacre." Yet almost eight decades later, important facts remained in dispute.

Crowds gathered after the shooting to view the carnage and the blasted windshields of two vehicles.

Adam Richetti

Hoover's men went after Miller, but the underworld got him first. In November 1934, Verne Miller was found dead in a drainage ditch in Detroit, savagely beaten to death by blow after blow to his head. Some mobster somewhere had ordered the job.

Since the 1930s that much of the story generally has been agreed upon by the Bureau and by various lawyers, reporters and authors.

The claims diverge, however, on two crucial matters — who killed whom that day, and who were Verne Miller's accomplices?

According to the Bureau's official account, a voice was heard shouting, "Let 'em have it!'" and a gunman who was crouched behind the radiator of another car about 15 feet away opened fire. That took the lives of the two Kansas City policemen who were standing guard. Then, shots from one or more of the gunmen killed Nash and Chief Reed inside the car. The Bureau does not mention who shot the fifth victim, agent Caffrey.

Not long after the massacre, doubts were raised in the press about that version of the deaths. In the 1990s, those doubts got a thorough examination in a book by Robert Unger, a teacher and former reporter for *The Kansas City Star* and *Times*. Unger had written a series of articles about the massacre for *The Times* in the 1980s, and as part of that effort had requested FBI documents under the Freedom of Information Act. Long after the series was published, the documents kept arriving from Washington. Unger catalogued them, studied them and came up with a book, *The Union Station Massacre: The Original Sin of J. Edgar Hoover's FBI*, first published in 1997.

In the matter of who killed whom, Unger pointed out that Nash was shot in the back of the head. The glass that shattered the windshield in front of Nash landed on the hood of the car, as if caused by a weapon fired from inside the vehicle. Unger found that agent Lackey, sitting immediately behind Nash, had mistakenly grabbed Chief Reed's short-barreled, 16-gauge shotgun as the prisoner escort left the train. The weapon was specially equipped to fire rapidly when pumped, and Lackey was unfamiliar with its working. It also contained shells loaded with ball bearings instead of buckshot.

Lackey, Unger says, probably grabbed the weapon when he saw the gunmen approach. Meaning only to pump it to prepare for firing, he unintentionally fired it, not once but twice, thus touching off the gun battle. It's likely that the blasts from the shotgun killed not only Nash in the seat in front of Lackey but also agent Caffrey, who entered the shotgun's line of fire as he rounded the front of the car. In fact, an autopsy showed Caffrey died from a wound caused by a ball bearing.

One of the Kansas City policemen in front of the car, the autopsy found, had a wound that also probably came from a shotgun. The same blasts, Unger says, struck the Plymouth parked alongside; one ball bearing landed on the floorboard.

The gunmen themselves were reported to have carried machine guns and revolvers, but not shotguns. The fourth victim, officer Grooms, was killed by two machine-gun bullets — definitely the work of Miller's crew. The fifth and final victim, Chief Reed, was hit in the head by a machine-gun bullet and also by a bullet from a .38-caliber handgun, suggesting he was shot by both gunmen and officers.

In his report to Hoover, agent Lackey said only that the shotgun he was carrying jammed and was rendered ineffective. In testimony at the only trial to take place after the massacre, he said he wasn't even sitting behind Nash, that instead he was on the right or west side of the back seat. That contradicted his own statements immediately after the massacre and also the evidence of witnesses.

As for the question about Miller's accomplices, the Bureau believed that they were the notorious Charles "Pretty Boy" Floyd, and his longtime ally, Adam Richetti. They based this on the statements of two sources. One was a minor underworld character from Kansas City

> Dear sirs:
> I— Charles Floyd want it made known that I did not — payticipate in the masacree of officers at Kansas City.
> Charles Floyd

Charles "Pretty Boy" Floyd denied any involvement in the Union Station "massacree."

whom the mob was trying to kill. A year after the massacre, perhaps in order to win favor and protection from the Bureau, he named Floyd and Richetti. Both were known to have been in Kansas City the weekend of the massacre. The other source was a girlfriend of Miller's. After a long interrogation by the Bureau, she, too, named Floyd and Richetti.

Hoover sent his agents after the two. In October 1934 in Ohio, Floyd was run to ground. He died at the hands of FBI and local police. Richetti was captured nearby and put on trial in Kansas City in the slaying of one of the policemen. Evidence against him included a fingerprint found on a beer bottle in the home on Edgevale Road where Verne Miller lived. Richetti was convicted and executed in Missouri's gas chamber in October 1938.

Unger lists various clues that bring into question whether Floyd was involved. One of the most prominent clues was that Floyd had never had dealings with Frank Nash, and thus little reason to try to spring him. Many of the same questions applied to Richetti, Floyd's sidekick. If neither actually helped Verne Miller that day, then it may never be known who did.

No matter which version is true, J. Edgar Hoover used the shocking events at Union Station to argue successfully for a bigger role for his agents in crime-solving. That brought greater power to his agency and himself. The massacre ignited the growth of the modern Federal Bureau of Investigation, the FBI.

For Kansas City, the massacre became the stuff of legend. A minor part of the tale was the long-held belief in some quarters that holes in the granite facing at the station were caused by bullets from machine guns fired during the massacre. The story, told entirely by word of mouth, was disproven in the late 1990s by tests showing that machine-gun bullets could not have penetrated the granite, but could only have grazed the surface.

Yet a central truth remained: A bloody event that rocked the country and propelled into being the modern FBI took place at Kansas City's doorstep, directly in front of its most recognizable building. The city was looking wide open, indeed.

"All hell broke loose"

The infamous Barrow gang tries to rest up at a motor court on the outskirts of town — without success.

THE CRIME

- » **When:** 1933
- » **What:** The Barrow Gang, hiding out in a motor court, shot its way out of a law enforcement assault
- » **Where:** Platte County, Missouri
- » **Status:** Bonnie Parker and Clyde Barrow escaped. They were shot to death in 1934 near Gibsland, Louisiana.

Late on a July night in 1933, a dark Ford sedan rolled to a halt at the Red Crown, a combination service station, tavern and café at the junction of U.S. 71 and a state road north of Kansas City. The business also had two guest cabins, available for $4 a night. There, in the rolling countryside of Platte County, the driver and his four passengers hoped to recover quietly from a grueling journey.

They had no such luck. They would have to shoot their way out.

They were the Barrow gang — leader Clyde Barrow, companion Bonnie Parker, brother Buck Barrow, and Buck's wife, Blanche. Along for the ride was W.D. Jones, a longtime friend of Clyde's. For months they had driven the highways and back roads of middle America, fleeing the law for past crimes and breaking more laws as they went. When they needed a car, they stole one. When they needed cash, they held up stores and service stations. When they needed a place to spend the night, they rented rooms if cash was available and camped in the country if it was not.

They trekked unendingly across the country, passing from jurisdiction to jurisdiction to elude the law. To make their trail hard to follow, the gang drove in great loops, motoring from their native Texas through Missouri and Oklahoma, Iowa and Minnesota, Arkansas and Louisiana.

The Barrows and other gangsters were much in the columns of newspapers and on the minds of Americans in the early 1930s. The availability of automatic weapons and fast automobiles helped outlaws defy poorly equipped local authorities. In Kansas City only one month before, emboldened hoodlums had ignited the Union Station massacre when they tried to free a convict. All escaped — except the convict.

The Barrow gang changed over time, but two members were constant — Bonnie Parker and Clyde Barrow. The five who rented two cabins at the Red Crown in Platte County on July 18, 1933, had been together since late March, when Buck Barrow was

Left, the Barrow gang's getaway car. Right, Bonnie Parker and Clyde Barrow, who loved to pose for snapshots.

released from a Texas prison.

At first, he and Blanche joined Clyde, Bonnie and W.D. Jones in Joplin, Missouri, where they rented an apartment. There they spent their days indoors and their nights robbing stores until the law became suspicious and tried to corral them. In April 1933, the gang shot its way out of an ambush, leaving two dead officers behind.

Afterward, the gang kidnapped an undertaker and his fiancee in Louisiana, held a Barrow family get-together near Dallas, wrecked their vehicle in the Texas panhandle and killed a town marshal in northwest Arkansas. Now the subject of national attention in the newspapers and among law enforcement, the Barrow gang continued wandering. Just before arriving at the Red Crown, they had been in Iowa, holding up three service stations.

The Red Crown, named for the brand of gasoline it originally sold, was built in 1931 to take advantage of the traffic along U.S. 71. It lay about 20 miles northwest of downtown Kansas City and five miles southeast of Platte City.

The gang member who needed rest the most was Bonnie Parker. She had been severely burned in June, when the Barrow vehicle crashed into a stream bed in the Texas panhandle. She was still recovering in late July, and the gang hoped a stay at the Red Crown would help. They checked in about 10 p.m. on July 18, a Tuesday.

But if privacy was what they wanted, they were sloppy about protecting it. On July 19, Blanche Barrow drove to a drugstore in Platte City to buy medical supplies to treat Bonnie. She wore a riding habit she had purchased in Texas, which drew the attention of the regulars at the drugstore's soda fountain.

Back at the Red Crown, these new residents stayed mostly inside their cabins, behind closed doors and windows even as temperatures reached the mid-80s on July 19. Blanche made most of the purchases and paid mostly in coin.

Red Crown employees grew suspicious and went to the sheriff of Platte County, Holt Coffey. The local highway patrol captain, William Baxter, was also

Blanche and Buck Barrow, Clyde's brother and accomplice in many of the gang's activities.

contacted. For various reasons, the officers suspected that this was the Barrow gang. They notified the Platte County prosecutor, David Clevenger, and began organizing a posse that numbered as many as 13 officers.

Knowing that the gang possessed military-grade weapons — Browning Automatic Rifles, or BARs, stolen in a raid on an armory in Oklahoma — the officers also persuaded the Jackson County sheriff's department to lend them its new armored car and some metal shields. The two cabins rented by the gang were built of brick and joined by a low, two-car garage for guests' automobiles. The cabin-garage structure was separate from the main Red Crown service station and café.

On the night of July 19, Coffey and his posse, having waited for a dance at the Red Crown to end, began moving in. Quietly, they parked a truck in a driveway to block an escape route and rolled the armored car up to the door of the garage containing the Barrows' car.

Holding a shield in front of him, Sheriff Coffey approached the cabin of Buck and Blanche Barrow, knocked and announced his presence. According to most accounts, Blanche replied loudly, using a phrase that tipped off Clyde in the other cabin. Although accounts vary widely on the events that came afterward, all were consistent with Sheriff Coffey's recollection reported years later:

"All hell broke loose."

Using their powerful Browning Automatic Rifles, the gang members opened fire from inside the cabins. Sheriff Coffey fell to the ground, wounded. Bullets slammed into

The Red Crown gas station and cafe, top, and the cabins and garage in back, where the Barrow gang tried in vain to spend a restful night, above.

Using their powerful Browning Automatic Rifles, the gang members opened fire from inside the cabins.

BATTLE WAY OUT

Midnight Police Net Fails to Hold Two Believed to Be Barrow Brothers.

THREE OFFICERS WOUNDED

Machine Gun Bullets Come From Cabin in Camp South of Platte City, Mo.

Sheriff Holt Coffey, His Son, and George Highfill of Kansas City Are Hit.

ONE FUGITIVE STUMBLES

Both Men and a Woman Companion Reach Car and Escape Amid Shots.

Two men, believed to be the Barrow brothers, notorious criminals, fought their way through a cordon of police officers at a cabin camp south of Platte City, Mo., early today, and escaped after wounding three men. They took a woman companion with them.

One of the outlaws was believed to have been wounded in the encounter. He stumbled several times as he left the cabin, and blood-soaked rags were found in the building.

After the shootout, newspaper accounts showed the Red Crown cabins, top, Sheriff Holt Coffey of Platte City and Capt. William J. Baxter of the Missouri Highway Patrol, who led the assault, above left; and shattered glass in one of the cabin doors, above right.

the walls of the main Red Crown structure, ricocheting off. The posse fired back.

The Barrows' BARs blasted through the armor of the special car, striking the driver in the leg and hitting the horn, which began to sound continuously. Fearing for their lives, the occupants of the armored car backed it away from the garage door. The posse, perhaps thinking the blaring horn was a signal, briefly stopped firing.

Buck and Blanche burst through the doorway of their cabin, heading for the Barrows' car. On the way, Buck was struck in the head by a bullet. Meanwhile, the burned Bonnie Parker made it to the vehicle, too, and the garage door was opened. With all aboard, Clyde behind the wheel and W.D. Jones on the running board firing his weapon, the Barrows rumbled out of the garage. They avoided the truck meant to block them, and sped off down the highway. In the process, bullets fired through the back window of the Barrows' vehicle shattered the glass. Slivers of glass lodged in Blanche Barrow's eye.

Neither Clyde Barrow nor W.D. Jones was injured in the battle. In the haste to leave, Bonnie Parker reopened some of her burn wounds. Blanche eventually would lose sight in her right eye. Buck Barrow's head injury was serious, but he would survive a few more days until July 23, when the gang was surrounded by a posse at an abandoned amusement park near Des Moines, Iowa.

The five outlaws saw the posse, which numbered more than 100, and began firing. Clyde, Bonnie and W.D. Jones disappeared into a nearby woods. Buck was struck again and Blanche stayed with him. The two were arrested. Buck was hospitalized but survived only six days. Blanche was returned to Platte City to face charges in the Red Crown shootout.

Ten months later, Bonnie and Clyde were ambushed on an isolated road near Gibsland, Louisiana, and died in a hail of gunfire. Thousands of people flocked to see the scene of their deaths and crowded around their bodies.

Three decades later, Hollywood revived their story with the motion picture, "Bonnie and Clyde," which won two Oscars and was nominated for others including best picture. Warren Beatty and Faye Dunaway played Clyde Barrow and Bonnie Parker as antiheroes, drawing rave reviews and also complaints that they had romanticized brutal killers.

As with most historical movies, facts were altered for the sake of the story. One of the most notable changes: Platte City, and thus the Red Crown incident, was placed in Iowa, not Missouri.

Today, the Red Crown is gone. Its site is near an exit off Interstate 29 leading to Kansas City International Airport.

On the spot

Riding home from an ice cream social, the sheriff comes upon a classic mob hit and kills two of the hit men.

THE CRIME

- **When:** 1933
- **What:** After mobsters knocked off a foe, they drove into the path of Sheriff Tom Bash, who shot two dead and arrested a third.
- **Where:** Near Armour and Troost, Kansas City, Missouri.
- **Status:** Bash was hailed as a hero but it took several years of prosecution to convict the arrested man, Charles Gargotta.

On the warm summer evening of August 11, 1933, the ladies auxiliary of the Co-Operative Club, called the Co-Operettes, gave a lawn party and ice cream social at a residence at 78th Street and Lydia Avenue, one block from what was then the southern boundary of Kansas City. More than 400 people listened to the music of Ray Stinson's six-piece orchestra — and opened their pocketbooks for charity. The event was an annual affair, a benefit for the Jackson County Parental Home for Girls, which cared for homeless, neglected and delinquent girls. The proceeds were handsome.

Several prominent Kansas Citians were members or friends of the local Co-Operative chapter. Among them was the sheriff of Jackson County, Tom Bash. He was a quiet, conservative-dressing 40-year-old from a well-to-do farming family who was a political choice of the Pendergast machine. Bash was a farmer, a horseman and an inventor, and also a skilled duck hunter.

His wife, Jennie Bash, was an active supporter of the Co-Operettes and a patron of the girls at the Parental Home. For several years she had brought young residents of the home to the annual lawn party. This year her guest was teenage Melva Taylor, whom she and the sheriff drove to the party in the sheriff's Dodge.

The party ended late, and the sheriff had agreed to escort the auto carrying the evening's proceeds, so the Bashes would give Melva a ride and let her stay overnight at their house. After midnight, the lawn party having broken up, the couple who would keep

Sheriff Tom Bash showed how a weapon was handled. Ferris Anthon, a/k/a Tony Kansas, right.

Scene of the crime: Armour Boulevard — a beautiful and heavily traveled thoroughfare in the 1930s.

By a stunning coincidence, the chief law enforcement officer of Jackson County had come upon a classic, movie-style mob hit as it happened.

the proceeds got in their car and headed north toward their home in the 3400 block of Troost Avenue. Right behind them went Sheriff Bash's Dodge, driven by deputy Lawrence Hodges and carrying the sheriff, who sat in front, and Jennie Bash and Melva Taylor, who sat in back. The Dodge was a department vehicle, so it had weapons aboard.

The first car pulled over and parked on Troost, half a block north of Armour Boulevard. The Bash auto paused while the couple in the first car carried the cash from the lawn party safely into their residence.

Security chores done, the Bash car circled the block, intending to return to Armour and use that thoroughfare

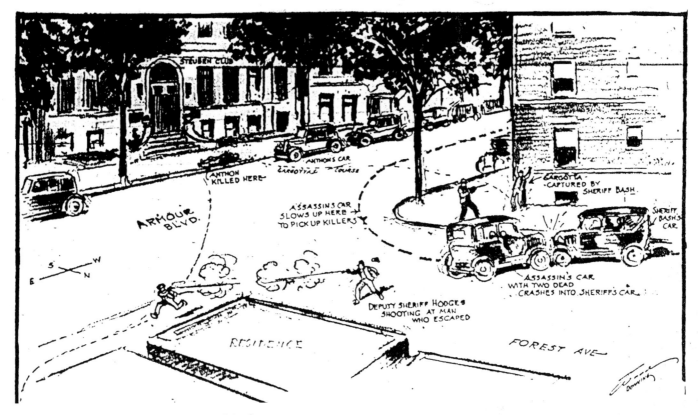

A Kansas City Star artist's conception of the fracas.

to drive to the Bash residence seven blocks east. Circling the block required a short drive north on Troost, a turn east on 34th Street, and then a turn south on Forest Street. The temperature was in the middle 70s. The time was 1:15 a.m.

Just then, the Bash party's pleasant and uneventful evening wrenched to an end.

Gunshots rang out from somewhere nearby. Then a woman screamed and still more shots exploded.

Bash gripped his deputy's arm.

Stop the car, he said, we're running into something.

The car halted on Forest about 100 feet away from its intersection with Armour. Bash reached into an overhead rack and pulled down a riot gun. The deputy drew his .38 revolver. Both men leaped out of the car and walked toward the noise.

Inside the car, Jennie Bash and Melva Taylor dropped to the floor. Mrs. Bash threw her arms around the girl and told her to be quiet and calm.

Suddenly, a Buick sedan turned from Armour north onto Forest, heading straight at the Bash auto. The passenger, his hand stretched outside the Buick, fired his pistol at Bash's Dodge.

Bash, striding down Forest, raised his shotgun to his shoulder and returned the fire. The blast from his riot gun crashed through the glass and blew off the top of the driver's head. Bash pumped a new shell into the chamber and fired again, this time at the windshield. That shot blew off the top of the passenger's head.

The gunmen's automobile, out of control, smashed into the sheriff's car. Huddled on the floor of the back seat, Jennie Bash and Melva Taylor felt the impact.

Outside, a third gunman ran at Bash, firing a revolver but missing with every shot. Bash leveled his shotgun at him. Just then, the gunman ran out of ammunition. He dropped his weapon, and instantly turned from attacker to beseecher.

"Don't shoot me!" he pleaded with Bash. "My God, man, don't shoot me!"

The sheriff, looking at what was now a defenseless

A crowd surrounded the hit men's vehicle after their bodies were removed.

man, lowered his gun, stuck its muzzle into his captive's stomach and backed him against the wall of a building. All the while, Bash kept an eye on the revolver that the gunman had dropped.

Meanwhile, a fourth man crossed Armour on foot, firing at Deputy Hodges, who fired back and followed him. The man ran between two houses, dropping his pistol along the way, and disappeared. Hodges gave up the chase and returned to Bash. He picked up the dropped revolver and handcuffed the gunman who had surrendered to Bash.

Bash returned to his car. Jennie Bash and Melva Taylor were both unharmed. Scores of residents, some in their pajamas, poured out of the apartments that overlooked the intersection and filled the scene of the crime. Traffic promptly clogged Armour Boulevard.

By a stunning coincidence, the chief law enforcement officer of Jackson County had come upon a classic, movie-style mob hit as it happened. By killing two of the hit men and arresting another, he had brought it to a crashing, cinematic conclusion — all in a matter of seconds. Because this was the heyday of machine corruption, however, years would pass in the attempt to bring the perpetrators to justice. In the end, justice would be little served.

The fireworks that summer night were touched off by swirling underworld allegiances that had left the intended victim, a minor gangster named Ferris Anthon, on the wrong side of a mob faction that was challenging the authority of John Lazia.

Ferris Anthon, who was 32 years old, had made something of a name for himself in mob circles as an arsonist and bootlegger. A considerable amount of his efforts took place in Kansas City, Kansas, and from them Anthon had won a nickname, Tony Kansas. Like many mobsters of the era, he also had interests in taverns and restaurants. Anthon was known to own a share of the Arena Buffet at 15th and Troost and the Il Travatore Café near Armour and Troost.

He fell in with the so-called East Side mob, headed by Joe Lusco and allied with a demi-boss, Casimir Welsh. The East Side group's upstart activities clearly annoyed Lazia's North Siders and Lazia was demanding payments. Also, The East Side was challenging Lazia's dominance in bootlegging.

Feeling a thorn in its side, the Lazia group decided it was time to act, and so Ferris Anthon's number was up. In the parlance of the day, Anthon had been put "on the spot." In the same parlance, the message for Anthon's allies was to "get right" with Lazia.

Like Sheriff Bash that evening, Anthon was heading home from a night on the town — a vastly different part of town. He and his 24-year-old wife, Evelyn, along with her mother, Ella Betz, and her 7-year-old brother, Elvin, had spent the evening of August 12 at wrestling matches. Then they dropped by Anthon's Arena Buffet. Like many "buffets" in that era, the proprietors made their big money selling alcohol.

Returning to their car and turning on the radio, the four took an evening ride around Kansas City. They drove as far south as 85th Street and Wornall Road. Anthon, his wife told police, "was in high spirits. He never gave any indication of being afraid of anything."

An hour after midnight, they headed for the Cavalier Apartments, where the Anthons lived. The building was on the south side of Armour Boulevard, just east of its intersection with Troost.

The nearest parking space was in front of the Steuben Club, which was next door to the Cavalier Apartments. Anthon pulled the DeSoto car in there.

His passengers got out and walked away. Anthon stayed to lock the car.

As he did so a Buick approached. A man, his face covered, walked toward him and raised a .45-caliber automatic pistol. He fired five times at Anthon. Evelyn Anthon began to scream. Then he fired three more times. Anthon dropped to the sidewalk, blood oozing from the eight wounds. His wife and mother, hauling the 7-year-old with them, ran toward the entrance of the Steuben Club. They were not hurt.

Whatever their part in the murder, the two men in the Buick sped away. Were they panicked about being seen by the many residents who ran to their apartment windows to see what the ruckus was about? At any rate, the two turned onto Forest and drove into the line of fire of Sheriff Bash.

They were identified as Sam Scola, a bootlegger and once part-owner of the Jewel Club at 18th Street and Baltimore Avenue, and Gus Fasone, operator of another nightclub. Scola was the driver and Fasone was sitting in the front seat.

The man who had run toward Bash, shooting, and who was arrested by him turned out to be Charles Gargotta, a heavy in the Kansas City underworld and an associate of John Lazia. Gargotta operated the notorious Chesterfield Club downtown, where waitresses wore only shoes and clear plastic aprons.

As for the man who escaped on foot, police suspected he was Gaetano Lococo, another ally of Lazia's. Hours before the night's violence began, Lococo had been seen sitting in a car alongside Gargotta not far from Anthon's Arena Buffet at 15th and Troost. The implication was that they were

Ferris Anthon's wife, Evelyn.

watching to see when he departed.

Gargotta gave an alibi. He claimed he had only been visiting a woman in the Cavalier Apartments and was on his way out when he stumbled upon the shooting of Anthon.

As Gargotta was being driven to a police station, a guard's elbow struck something in his coat pocket.

"Go ahead and take it," Gargotta said. It was a .45-caliber pistol, fully loaded, one he had not drawn on the sheriff.

Authorities collected five U.S. Army .45-caliber automatic pistols from the scene. Ballistics test showed several had been used in the murder of Anthon and in the shootout with the sheriff and his deputy. The weapons had been stolen from a National Guard Armory in Kansas City, Kansas, a year before.

From all this, Sheriff Bash emerged a local hero, a man who had stood toe to toe with mobsters and won. Despite his ties to the machine that controlled both City Hall and the Jackson County courthouse, Bash showed he meant to enforce the law.

The presiding judge of the Jackson County administrative court, Harry S. Truman, also a Pendergast favorite, called to say, "The county court is proud of you."

As for Mrs. Bash, who endured the massacre from inside the car, she said, "In my husband's business, there are things to cause a wife to think."

After things quieted down that night, she drove Melva to the couple's home for the rest of the night, and then after daybreak returned her to the Parental Home for Girls.

"Melva kept her courage up," Mrs. Bash said the next day. "She didn't cry out once."

As the sheriff's wife sat on her porch, talking to reporters, a telegram arrived from the host of the previous night's garden party.

"Congratulations on your brave act," it said. "We will have another garden party sometime."

The murder of Ferris Anthon had more stunning aftereffects. The outcome of Gargotta's prosecution was nearly as outrageous as the slaying itself.

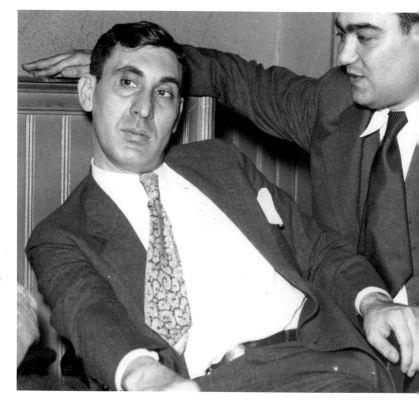

Charles Gargotta, top, with his lawyer, Jasper DeMaria; above left, in his prison mugshot. Sam Scola, above right, bootlegger, club owner and first victim of the sheriff's riot gun.

Despite ballistics evidence that the pistol used to kill Anthon was the same as the one Gargotta dropped in the street, a jury in May 1934 accepted testimony from a police detective, Leonard Claiborne, that evidence tags had been switched on pistols recovered at the scene. That left too much doubt in the jurors' minds that Gargotta had been carrying the murder weapon. Gargotta was found not guilty.

Later, federal agents prosecuted Gargotta for having stolen government property — the .45 that he had kept in his pocket. In the process, Detective Claiborne was shown to have lied about the evidence tags. The tag in question, the agents found, hadn't even been manufactured when Claiborne said he put it on the wrong pistol.

At his perjury trial, Claiborne testified that he had been promised a department promotion by a "higher up," perhaps John Lazia, for his testimony that helped free Gargotta. In July 1934 Claiborne was convicted and sent to prison for four years.

Gargotta was convicted on the firearms possession charge in June 1934, but the verdict was overturned on appeal.

As for the assault on Sheriff Bash, Gargotta was charged but his trial was delayed again and again. The Jackson County prosecutor, W.W. Graves, an ally of Pendergast, repeatedly asked for continuances — 27 in all. In late 1938 Graves asked that the charges against Gargotta be dismissed.

Outraged, state officials launched a far-reaching investigation of crime in Kansas City. That led to appointment of a grand jury that not only indicted Gargotta but also the recalcitrant

W.W. Graves, prosecutor

Sheriff Bash, right, examined the crime scene weapons as they were entered into evidence.

prosecutor, Graves. The state attorney general took over prosecution.

In June 1939, six years after Anthon's murder and one month after the Pendergast machine saw its leader sentenced to federal prison, Gargotta pleaded guilty just as his trial began for the assault on Sheriff Bash. He was sentenced to three years in prison. After serving only seven months, Gargotta was released from the penitentiary, his sentence commuted by Gov. Forrest Donnell.

Gargotta's run ended in 1950, when he was gunned down alongside Kansas City's newest boss, Charles Binaggio.

Thomas Bash died of coronary disease in 1952. By then, he had returned to farming in rural Chariton County, Missouri. *The Star* remembered him by saying that Bash "gave the public one hero in sordid times,"

Ghosts & gore

Boss rule and reform movements clash in city elections. The results: beatings and murders.

THE CRIME

» **When:** 1934

» **What:** Four people killed in violence associated with Kansas City elections.

» **Where:** Kansas City, Missouri.

» **Status:** Only one person was convicted.

Kansas City's bloodiest election day came in March 1934, when the organization of democracy seemed simply to break down.

The election was expected to be the first test of an anti-machine reform effort. In a stunning outburst of violence amid waves of "ghost voters" the Pendergast machine showed it was not going to give in to the reformers. Yet there was more going on that day — battles fought among competing factions within the machine and ending in death. Some of the internecine warfare evidently was aimed at weakening Thomas J. Pendergast and promoting other bosses. Some of it amounted to squabbling among allies.

As the election neared, most of the public attention was paid to the efforts of a group of young reformers — most from the upper-income South Side of town, many well-educated and many rather conservative. One of the group's arguments was that the Pendergast machine enriched its friends at the expense of the rest of the city.

The reformers banded together as the National Youth Movement. They boasted as many as 400 members, although they used tricks to inflate their image. For one, the movement was not "national" but local to Kansas City. For another, movement membership cards began with No. 2,301. The NYM dedicated itself to a ticket of candidates under a single banner, Citizens-Fusion. The "citizens" part hinted that it arose from the grass roots, and the "fusion" recognized that Republicans and anti-Pendergast Democrats had fused for the purpose of this election.

As the March 27 city elections neared, NYM candidates busily denounced the Pendergast machine for padding payrolls, playing favorites among contractors and using taxes and licenses to cajole cooperation from people and businesses.

Repeat voters were reputed to be one of the machine's methods of winning elections, so the NYM sent members with cameras to voter registration sites before the election. Because of that effort, nearly 90,000 names were stricken from the rolls as "ghost" voters. Despite that, the machine created yet more names and drove registration to the highest in

Star cartoonist S.J. Ray depicted "dishonest elections" at the Kansas City polls, right.

Kansas City history.

With tensions clearly growing, the reformers called on Governor Guy Park to send National Guard troops to help keep the Election-Day peace. He declined.

On Election Day, someone fired shots into Citizens-Fusion campaign headquarters. Meanwhile, the machine sent cars with no license plates but filled with supporters to patrol polling places, intimidating voters. The mob under John Lazia was known for importing toughs from Chicago to work the polls, using their fists and firearms if necessary. The Citizens-Fusion reformers arrived with cars of their own to document the thugs' work.

A reporter for *The Kansas City Star*, Justin Bowersock, gave a ride to two Citzens workers as they checked reports that machine workers were carrying people from place to place to vote over and over. At one point, Bowersock realized he was being followed by a car full of thugs; they fired at Bowersock's car, brought it to a halt and began striking the three occupants. The reporter fled, hitched a ride with a car belonging to another Citizens supporter and headed for *The Star* with the thugs' car right behind. At the McGee Street entrance to the building, he jumped out and was followed to the door. Then, the enforcers retreated.

Worse, a gang of hoodlums came to a polling place on 24th Street to beat an election judge. When a Democratic precinct captain, 56-year-old William Finley, pulled a revolver to try to defend the judge, the gang shot Finley in the chest, killing him.

Telegrams went to the governor, but still he refused to intervene.

The violence continued, the next event evidently having nothing to do with the reformers but with a dispute among a machine faction within a faction. That afternoon, a squadron of cars under the command of one of the factions drove to a grocery on Swope Parkway to get revenge against a deputy sheriff, a fellow faction member who was not deemed to be working hard enough against a certain opponent. The deputy, 35-year-old Lee Flacy, had been guarding a polling place next door. On a break, Flacy was eating a sandwich at a delicatessen next door when his assailants found and shot him. Flacy struggled to the door as the thugs fled. He fired at the fleeing cars, and their occupants fired back, mortally wounding Flacy.

Their fire also struck a 78-year-old hardware store owner, P. W. Oldham, who was closing up for the day. He died instantly.

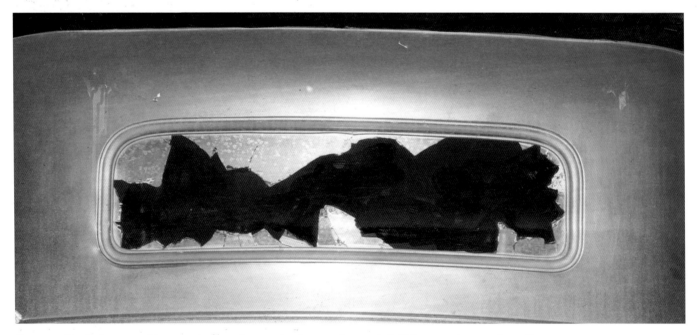

Reporter Justin Bowersock's rear window, shot out by thugs as he carried Citizen workers to the polls.

Machine thugs damaged reformer headquarters, above, and later shot and killed an uninvolved hardware store owner, P. W. Oldham, below, on Swope Parkway. Nearby a gunmen's car crashed and one occupant died, right.

As it sped away, one of the gunmen's cars failed to negotiate a high-speed turn and crashed. One of its occupants, who was found to have been shot, died in a hospital, as did Deputy Flacy.

All this occurred in the same block as a polling place.

The Election-Day results: Four dead, Bowersock and 10 others severely injured, and dozens suffering bumps and bruises from rough stuff at the polling places.

Meanwhile, almost 224,000 votes were cast of some 244,000 registered voters — an amazing turnout that probably had more to do with fakery than with civicmindedness.

When all was said and done, the young reformers and their Citizens-Fusion ticket won two council seats but the machine won seven, and also kept the mayor's position.

The election marked the end of a period in which East Side political boss Casimir Welch had tried to flex his muscle. Allied with certain gangsters against the dominance of Pendergast and John Lazia, Welch had seen

Election Day Murders

things blow up in his face.

In a wiretapped telephone conversation after the election, Pendergast put him in his place:

"Now if you want to talk sense, if you want to get along with me, I'm perfectly willing. But if you don't, there's no use….Do what I ask you to do and don't be raising hell all the time…and we'll get along."

Welch replied, "You won't have no trouble with me from now on."

In a separate conversation with Mayor Bryce Smith, also wiretapped, Welch acknowledged that there had been no need for most of the tens of thousands of padded votes; Smith's margin was 59,000. Things would have to cool down in November, Welch said.

Casimir Welch

Beset by complaints that police had done nothing to quell the violence, the Pendergast machine fired its handpicked police chief, Eugene Reppert, and replaced him with one named Otto Higgins, a former *Star* reporter.

As for all the deaths that day, only one person was convicted of murder. He was a member of the gang that assaulted deputy Flacy. He served only three years for the crime. One other man was charged but the charges were dropped by the Jackson County prosecutor's office, an agency known as friendly to Pendergast.

Toppling the Pendergast machine at the polls would take half a decade more.

Crowds gathered outside the deli where Deputy Flacy was shot and killed.

Gangland style

The Kansas City mob's dapper No. 1 is gunned down in front of his home, and the outfit gets its revenge.

THE CRIME

» **When:** 1934

» **What:** Mob boss and charmer John Lazia was slain in a hail of machine-gun fire.

» **Where:** In front of his home on East Armour Boulevard, Kansas City, Missouri.

» **Status:** Lazia's killers remain unknown.

Well-spoken, amiable, a snappy dresser — John Lazia used abundant charm to work his way to the apex of the Kansas City mob. He also used his intelligence, management skill and willingness to employ force.

Lazia was born in 1895 in Brooklyn, New York. His parents, who had come to the United States from Sicily, soon moved to Kansas City and its Little Italy, situated in what was then the north end of town. Nearby was the old City Market, and many Sicilian immigrants called the area home. As a youth, Lazia ran with a gang of holdup men and burglars. After a stint in prison, he moved up the ladder to bootlegging and gambling.

In the late 1920s, he elbowed aside the Irish-descended boss of the city's north ward, a Pendergast man, and reached an accommodation with boss Thomas J. Pendergast. The Pendergast political machine would profit from the gangs' skills at voter turnout and intimidation, and Lazia would keep a lid on mob violence. The mob would operate its rackets — gambling, bootlegging and prostitution — and city police would look the other way.

Further, the machine would take a cut of the proceeds.

In 1932, the Missouri Supreme Court struck down the decades-old system by which the police were managed by a state-appointed board. Now, so-called home rule of the police was turned over to City Hall. There, Pendergast's hand-picked city manager, Henry F. McElroy, insured that the city force would operate the way Lazia wanted.

Lazia took advantage. He visited City Hall frequently, offering his opinions about

The stylish John Lazia leaving his income tax evasion trial, above.

His clothes were fine, and his acquaintances were many. Lazia spoke with factional boss Casimir Welch as two judges looked on, smiling.

which policemen to hire and about how crime should be handled. As a result, ex-convicts began to populate the force, a former car salesman and pal of Lazia's was chosen as police director, and the law kept its hands off the mob's gambling and bootlegging businesses.

Lazia's pleasant looks and good command of English made him the perfect front man for the mob. To the public he was No. 1, an intriguing amalgam of smooth manners and potentially dark deeds. He spent a lot of time as a man-about-town, on downtown corners where he handed out dollar bills, or at his Cuban Gardens nightclub north of the Missouri River, where gambling brought in thousands of dollars each night. He had a vacation home and a speedboat on Lake Lotawana in southwest Jackson County. That was fine by the shadowy figures who shared power with him and, some believed, ran the show from the background.

Lazia was not without concerns. In 1934, for instance, he was convicted of federal income-tax evasion. Nevertheless he remained free, living the good life, while he appealed a jail term in the case.

Kansas City was shocked, then, when it awoke on July 10, 1934, and found that John Lazia had been gunned down, gangland-style.

The slaying happened about 3 a.m. that morning, as Lazia and his wife, Marie Lazia, arrived at the door of their fashionable apartment building at 300 East Armour Boulevard.

Lazia's driver, Charles Carrollo, had brought the Lazia limousine to a halt on the drive. Marie was sitting in front with Carrollo, Lazia in back. The mob leader got out and was about to open the door for his wife when two

Lazia's Lake Lotawana vacation home, above, and the East Armour Boulevard apartment building in which he and his wife made their city home. Marie Lazia, below, in February 1934.

men stepped out of the shrubbery. One had a submachine-gun, the other a shotgun. They blasted away at Lazia.

"Get Marie out of here," Lazia told Carrollo. "Step on it, Charlie."

Carrollo wheeled the limousine carrying him and Marie Lazia out of the driveway and into the street. The gunmen, who ended up firing eight times into their victim, raced to their own car, where a third man sat behind the wheel. As they sped north, their vehicle nearly collided with the fleeing Lazia limousine.

At St. Joseph's hospital, Lazia lingered for hours, receiving two blood transfusions. A steady stream of important visitors came to his room, among them Thomas J. Pendergast. Occasionally, Lazia came to consciousness, and was said to have asked, "Why me, who has only been good to people?"

At 2 p.m. that afternoon, he died of his wounds. He was only 38 years old, according to his death certificate. Lazia's slaying occasioned a massive funeral procession from his sister's home at 55th Street and Tracy Avenue, where the casket had been placed for viewing, to Holy Rosary church at Missouri Avenue and Campbell Street in the city's North Side. Riding in the long line of automobiles were Thomas J. Pendergast, City Manager McElroy and other Kansas City notables.

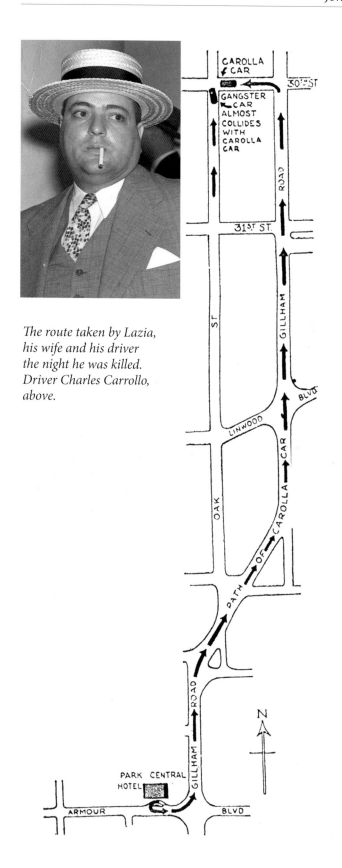

The route taken by Lazia, his wife and his driver the night he was killed. Driver Charles Carrollo, above.

> "Why me, who has only been good to people?"

Who killed John Lazia? Officially, the answer remains unknown. No one was ever charged with the crime although theories ranged from members of the Ma Barker gang to Pendergast himself. None was plausible.

Unofficially, signs pointed to two men. The slain bosses' mob associates aimed to get retribution. They focused on James Michael LaCapra, a minor mob figure with big ambitions who had suffered rebuffs from Lazia, and his associate, Jack Griffen, also known as Jack Gregory.

Twenty days after Lazia was killed, Gregory was entering his hotel when a man emerged from a car across the street, and shouted, "Hey, Jack." Gregory stopped, turned and was shot three times. He survived, only to be spirited out of General Hospital in mid-August by a police lieutenant with purported mob ties, and taken before a mob-connected justice of the peace. Charged in a 1933 bank robbery and then freed on bond, Gregory was never heard from again.

About the same time Gregory was shot, LaCapra had to use his gun to fend off attackers as he walked along Independence Boulevard. By late August, he had left town to visit relatives in tiny Argonia, Kansas, about 40 miles southwest of Wichita. On August 30, a car carrying three men pulled beside his car on a country road and a shotgun blast was fired at LaCapra. He survived, and happily was taken to jail in Anthony, Kansas. The three gunmen, who had once been associated with LaCapra, were taken to the same jail. They were charged with attempted murder, freed on bond and disappeared. Then the same mob-allied Kansas City police lieutenant appeared on the scene to take custody.

By then, news of the attempt on LaCapra's life reached agents of the Bureau of Investigation in Kansas City. On August 31 two of them headed for Wellington. LaCapra, desperate to win their allegiance and protect himself, spun them a tale — not about the slaying of Lazia but about the massacre at Union Station. He told the agents that Lazia had put Verne Miller with Charles "Pretty Boy" Floyd and Adam Richetti to free Frank Nash. After the massacre, LaCapra told the agents, Lazia had overseen efforts to spirit Floyd and Richetti out of town.

With Miller already dead, the story set the Bureau and its dogged chief, J. Edgar Hoover, on the trail of Floyd and Richetti.

In Anthony, Kansas, meanwhile, the federal agents, believing they would never see LaCapra again, won custody of him and took him to the Jackson County Jail, where he would be the prisoner of Sheriff Tom Bash and out of the control of the suspect and vindictive Kansas City police. After testifying to a grand jury, LaCapra was freed and headed east.

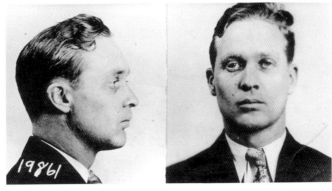

Jack Griffen, alias Jack Gregory, above, and James Michael LaCapra, below. Both men were regarded by authorities as suspects in Lazia's killing. The mob considered them the culprits.

By sending three gunmen after LaCapra, the underworld showed it believed LaCapra was responsible for the death of John Lazia. Evidently, the mob had its way. On August 21, 1935, LaCapra was found shot to death alongside a highway west of Poughkeepsie, New York.

The Kansas City mob's new front man was Charles Carrollo, who had been Lazia's driver on the fateful night. Carrollo, however, was nowhere near as polished as Lazia and would never match his former boss's legend. In 1939, as the Pendergast machine crumbled, Carrollo was sent to prison. By the time he got out, a new front man had emerged for the Kansas City mob. Charles Binaggio would be the face of the underworld through the 1940s — all that Lazia was and more. Unlike Lazia, Binaggio would try to control an entire state.

Unsolved

The gruesome murder of a young Kansas Citian remains a mystery after seven decades. So does the investigation.

THE CRIME

- **When:** 1941
- **What:** A 24-year-old woman was murdered in her bedroom, her body marked and mutilated.
- **Where:** Kansas City, Missouri.
- **Status:** Her brother was tried and acquitted. The culprit was not caught.

The crime riveted Kansas City.

For one thing, there was no apparent motive.

The victim was an attractive and well-liked 24-year-old from a well-set family who lived at home with her mother and brother. She went to church, went out with her boyfriend and had no enemies.

Or so it appeared.

In the dark, early hours of March 9, 1941, someone entered her bedroom as she slept, slit her throat from one ear to the other and bashed her head until her skull broke into pieces. The assailant waited in the room about 30 minutes, until the victim's bleeding slowed, and then sliced a circle of flesh out of her buttock and marked an initial — "G" or "S" — in blood on her leg.

A heavy hammer was left on the floor next to her bed. Just outside her window, a kitchen knife was stuck in the ground.

There was no sign of sexual assault. No money or valuables were missing from the room.

The fiendishness of the crime demanded attention. Also, there was the place — a quiet, middle-class and mostly crime-free neighborhood in what was then known as the city's South Side. Finally, there was the simple pointlessness of it: murdered and mutilated, and for what?

Nearly seven decades later, the murder of Leila Welsh in her home on Rockhill Road remains unsolved. Her killer was never brought to justice.

For tense days and weeks after her murder, Kansas Citians feared the assailant might strike again. The event was the talk of the town, and locksmiths reported a brisk business. Today, compared with the Union Station massacre or the kidnapping of Nell Donnelly, the murder of Leila Welsh is barely remembered, except among longtime Kansas Citians. In the early 1940s it held center stage.

Leila Welsh grew up on a farm near Lee's Summit, on land purchased by her grandfather, James B. Welsh. He had amassed substantial wealth from real estate dealings in Kansas City at the turn of the century.

The faces of Leila Welsh. From left: photo for a 1937 University of Kansas City beauty contest; her senior picture from the 1938 yearbook; in the final weeks of her life.

She was the third child born to George Winston Welsh and Marie Fleming Welsh. Her parents married in 1905, lived in Kansas City with Welsh's father for about five years and then headed for Oklahoma, where George Welsh practiced law. After Welsh's left side was paralyzed, he quit the law and the family returned to the Kansas City area.

The family's primary support came from proceeds of a $200,000 trust from the estate of James B. Welsh. In 21st-century dollars, the trust would have totaled nearly $3 million.

They set up housekeeping on a farm donated to them by James B. Welsh southwest of Lee's Summit, which was then a country town.

The Welshes had four children. The first died when he was 11 months old. Mary Frances was the second and then George Winston Jr. In 1916, they had their fourth child and named her Leila Adele.

The oldest surviving sibling, Mary Frances, married an Army officer about 1938 and moved out of town. At the time of Leila's death, they were at Scott Field in southern Illinois.

George Jr., who was three years Leila's senior, and Leila attended a country grade school near their house and graduated from high school in Lee's Summit. In the middle 1930s, Leila enrolled at the University of Kansas City and George Jr. found work at a real-estate company. Commuting from the city over two-lane country roads to Lee's Summit proved time-consuming, so in 1937 Marie Welsh rented an apartment just east of the Country Club Plaza. The three lived there and later in a house at 60th and Charlotte while Leila finished school; she had already earned credits toward graduation from a women's college in Ohio.

At the university she joined a sorority and frequented dances. She was an above-average student and well-liked with a sunny disposition and quick, flashing smile. In 1937, she was a finalist in a campus beauty contest.

George Jr. sometimes traveled in the same social circle, occasionally dating friends of Leila's.

Often, Marie Welsh, George and Leila visited their husband and father at the farmhouse near Lee's Summit, where he was cared for by the couple who operated the farm for him. Once a week, the farmer drove the senior Welsh to a hospital in Kansas City for treatment.

In 1938, Leila finished her degree and that fall moved to Knoxville, Illinois, where she taught school. In October 1939, she met and dated a man named Gabby Boynton. He told her he loved her and she received his pin, a step on the road to engagement, in November. Yet in June 1940 she broke off the relationship and moved back to Kansas City.

Two weeks before her death, Leila, her mother and brother drove to Illinois to visit Leila's sister and her husband at Scott Field. For some unrevealed reason, Leila and George made a side trip to Knoxville, Illinois to see Boynton, her ex-boyfriend.

Upon returning to Kansas City, Leila Welsh had done volunteer work with poor children on the West Side and in the North End, and had also spent one day a week preparing bandages at the Red Cross. In the Christmas season in 1940, she worked at Chandler Floral.

In the first week of March 1941, she applied for a job as receptionist at the photo studio at Kline's clothing store downtown. She told her prospective employer, "I want to keep occupied."

Asked about any marriage plans, which job interviewers did in those days, she replied:

"No, positively not. I have no intention of being married. I don't want to get married."

By then Marie, Leila and George Jr. were living in a house at 6109 Rockhill Road. It had three bedrooms

Leila's was on the northeast corner of the first floor. Her mother had a bedroom at the northwest corner; her brother's was upstairs.

George Jr. had briefly attended Westminster College and taken a business college course, worked at a Kansas City law office and sold furniture. By the time of Leila's death, he had switched to the real estate department of City Bank & Mortgage Co., where he sold houses.

He had plenty of money, but reportedly little ambition and ran with an easygoing crowd, frequenting nightclubs. At Dierks tavern, he wrote checks — several of them, totaling $1,500 — that mysteriously remained uncashed by the tavern owner.

George and Leila were close, so close that Leila dipped into her savings to help George make a loan of $900 to a friend of his who ran a gasoline station. She also lent George $300 for his own use.

On the eve of her death, Leila Welsh had a date for the evening with Richard Funk, who at the time was working as an accountant for Skelly Oil. She and

The home at 6109 Rockhill Road occupied by Leila, her mother and brother. Arrow marks Leila's bedroom.

Funk had met at a university-sponsored dance in 1936 at a Kansas City-area country club. They had seen each other off and on ever since; even when Leila worked and in Illinois, they got together when she came home on vacation. After her return to Kansas City the previous summer, Funk often invited her to spend weekends at his parents' home at Lake of the Forest in Wyandotte County, Kansas.

For a year or so, they had gone out several times a week.

On the night of March 8 the two planned to go to the 8:20 p.m. performance of the police circus, which was in its final day at Municipal Auditorium.

That afternoon, Leila and her mother went shopping. George, meanwhile, worked part of the day and came home, showed a house to a potential client at 5 p.m., and then he, his sister and mother gathered for supper. Afterward, George lay on the satin-covered davenport in the living room to nap. Richard Funk, Leila's date, arrived about 7 p.m., and the two left within 10 minutes.

When the circus performance was over, Leila and Funk left the auditorium and walked north. About 10:30 p.m. they stopped for Rum Collinses in the Tropic Room of the Hotel Phillips. They returned to the Welsh residence about 1 a.m., parking along Rockhill. They sat in the car for a while, talked and hugged and kissed. Then

George Welsh, Leila's brother, at his trial for her murder. Far right: Ad for the police circus that Leila attended with a date.

Funk walked her up the steps to the door of the Welsh home, where he kissed her again and said good night.

Leila's brother, still asleep on the davenport, came out of his snooze long enough to say hello. Leila knocked on her mother's door to exchange greetings. She told her she wanted to be awakened by 9 a.m. the next morning so she could go to church.

Then Leila went to her own room and closed the door.

About 3 a.m., her mother was roused from bed by the sound of two thuds. She looked into the living room and saw George there, still on the davenport, asleep, so she thought nothing more of it and went back to sleep.

The next morning, George arose about 7 a.m.. He had placed classified advertisements for several houses in *The Star* and a couple was interested in seeing them that morning.

He and his mother ate breakfast and by 9 a.m. he was gone. Minutes later, Marie Welsh went to Leila's room to awaken her daughter. She tried to open the door, and struggled to swing it wide. The door, she found, had been blocked from inside by a chair. Both windows of Leila's bedroom were up, letting in cold March air. Marie Welsh closed one and then her eyes fell on her daughter's bed, where she saw the covers pulled close around Leila's face. There appeared to be blood on it. She spoke to Leila, who did not wake up. She touched her.

Leila's body was cold.

Marie Welsh ran from the room, screaming, leaving the house to look for a neighbor.

She and the neighbor returned and went into Leila's room. Her throat, they saw, had been slit and a shirt stuffed in it. They called a doctor and shortly police were called. They arrived about 9:45 a.m.

Investigators discovered more. Leila's head had been bashed, a six-inch disc of flesh sliced from her buttock and an initial marked on her leg.

Beside the bed was a blood-soaked cloth, lying in a pool of blood. Her throat had been cut from ear to ear and back to her neck, nearly beheading her. Blood had dripped through the floor to the basement below.

The family began to look for George. Not knowing which house he would be showing at what time, Marie Welsh's brother pored through classified advertisements in *The Star* that bore George's name. At each house, he left a note for his nephew. About 11 a.m. George

> Her throat had been cut from ear to ear and back to her neck, nearly beheading her. Blood had dripped through the floor to the basement below.

found one of the notes and rushed home. When he arrived, his mother was being helped to a car by her doctor and her brother's wife, who told George to get in the car.

At Marie's brother's house, a few blocks away, George was told what happened.

Meanwhile, police, sheriff's deputies and staff from the Jackson County prosecutor's and coroner's offices swarmed the residence and the neighborhood.

On the floor of Leila's bedroom lay a heavy railroad hammer, muddy and with leaves stuck on it. There, too, were blood and muddy footprints. The drapes and curtain rod had been detached and laid across the window sill. Outside, about a foot from the window, a kitchen knife stuck halfway into the ground. Footprints were visible, though they were indistinct in the muddy soil left by melting snow. They led toward an alley behind the house.

In a backyard about 300 feet away, police found the chunk of flesh carved from Leila's body. A couple of backyards beyond, they found blood-soaked cotton gloves.

George Welsh, who had been sleeping so close to where the murder happened, was questioned closely. Police asked about his sister, about her past and her acquaintances, about him and about the case in general. George took two lie-detector tests and passed both.

Authorities also spoke with Gabby Boynton, the man whom Leila had dated when she taught school in Illinois. By then Boynton had married. He turned over to the police all the love letters Leila wrote to him.

FIEND SLAYS GIRL

Miss Leila Adele Welsh, 24, A. C. U. Graduate, Is Murdered in Bed.

HER BODY MUTILATED

Killer, Who Escapes, Entered Bedroom Window of Home, 6109 Rockhill Road.

Throat of Victim Had Been Slashed and Head Crushed With Hammer.

FOUND BY HER MOTHER

Young Woman Had Asked to Be Called for Sunday School— Intense Police Probe.

Miss Leila Adele Welsh, 24 years old, granddaughter of the late James B. Welsh, pioneer Kansas City realtor, was killed in the bedroom of her home 6109 Rockhill road, early yesterday morning in one of the most brutal murders ever recorded here. The slayer

The inquiries continued for months and became tortuously embroiled in the charged politics of the era. Pendergast domination of city government had ended in 1940 with the election of a reform mayor and council. City police, now under the control of the reformers' hand-picked chief, former FBI agent Lear Reed, conducted one investigation of the Welsh murder. But the Jackson County Sheriff's Department, headed by Sheriff Granville Richart, still was controlled by Pendergast allies. The sheriff conducted his own inquiry. Both sides tried to boost their credibility with the public — and thus their prospects in the next election — by solving the case of Leila Welsh.

In the competition, both sides continued to focus on Leila's brother. Often, one agency interviewed George and the other, on finding out, called him in right away for its own interview. Still, no charges were filed against George or anyone else.

In fall 1941, George quit his job at City Mortgage and moved to California, where he kept books for a drive-in restaurant. He wrote Funk, Leila's last boyfriend, as late as December that year, chatting about social matters in Kansas City.

On December 9, 1941, Jackson County empaneled a grand jury to look into the crime. According to *The Kansas City Times*, it contained Pendergast precinct captains. The grand jury existed for three months and in that time its work ranged far afield. Among the social strata it scoured was the Kansas City demimonde and eventually the grand jury claimed to be trying to root out what it called perversion in Kansas City. It tied that world to the world of George Welsh.

By many accounts, the grand jury went overboard in its reach and its tactics, too. Witnesses told reporters that grand jurors suggested George Welsh was a drug user and a pervert. His lawyer said the grand jurors had asked George to roll up his pants legs and sleeves so they could look for needle marks, had kept him on the stand for hours and had used physical force on him, all in an attempt to get him to confess to the murder. It was reported that copies of *Spicy Detective* and *Spicy Western* magazines, a series that typically carried cover illustrations of scantily clad women under threat from menacing-looking men, had been recovered from the Welsh home.

Jurors told witnesses that George was a marijuana user. When witnesses tried to deny it, jurors browbeat them.

One witness said that she was called "the worst liar I ever had in all my experience," by the prosecution team, headed by no less than Missouri Attorney General Roy McKittrick.

"They seemed to be in a rage, shouting and hollering," said another witness, a 23-year-old University of Kansas City graduate. "They shouted at me so even my sister seated in a hall outside could overhear."

The grand jury sent investigators to California, where they found George, packing for a Christmas holiday trip to visit his mother in Kansas City.

On December 27, he testified before the grand jury and then remained in town, moving back in with his mother in her new home at 55th and Charlotte streets. She had moved out of the Rockhill residence after the murder

On January 28, 1942, the county grand jury indicted George Welsh in his sister's murder. Sheriff's deputies arrested him at his home. But the jurors weren't done. They continued their purported moral crusade.

John T. Barker, one of George Welsh's lawyers, showed jurors how the knife found at the scene was too dull to cut anyone's throat.

On March 8, the grand jury issued a report saying it had found "a widespread, contagious and crime-breeding condition of moral degeneracy and perversion that exists in the community."

Perversion, it said, endangered America. The condition played into the hands of the country's enemies and would bring down the United States just as it had brought down ancient Greece and Rome, the jury believed.

The jury also blasted the competing police investigation of Leila's murder. It referred to Lear Reed, who by that time had moved on to another job, as a "dime store detective."

Having indicted George Welsh in January, the grand jury took the opportunity to slam him again in March. At least twice before his sister's death, it claimed, he had committed acts of indecent exposure but was never prosecuted.

An editorial in *The Kansas City Times* belittled the grand jury's strenuous and curious efforts, saying the jurors seemed to have approached their task "in the spirit of small boys talking about sin behind the barn."

Lawyers for George Welsh, fighting the indictment, protested. They won an early round.

On May 4, 1942, a circuit judge set aside the grand jury indictment against George. Among other things, the judge cited an instance in which the foreman of the grand jury "made utterly shocking accusations against the murdered girl" and also against her brother "without any reason for so doing, as far as the evidence discloses." The jury's final report, the judge said, "gratuitously charged the man they already had indicted with low and revolting conduct."

Marie Welsh with her son at the defense table in his trial.

After funeral services in Kansas City, Leila Welsh's casket was taken to Carrollton, Missouri, for burial.

The county prosecutor's office, however, was unwilling to let the matter go. It went to a cooperative justice of the peace with the charge against George Welsh, and the justice ordered Leila Welsh's brother to stand trial in the murder of his sister.

Finally, two years after the murder and all the warring investigations and political posturing, a trial for the death of Leila Welsh got under way.

Before courtrooms crowded with spectators, the prosecution brought forth a Kansas City hardware dealer who identified George as the man who bought a kitchen knife from him the day before Leila Welsh's murder. A clerk in another store said he had sold George a pair of cotton gloves. The prosecution also produced fingerprints of George's that were found on Leila's windowsill.

They offered a motive for George to kill his sister: a large life-insurance police left by Grandfather Welsh for the three grandchildren to share. With the death of one, the remaining two would split what was left.

On George's behalf, defense lawyers challenged the recollection of the witnesses who said they sold the knife and gloves, and also cast doubt on the skill and the character of fingerprint expert brought forward by the prosecution. They cast doubt that the knife found in the ground was sharp enough to cut much of anything. Also, the defense challenged the insurance accusation, saying that the elder siblings had attempted to turn down the share of their sisters' money and to take only the interest on it.

The trial continued for two weeks. The jury took five ballots to reach a verdict:

George Welsh was not guilty.

When the verdict was announced, the courtroom erupted in cheers and applause. Some of the spectators climbed onto their seats and attempted to reach the defendant, now 29, and his mother at the counsel table.

"I wasn't guilty," Welsh said, "and that was the only verdict they could reach."

His lawyer condemned a "campaign of slander" against George, saying it "failed to produce the results which its proponents circulated but could not sustain."

On May 14, George went to Fort Leavenworth for induction into the Army, and afterward sent to Camp Robinson, Arkansas. By the end of July, however, he was discharged. His mother said the Army cited physical reasons.

Over the years, perhaps because of what his lawyer had called the campaign of slander in Kansas City, George Welsh melted into obscurity. In the late 1960s, Walt Bodine, reporting in *The Town Squire*, said Welsh occasionally visited Kansas City on family business. He turned down a request for an interview.

Leila was buried in a cemetery in Carrollton, Missouri, east of Kansas City, alongside several generations of her family.

The identity of her assailant — and why that person committed such an act — remains undetermined.

Getting behind schedule

Charles Binaggio lost favor with the mob when he couldn't deliver what he promised. It cost him his life.

THE CRIME

- **When:** 1950
- **What:** Charles Binaggio and Charles Gargotta were shot to death.
- **Where:** First District Democratic Club on Truman Road in Kansas City, Missouri.
- **Status:** No one was ever arrested in the murders.

On the first Tuesday in November 1948, the attention of the country focused on the presidential race — the embattled incumbent, Harry S. Truman, against the seemingly invincible New York governor, Thomas Dewey.

Yet all politics, it has been said, is local. That was nowhere more true than at the First District Democratic Club on Truman Road just east of downtown Kansas City. On election night, folks there watched the wall-size blackboard for a race that appeared down the ballot from Truman-Dewey — the race for governor of Missouri. At the center of that crowd stood the well-dressed, calm, 30-something Charles Binaggio, leader of the First District and the front man for the mob in Kansas City.

Binaggio's man that night was Forrest Smith, a Democrat. If Smith won, he'd be expected to appoint the outfit's friends to the Kansas City Police Board. Control of the Police Board meant nothing less than control of the Kansas City Police. The department could crack down on taverns, gambling houses and prostitution — or it could look the other way. The police determined how much vice would be tolerated — and whose. That much had been demonstrated in the 1930s, when the department was run by John Lazia and his North Side colleagues.

Forrest Smith, Binaggio's favorite for Missouri governor. Facing page: Binaggio at his headquarters on election night 1948

But those days of the wide-open town were dampened when the Police Department was returned to what was characterized as state control — run by a police board named by the governor. Binaggio, however, knew that a friendly enough governor could hand control back to his friends in Kansas City. St. Louis had an appointed police board, too. If Binaggio's man handed him the right appointments, the underworld could flex its muscle, open up lucrative gambling joints and line its safes in both of Missouri's major cities.

Binaggio assured his backers this could be accomplished, and the backers —

from inside Missouri and out — invested hundreds of thousands of dollars in his work.

Election night turned out happy. Forrest Smith, Binaggio's candidate, handily beat his Republican opponent, and Binaggio, surrounded by his supporters, smiled serenely for the photographer. In January 1949, Smith was inaugurated.

Then reality set in. The new governor was not as cooperative as Binaggio had imagined. Soon after Smith entered office, word spread that the new appointments were going to take a while. Six months later, Smith gave the mob only some of what it wanted — a couple of posts on each police board. Falling short of control, the Kansas City outfit and its pals in St. Louis began to grow disappointed with Charles Binaggio.

By the end of 1949, friends noticed that his air of confidence was fading, that he seemed anxious. Binaggio had scaled the heights of the Kansas City mob, and the way down was uncomfortable.

Charles Binaggio's rise came as the dust settled from the fall of the Pendergast machine in 1940. Charles Carrollo, the front man for the Kansas City mob since the slaying of his boss, John Lazia, was sent to prison in 1939, the same year as Pendergast. Afterward the mob eased away from politics and into the area in which it felt comfortable — liquor, gambling and the rackets.

Soon the new face of the Kansas City mob was a smooth operator named Charles Binaggio, who had run

Binnagio's home on West 70th Street. Below: Cecilia Binaggio.

with Lazia and his allies in the 1930s. Binaggio, Texas born, had a record of minor police violations as a youth. Among them were an auto theft charge in Denver when he was 18 and a weapons charge there when he was 21. At some point, he joined Lazia's North Side group and advanced quickly: at 25, he was chosen to be one of the pallbearers for the fallen boss. Binaggio became a mainstay of the organization under Carrollo, and when Carrollo went to prison at the time of the Pendergast fall, Binaggio went to work to become No. 1. Although he fancied himself capable of the big time, he was rather quiet and unassuming. Gardening was a favorite hobby at his home off Ward Parkway.

In the inner circle of the local mob, he was one of several rulers and not the most important at that, but to the public he represented the Kansas City outfit.

In 1946, Binaggio's name was linked to an infamous vote-fraud investigation that was literally blown up when a safe at the Election Board was blasted and the evidence stolen.

> He wanted all of Missouri as his apple, namely to operate as he wished not only in Kansas City but also in St. Louis. That was where the governor's race in 1948 came in.

Those events hinted that Binaggio was an important man in the Kansas City underworld, but he had bigger aspirations. He wanted all of Missouri as his apple, namely to operate as he wished not only in Kansas City but also in St. Louis. That was where the governor's race in 1948 came in. For the mob, politics would be back in vogue.

Reportedly, Binaggio received hundreds of thousands of dollars from St. Louis and also from interests in Chicago and New York. That money would grease the skids in the 1948 race. The investors' return would be a Missouri where gambling could thrive unmolested by police in the two major cities.

The first step went well for Binaggio: Forrest Smith was handily elected.

As bidden, Smith named two Kansas City allies of Binaggio to the Police Board. They joined two holdover members named by the previous governor. Binaggio was on his way; he had even selected the man he wanted as the new chief of police, a policeman once disciplined for running a crap game at his station house.

But three votes were necessary to make Police Department policy. The two incumbent police commissioners, one a Republican, one a Democrat and both appointed by Forrest Smith's predecessor, refused to budge. Binaggio's allies and Binaggio himself brought pressure on them, including offers of money and telephoned threatens, but the two held their ground. The new governor made no great effort to remove them, either. Similar impediments arose with the St. Louis Police Board.

In addition, Binaggio failed to gain control of the state-appointed Kansas City Election Board and could not win passage in the General Assembly of measures that would have lined up jobs for Binaggio allies.

In sum, Kansas City and St. Louis were not opening up the way he promised, and Binaggio's big-money backers in-state and out were growing frustrated.

By the end of 1949, besides having failed to open all of Missouri to gambling, Binaggio was annoying other local crime leaders. He was questioned in the gangland-style slaying of Wolf C. Rimann, who had operated liquor distributorship and placed coin-operated games in many

Election-day party at Binaggio's political club. Binaggio is in the center, below the Truman photograph.

a tavern, sometimes intimidating the owners to do so. A federal grand jury was created in early autumn, and Binaggio's activities were studied closely along with those of others in the mob. Binaggio, it was later reported, talked openly before the grand jury. So did Binaggio's second-in-command, Charles Gargotta, the much-arrested mobster who had surrendered to Sheriff Thomas Bash the night of Ferris Anthon's murder in 1933.

All the while, Binaggio was telling his colleagues in the Kansas City outfit that, with the grand jury in session, this was no time to try to open up Kansas City again to the profitable rackets. He got busy trying to raise money to pay off the investment made in him for the 1948 election. He also began laying plans to leave town and his troubles behind.

Charles Binaggio would not get away fast enough.

On April 5, 1950, after spending part of the day at the Democratic Club on Truman Road and part tending his yard, Binaggio instructed his chauffeur to take him to

The bloody scene inside the First District Democratic Club. Charles Binaggio was shot four times as he sat in his chair, above. Charles Gargotta lay in a pool of blood, left, near the door.

the Last Chance tavern on Southwest Boulevard at the Missouri-Kansas line. There, he would meet Gargotta. At 8:15, they asked the manager to lend them his car. Telling his chauffeur to wait because they'd be back in 20 minutes, Binaggio and Gargotta headed to the Democratic Club.

Hours later, when the men had not returned, the chauffeur assumed they had found another ride and went home to bed.

Meanwhile, a cab driver who had parked his vehicle near the Binaggio headquarters walked past the club on his way to a cafe. He heard water running inside and called the police, who came expecting to deal with a plumbing matter. Instead, they found a much bloodier scene.

Just inside the door, Charles Gargotta lay on his back in a pool of blood, shot four times, evidently from close range. At the rear of the room, behind a railing, slumped in a chair, was Binaggio. He was covered in blood, also having been shot four times at close range.

It was clear to authorities that Binaggio must have been comfortable with his killer or killers because he dropped his ordinary caution enough to let them enter for a talk. Gargotta may have been similarly tricked and shot as he tried to escape. It's possible, investigators believed, that Gargotta may have set up Binaggio for assassination and then been surprised that he, too, was marked.

The double murder of mob chieftains on the home turf of the President of the United States created national news, and quickly U.S. Sen. Estes Kefauver scheduled a hearing of his crime commission in Kansas City. Among the 48 witnesses called by the commission, which included many members of the Kansas City organized crime family, was Police Board member Robert Cohn, one of the two incumbents who refused to move from their posts under Binaggio's urging. At his last meeting with Binaggio in June 1949, Cohn testified, Binaggio appeared to be disturbed by his inability to open up the town. He

Binaggio's funeral drew hundreds to the streets of Kansas City's Little Italy.

quoted Binaggio as saying, "The boys were behind in their schedule and making it hot for him."

No one was ever arrested in the murders, and various theories have been advanced as to who carried them out. Veteran Kansas City FBI agent William Ouseley, in his book, *Open City*, indicated that the Kansas City outfit handled the matter. Quoting the theory of an unnamed source in federal law enforcement, Ouseley pointed to how the killings could have been considered acts of "special merit."

Who would have wanted to orchestrate such acts? It would have to be someone with brains and abundant ambition to rise in the organization. There was, indeed, someone who had actually resisted joining the mob, a longtime petty criminal who had been enlisted only recently. Within three years, he would be head of the Kansas City outfit and remain that way for more than two decades. His name was Nick Civella.

Where is my son?

Looking for an easy payoff, two losers kidnap and murder a 6-year boy, son of a prosperous Cadillac dealer.

THE CRIME

» **When:** 1953.

» **What:** Kidnapping and murder of the 6-year-old son of auto dealer Robert Greenlease.

» **Where:** Kansas City, Missouri and Johnson County, Kansas.

» **Status:** Carl Austin Hall and Bonnie Heady were tried and convicted of murder. They were executed at the Missouri State Penitentiary in December 1953.

About 11:30 a.m. on the warm autumn morning of September 28, 1953, the telephone rang in the Mission Hills home of Robert and Virginia Greenlease. On the line was Mother Marthanna, second in charge at the French Institute of Notre Dame de Sion, an exclusive elementary school run by an order of French nuns. The Greenleases' son was enrolled there. She asked Mrs. Greenlease a simple question: How was she feeling?

From that moment on, life for the Greenlease family would never be the same.

That same morning, as he had most school mornings, Robert Greenlease dropped off the couple's 6-year-old son, Bobby, at Notre Dame de Sion, which is in midtown Kansas City. Then he headed to work at Greenlease Cadillac, the dealership he had owned since 1918 at Gillham Road and McGee Street Trafficway, a mile north of Bobby's school.

In decades of selling high-end cars through his Kansas City dealership and other Midwestern dealerships in which he was a partner, Robert Greenlease had accumulated impressive wealth and become one of Kansas City's richest men. He had not, however, had a biological child until he divorced his first wife and married Virginia Pollock, 27 years younger than Greenlease, in 1939. The couple had a daughter, Virginia Sue, in 1941, followed by Bobby in 1947, when the elder Robert Greenlease was 65 years old.

Robert and Virginia Greenlease. Right: Bobby.

Mother Marthanna quickly told Virginia Greenlease the reason for her call. Only a half-hour earlier, just before 11 a.m., a woman claiming to be Virginia Greenlease's sister had entered the school. The woman told a nun who was stationed at the school's main

Bobby Greenlease

The Greenlease home in Mission Hills, above. Bobby and his father on a visit to Europe in summer 1953, right.

door that she and Virginia Greenlease had been shopping at the Country Club Plaza nearby when her sister had fallen ill. Virginia Greenlease, she went on, had gone to a hospital and now wished that her children could come to her side. According to the woman's story, she had been dispatched to pick up Bobby.

The nun believed her. Promptly, she delivered Bobby from his classroom. The boy was wearing a Jerusalem Cross, given for exceptional school work the previous week. It was pinned with a red ribbon on his shirt. Cooperating and cheerful, Bobby took the woman's hand and the two walked out the door to a waiting taxi.

The nun told Sister Marthanna about Bobby's departure, and Sister Marthanna became curious. She called the Greenlease home. Virginia Greenlease, it turned out, was not ill, and had sent no one to pick up Bobby. She had only one, excruciating question:

Where is my son?

She called her husband, who telephoned the police, reaching Chief Bernard Brannon. Brannon accompanied Greenlease to his home. At 3 p.m., police announced the kidnapping. Probably, whoever did it would soon try to get a piece of the Greenlease fortune in return for handing over Bobby. The police alerted the Post Office to watch for letters addressed to the Greenleases. That evening, postal authorities intercepted a special-delivery letter and took it to the Greenlease home. The envelope contained the wrong address. Bobby, the letter said, was in good hands. If the Greenleases wanted him back alive, it would cost them $600,000. In 21st-century dollars, that ransom amount would have been worth about $4.8 million.

The note was signed only with the initial "M." To show that the family had received the letter, Greenlease was to drive up and down Main Street between 29th and 39th streets with a white T-shirt tied to his car aerial. At midnight, he and a friend did so.

According to his friends, there was never any doubt that Robert Greenlease would meet the ransom demand. The next morning, September 29, he and associates went to Commerce Trust Company and asked bank executive Arthur Eisenhower, a brother of U.S. President Dwight D. Eisenhower, to draw the ransom money from Greenlease accounts. The ransom letter asked for bills directly from each branch of the Federal Reserve — the better to avoid being traced — and the task would take several days.

That day, Robert Greenlease tried to talk to the press but could not utter more than a sentence. By then, the news of the kidnapping had spread around the country and soon it would be known around the world. The taking of Bobby Greenlease was the biggest kidnapping story since the abduction and killing of Charles Lindbergh's baby boy more than two decades before.

Not only did it draw sympathy for the Greenleases and concern on the part of every parent of a young child, it also drew fake ransom demands.

That night, the family received its first telephone call from "M." Stewart Johnson, a business associate, spoke with the man on the line, but learned nothing new. The next morning, September 30, a second ransom demand arrived from the Post Office. The kidnappers had realized that they had written the first letter to the wrong address. Inside the envelope this time was proof that "M" was the real kidnapper: the Jerusalem Cross that Bobby wore as he walked out of Notre Dame de Sion two days before.

That night, "M" called again, leaving word that the ransom should be ready by the next night, though he gave no clue where it should be taken.

On October 1, the Greenleases heard nothing. The family was living, an associate said, "on faith and prayer."

On the evening of October 2, a Friday. Norbert O'Neill, Greenlease's partner in a Kansas City Oldsmobile dealership, answered the phone. Again it was "M." Again the man gave little information but said he would call back later that night. Bobby, he said, was fine but

Circuitous directions for ransom drop-offs began with one midtown mailbox, above, led to another, right, and finally to a church at 40th and Harrison streets, below. That failed. The actual drop point was near a bridge in Jackson County, bottom.

homesick.

October 2 turned into Saturday, October 3. The phone rang again at the Greenlease home and O'Neill answered. It was 1:35 a.m. and now "M" was going to give directions for delivery of the money. When he spoke, he spoke deliberately, sometimes sounding confused and sometimes sounding simply drunk. Bobby, he said, was doing well and would be returned 24 hours after the ransom was received.

The ransom would not be ready. As "M" spoke, the bills were being recorded and photographed.

Nevertheless, it was decided to follow the caller's directions.

First, "M" said, go to 29th and Holmes streets, where a note would be fixed under a mailbox. In the predawn darkness of that Saturday morning, O'Neill and Johnson drove there, first failing to find the note and then seeing it taped to the bottom of the mailbox. The note said for them to go to another mailbox. There, a note directed them to leave the money at a church at 40th and Harrison. All the locations were in midtown Kansas City, none very far from the school where Bobby was abducted.

Not having the ransom money yet, Greenlease's associates left a note in an alcove at the church. It said that the money would be available soon. Three hours later, a passerby saw the note and took it straight to police. Meanwhile, "M" had called back and was told about the first failure to find the note under the mailbox. Still sounding confused, he said he would call back the next day with more instructions.

That afternoon the ransom money was delivered to the Greenlease home. It was packed in a duffel bag, as requested by "M."

In the early hours of Sunday, October 4, "M" called with new instructions, directing Greenlease's associates to 13th and Summit on Kansas City's west side. Instructions left there told them to drive north of the Missouri River. After finding what they believed, according to the vague instructions, was the spot, O'Neill and Robert Ledterman, another friend of the Greenlease family, dropped the duffel bag full of bills. But "M" called, unable to find the ransom. At mid-morning, "M" acknowledged that it was his fault and promised to call again with a third drop site.

The body of Bobby Greenlease was buried in Bonnie Heady's garden in St. Joseph, above.

This time, Ledterman told him, make the instructions simpler. Meanwhile, the bag was retrieved.

All along, the Greenleases and their associates were told, Bobby was fine. That night, a confused "M" called again, giving muddled instructions to go to a hotel and wait for a call at a pay phone. Eventually, Greenleases' associates figured out which hotel he meant: the Berkshire, at yet another midtown location. The pay phone rang and "M" directed the Greenlease friends to take the money to a deserted spot in eastern Jackson County next to a bridge. That was the final call from "M."

O'Neill and Ledterman found the spot, where Lee's Summit Road crossed the Little Blue River by a wooden bridge. There they dropped the duffel bag containing $600,000.

Not long afterward "M" called to report that he had the money. Bobby, who was fine, would be returned in 24 hours.

The kidnapper told Greenlease's associates that directions would arrive at the Western Union telegraph office in Pittsburg, Kansas, about 100 miles south of Kansas City. A tired O'Neill and Ledterman drove there, arriving Monday morning, October 5. They stayed two days, checking at Western Union and hearing nothing, before returning to Kansas City.

On Wednesday morning, October 7, the nightmarish wait ended. Word arrived from St. Louis that a man and woman in police custody there had confessed to kidnapping Bobby Greenlease.

Also, the reports said, Bobby was dead.

That same morning, authorities had dug up a shallow grave in a flower bed at a house in St. Joseph, Missouri. There they found Bobby's body.

At the Greenlease home, Ledterman confirmed the news. The boy's funeral would take place two days later at St. Agnes church in Roeland Park. He would be buried in a family crypt at Forest Hills cemetery.

In retrospect, it was no surprise that the kidnappers were captured. The surprise was that they had remained on the loose so long. Through the entire episode, Carl Austin Hall — that was the real name of "M" — and Bonnie Brown Heady stayed drunk or drugged almost constantly.

When they met at a hotel bar in St. Joseph in late May 1953, he was a 33-year-old smalltime crook on parole from prison. She was 40, plying her trade as a prostitute out of her home.

Both had been born into comfortable circumstances. Hall was the descendant of a pioneer family in eastern Kansas. His father, a successful lawyer in Pleasanton, Kansas, had created a sizable estate, and in 1946 Hall inherited an amount worth more than $1 million in 21st century dollars. He quickly spent the inheritance on a residence just off Ward Parkway, on bad business ventures, on booze and on gambling. By the early 1950s he was reduced to robbing taxicabs.

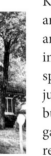

Heady owned a 316-acre farm near Maryville in northwest Missouri. She inherited it from her father. She had been married for 20 years to a successful livestock merchant, and become an accomplished horsewoman. After a mental breakdown and after divorcing her husband in late 1952, she turned to prostitution and heavy drinking.

Early photos of Carl Hall and Bonnie Heady. Left: The comfortable Hall family home in Pleasanton, Kansas.

Hall was looking forward to a payoff that would set them up for life, he told Heady, and a kidnapping seemed the perfect means to that end. The Greenlease family had the money, he knew. And they had a child small enough to be easily carried away and also young enough to trust

> Hall was looking forward to a payoff that would set them up for life, he told Heady, and a kidnapping seemed the perfect means to that end.

adults. In early September, Hall and Heady drove past the Greenlease home in Mission Hills, and then followed the elder Greenlease as he dropped his son off at Notre Dame de Sion. Now they had the timing. What would they do with their victim? He would have to be killed, Hall told Heady, to keep him from identifying them.

So on the morning of the kidnapping they left Heady's St. Joseph home and headed south, stopping at an early-opening bar along the way, then watching Robert Greenlease drop his son off at school, and finally driving to the Katz drugstore at Westport Road and Main Street. After Hall handed Heady breath mints to remove the scent of alcohol, she walked two blocks north to Toedman cab. From there a taxi took her to the school, where she spun her story to the credulous nun at the door. The taxi returned her and Bobby to the drugstore parking lot. Hall and Heady drove away with their victim. Bobby, they recalled, happily told them about his family, his pets and the two Cadillacs they drove.

The kidnap vehicle, Heady's Plymouth station wagon, crossed the state line from Missouri into Kansas and headed south to a farm field off a road that today is busy 95th Street. Unable to watch the bloodshed that was about to happen, Heady walked in the field with her dog. Inside the car, Hall grabbed a piece of clothesline and wrapped it around Bobby's neck. It proved too short for him to strangle his victim. Bobby put up a fierce struggle. Hall pulled out his .38-caliber revolver, held Bobby down and fired. He missed. He fired again, and the bullet went through Bobby's brain. He wrapped the child in a piece of blue plastic. Cleaning up the car as well as he could, he drove Heady and his victim to her home in St. Joseph, where he had already dug Bobby's grave in a flower bed.

For six days, Hall and Heady drank, mailed ransom letters and placed often-incoherent calls to the Greenlease home. They spent time in St. Joseph and in various spots in Kansas City.

On Sunday morning, having retrieved the duffel bag of money from the rural dropoff point, they headed east along U.S. 40 through Missouri, winding up in St. Louis. Hall and Heady hit bar after bar. Using some of the ransom money, they rented an apartment near Tower Grove Park where Heady stayed, too drunk to continue. Hall found a taxicab driver who provided him a prostitute. The driver, realizing how much money

Bonnie Heady and Bobby Greenlease got out of a cab at the Katz drugstore, Westport Road and Main Street, and walked to the spot marked by two x-marks. They entered a car driven by Carl Austin Hall and headed for rural Johnson County.

Kansas City Crime Central

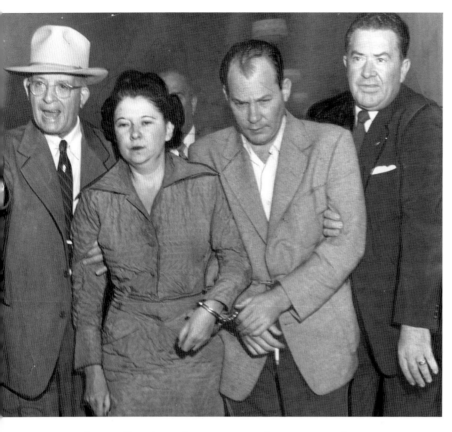

When Hall and Heady were captured in St. Louis, deputy U.S. marshals led them to jail. Below: After the kidnappers were sentenced to death in a Kansas City court, they were escorted out the back past a score of onlookers.

Hall was throwing around, notified a friend. Soon a St. Louis policeman, known to be corrupt, and another detective arrested Hall at the Coral Court, a notorious motel along U.S. 66, on Tuesday night, October 7.

Hall confessed to kidnapping Bobby Greenlease and led the police to Heady. At first, the two denied killing him, blaming that on an associate who they said had left Bobby's body for them to bury.

Eventually, they admitted the murder, too. Hall and Heady were returned to Kansas City, where they were tried, convicted and sentenced to death in the Missouri gas chamber in Jefferson City. There, just after midnight December 18, 1953, barely two months after their capture, the two were executed.

When authorities counted the ransom money taken with Hall, they found less than $300,000 of the original $600,000. Where the rest went remains a mystery a half-century later, although officials and students of the kidnapping believe it went to a St. Louis mobster who had it laundered through associates in Chicago. A few of the bills eventually turned up in the upper Midwest.

Robert Greenlease, who with his wife donated money and land to Rockhurst College and high school in Kansas City, died in 1969. Virginia Greenlease died in 2001, leaving $1 million each to the college and high school in the names of her husband and son.

Remorseless

The brightest boy in Wolcott, Kansas, murders his father, mother and sister — and remains so very calm.

THE CRIME

- » **When:** 1958
- » **What:** College freshman killed his mother, father and sister.
- » **Where:** Wolcott, Kansas
- » **Status:** Lowell Lee Andrews was found guilty of murder and executed November 30, 1962.

The nonchalance of Lowell Lee Andrews struck everyone who met him. His father, his mother and his sister had been murdered in the living room of their home, yet he seemed not to care.

First to notice the 18-year-old's air were the Wyandotte County sheriff's deputies called to the Andrews home on the weekend after Thanksgiving 1958. They found Lowell Lee Andrews sitting on a glider on the porch, playing with the family's pet Pekingese dog.

"What's the trouble?" one deputy asked. The boy pointed to the kitchen door and rubbed the dog's back, the deputy recalled, "as though the matter was something trivial."

The four deputies had trouble opening the door. Once inside, they found why: Pressed against the door was one leg of Andrews' father, William Lowell Andrews. The 50-year-old aircraft mechanic was dead, shot 17 times in the face and the heart.

Looking into the living room, they found Andrews' mother, Opal Andrews, 40, lying on her back, shot four times. Evidently she had been sitting in an easy chair when she was slain. Nearby, face down, was the body of her daughter, Jennie Marie Andrews, 20, shot three times.

The brutal crime was particularly remarkable for having happened in tiny Wolcott, where the Andrewses and about 150 other people lived. The community lay in the lowlands near the Missouri River in rural Wyandotte County.

Lowell Lee Andrews, who like to be called Lee, told the deputies that he thought burglars had killed his three family members. Dubious about that story, the deputies escorted the teenager to a sheriff's vehicle and drove him 15 miles to the County Jail in Kansas City, Kansas.

Along the way, Lee showed emotion only once, when he was told that the authorities would take his fingerprints and give him a lie-detector test.

He mentioned that his family regularly attended church in Kansas City, Kansas, so deputies called the minister. By then it was about 2 o'clock on a Saturday morning, but the minister came right away. The Rev. V. C. Dameron of Grandview Baptist Church at Grandview Boulevard and North 24th Street had been a lifelong friend of Lee's father since the two grew up near Moberly in rural north Missouri. William Lee Andrews was a deacon at the church.

Dameron and Lee were left alone in a lieutenant's office.

After some small talk about Lee's classes at the University of Kansas, where he was a sophomore, the minister asked:

"You want to help find who did this, don't you? You didn't do this, did you?"

Calmly, Andrews replied:

"I did it."

Then, to the minister and later to a prosecutor, he told the story. Never did he show emotion.

About 7 p.m. on November 28, the Friday night after Thanksgiving, the Andrews family was finished with dinner. Lee was picking walnuts in the kitchen, his mother was washing dishes and his father was reading a newspaper.

Leaving the walnuts, Lee went to his bedroom. There he loaded a .22 automatic rifle and a German Luger revolver. He opened a window, pushed out the screen, pulled open a dresser drawer and disturbed things inside. The idea was to make it look as if burglars had ransacked the place.

By this time, his mother, father and sister, a 20-year-old senior home on holiday break from Oklahoma Baptist University, had gone to the living room, where they watched television.

With the Luger in his belt, Lee went to a center hallway with entrances to the living room, raised the rifle and began shooting at his next of kin. His mother and sister fell to the floor. His father rose and ran to the kitchen, where Lee followed him, still shooting. When he had emptied the rifle, he began shooting with the Luger. He kept firing, he said, until no one moved.

He put on a parka against the cold, got into his father's Chevrolet and headed for Lawrence. At the north end of the Massachusetts Street bridge over the Kansas River, he dumped the two firearms into the water, then returned to the car and drove to a house on Tennessee Street where he roomed. He and a fellow roomer talked about the weather. Lee took his typewriter, which he needed for a weekend English assignment, put it in his car and drove to the Granada Theater in downtown Lawrence, where he watched a late showing of "Mardi

The Andrews home in Wolcott in Wyandotte County. Jennie Marie Andrews, Lowell Lee's sister, below.

Gras." The movie starred Pat Boone and featured musical numbers based on the annual New Orleans festival. Lee told the deputies he liked the show.

Then, he drove back home to Wolcott. About 12:45 a.m. November 29, he called the telephone operator, telling her to notify the sheriff's department about a shooting.

As his story ended, deputies asked Andrews why he did it.

"I don't know," he replied, and shrugged his shoulders.

Did he feel remorse?

"I don't feel anything — period," he said.

As unlikely as Wolcott seemed for such a massacre, so was Lee Andrews unlikely as a perpetrator. The youth — who stood 6 feet 2 inches tall, weighed 260 pounds and wore glasses to combat astigmatism — was known as a "brain." In high school, he had scored high on national merit examinations and, like his sister, was an honor student.

At KU he majored in zoology and played bassoon in the university band. People who knew him described him as mild-mannered, but with a touch of know-it-all in his personality. They said he had few friends. Some called him a nice boy.

His father had sold crops to pay for Lee's first year in college, authorities found. Now, after a poor crop and after his father's paychecks stopped because of a machinists' strike at TWA, where he worked, Lee was worrying about finances.

Prosecutors settled on Lee's motive: He was hoping to inherit the 250-acre farm his father owned and about $50,000 worth of other property. He was aware, they said, of suggestions that an industrial park might be built near Wolcott, and that he would make substantial profits from selling that land.

The teenager's own lawyers argued that he had gone temporarily insane.

He was tried for the murders in late 1959. A psychiatrist from the Menninger Clinic in Topeka testified that Andrews suffered schizophrenia, but two other psychiatrists said they thought he could tell right from wrong.

The jury took three hours and 40 minutes to find him guilty and sentence him to death by hanging at the Kansas State Penitentiary.

In late January 1960, he was moved to a cell on death row at the penitentiary in Lansing. Next door were Dick Hickock and Perry Smith, the murderers of the Clutter family in Holcomb, Kansas. Hickock and Smith often were visited by author Truman Capote, who was preparing a book about them. Capote also took an interest in Andrews' story, and described his case in his book, *In Cold Blood*.

> "The people who crossed his path, well, to his way of thinking, the best thing to do with them was just to put them in their graves."

When his appeals were exhausted he was hanged on November 30, 1962. An uncle and aunt were the last people to see Andrews before his execution. His remorseless attitude, they said, had never changed.

Four years after Lowell Lee Andrews was hanged, Capote acknowledged in an interview that Andrews' case might have been an equally good topic for *In Cold Blood* as that of Hickock and Smith.

"A nonfiction novel would have been written about any of the other prisoners in Death Row," Capote told his interviewer, "especially Lee Andrews.

"Andrews was the most subtly crazy person you can imagine — I mean there was just one thing wrong with him. He was the most rational, calm, bright young boy you'd ever want to meet. I mean really bright — which is what made him a truly awesome kind of person.

"His one flaw," Capote said, "was it didn't bother him at all to kill. Which is quite a trait. The people who crossed his path, well, to his way of thinking, the best thing to do with them was just to put them in their graves."

Cold blood

A local crook and his pal go looking for a big score. Their plan ends in bloody failure — and literary fame.

THE CRIME

- » **When:** 1959
- » **What:** Four members of a prosperous farming family died in a botched robbery conceived by a Kansas City-area man.
- » **Where:** Holcomb, Kansas.
- » **Status:** Dick Hickock, with his accomplice Perry Smith, were found guilty of murder and executed April 14, 1965.

Just before Thanksgiving 1959, in a tiny community in southwest Kansas, four members of the Herbert W. Clutter family were murdered in a bloody, seemingly mindless rampage. The Clutters — farmer Herbert, his wife, Bonnie, and high-school students Kenyon and Nancy — were known around Finney County as upright, honorable and well-to-do.

Why would anyone kill them? Was it robbery? If so, whoever killed the Clutters took only $40 and a portable radio.

How could such a thing happen in Holcomb, Kansas, amid the mostly good folks of the sparsely settled High Plains?

In those parts, the murders stirred fear that the perpetrators lived right there in wheat and cattle country. Rumors pointed to this or that local person, someone now living nearby and bearing a terrible secret.

In New York City, author Truman Capote read about the murders, wondered at the horror acted out in far-off rural Kansas, and found the seed for a novel.

In the end, when rumors were swept aside and Capote's work was done, the world would learn that the Clutter murders were the brainchild not of someone from the High Plains, but of one Richard Eugene Hickock, who had spent his life in the metropolitan orbit of Kansas City.

In and around Kansas City, Hickock learned the arts of petty crime. Up the road in the state prison, Hickock learned about the possibility of a big payoff sitting 400 miles away on the windswept plains.

Hickock was born in Kansas City, Kansas, in 1931, and lived there until he entered high school. His father, Walter Hickock, an auto mechanic and bodyworker, moved from job to job through the Depression years, working for a while at Marmon Service on North 18th Street, and then at the Clover Leaf garage on North 13th, at a filling station on State Avenue, and at Perry Motor Co. and then Markl Buick on Minnesota Avenue.

Meanwhile, Walter Hickock moved his family from place to place in the northern part of the city. Many of Dick Hickock's early years were spent in the Quindaro neighborhood. At one point, Hickock attended Sunday School at a Quindaro church.

Dick Hickock, in his 1949 high school senior picture, left, and in prison.

By Dick Hickock's own account, his father treated him and his brother, six years younger, strictly. The boys were often kept at home and away from playmates and made to do chores. His parents rarely argued, he recalled, and he was adequately provided for, despite the family's being "semi-poor" in those days of the Great Depression.

In 1946, when Hickock was about to enter high school, his parents left the city and moved to a 44-acre farm about 1½ miles southeast of Edgerton in southern Johnson County. Their new home had only four rooms, no running water and no telephone. They did little farming. Walter Hickock hired on for various jobs, among them working at auto shops and driving a school bus.

Around the Hickocks' new town, word was that the family had moved to try to separate young Dick from corrupting influences. However, the teenager soon showed he had brought some of those influences with him. At Edgerton's new pool hall, he quickly showed the locals his mastery with a cue. Occasionally, he did odd jobs for area farmers who discovered afterward that their wallets were missing. One day, he stole the school principal's pocketbook.

Hickock's parents, according to some, invariably defended him. One person quoted in a retrospective published in 1984 in the *Daily News of Johnson County* said the smooth-talking youth "had his family conned."

"When he took his mother into town," a neighbor recalled, "he always opened the car door for her and was a polite gentleman."

> He remained obsessed ... with the idea of a big score that would set him up in luxury. Hickock decided he would go to southwest Kansas, rob the Clutter safe and then disappear.

Edgerton Rural High School, where Hickock graduated in 1949.

Ray Braun, a service station operator who served as a sheriff's deputy in Edgerton and later mayor, recalled that no one was willing to prosecute the teenage Hickock for his petty crimes. A warning, it was hoped, would do the job.

One man who knew Hickock in his teen years told the newspaper that he had "the kind of reputation that you didn't really want to run around with him and become known as an associate."

Hickock laughed a lot, said another man who knew him, but usually he was laughing *at* someone:

"He had a mean streak. He was always pulling cruel pranks and then standing back and laughing at his victims."

Hickock attended Edgerton Rural High School. Becoming a good athlete as he grew, the 5-foot 10-inch Hickock played on the football and basketball teams. In a basketball game against nearby Gardner in early 1946, he was Edgerton's leading scorer, accumulating 15 points. He served on the Student Council one year, on the school newspaper and on the yearbook. He showed above-average intelligence, but it translated into only average grades.

Hickock graduated in May 1949, one of six in his class; the *Edgertonian* yearbook reported that he was class vice-president.

He also began to get into serious trouble. The

Kansas City Crime Central

same year he graduated, Hickock's name was associated with thefts from a service station, the grain elevator and a drugstore in Edgerton. Still, he was not prosecuted.

His first job out of high school in 1949 was with the Santa Fe Railway in Kansas City, Kansas. By winter, he was laid off.

In 1950 Hickock went to work for a body shop operated by Roark Motor Co. in Gardner, Kansas, about six miles northeast of Edgerton. A few months into the job, he took a company car out for a spin; one version of the story says he was sent to pick up auto parts in Olathe. Returning to Gardner in the rain, Hickock tried to pass a bus on U.S. 56, but lost control on the slick highway. The car began to roll; Hickock was thrown out and into a drainage ditch. He suffered a concussion, and the wreck also cost him some of his looks; a head injury left one side of his face out of alignment with the other.

Unemployed while he recovered, Hickock met a 16-year-old girl, Carol Bryan, who was a minister's daughter. He got her pregnant and in July 1950, over the objections of her father, married her. In Kansas City, Kansas, he and Carol eventually would have three sons.

For a while, Hickock worked 12-hour days as an attendant at a gasoline station. Then he landed a mechanic's position at Perry Pontiac, a dealership at 12th Street and Minnesota Avenue in Kansas City, Kansas. He and his wife, who worked at a dime store, needed all the money they could muster. For one thing, there were the children. For another, they habitually spent beyond their means. Hickock turned to gambling and also learned the technique of persuading salespeople to take his checks, which often turned out to be bad.

In the middle 1950s, Hickock quit working at Perry Pontiac and went into the auto repair business for himself, renting a garage. He met his landlord's daughter-in-law, began seeing her and got her pregnant. Eventually, Hickock's first wife, Carol, divorced him and he married

Hickock's prison record

his latest love. He went to work as an auto body repair man at Markl Buick, working for a while side-by-side with his father.

"I started drinking," he recalled, "and was drunk for almost a month. I neglected my business, spent more money than I earned, wrote bad checks, and in the end became a thief."

That career would lead him to the Clutter farm. First, however, Hickock stole a hunting rifle and other firearms from a farmer who lived not far from his parents' home. Caught and convicted, Hickock was sentenced in March 1958 to a term in the state penitentiary at Lansing. His second wife divorced him.

While in prison, Hickock briefly shared a cell with

The Clutter family, left to right, Nancy, Bonnie, Kenyon and Herbert.

Perry Smith, who had spent his life wandering from place to place in the United States and various parts of the world. Smith was serving time for a bank robbery in northwest Kansas.

In early July 1959, Smith was paroled and Hickock got a new cellmate. Floyd Wells was an itinerant who regaled Hickock with tales of a fabulously wealthy farmer for whom Wells once worked — Herbert W. Clutter of Holcomb, Kansas. Wells told Hickock about a safe inside Herbert Clutter's office. Hickock's imagination embroidered the tale. A safe, he reasoned, would contain cash for Clutter to pay his help.

With thoughts of Perry Smith and of the Clutter safe fresh in his mind, Hickock was paroled in middle August 1959. He moved back in with his parents at the farm near Edgerton, and went to work at a body shop in Olathe.

He remained obsessed, however, with the idea of a big score that would set him up in luxury. Hickock decided he would travel to southwest Kansas, rob the Clutter safe and then disappear. For that he would need an accomplice, so he began writing letters to Perry Smith, whom he found in Idaho. Smith agreed to return to Kansas. That was an uneasy proposition because his parole on the bank-robbery sentence required him to stay away from the state.

Smith arrived by bus on Thursday, November 12, 1959; Hickock met him at the depot, took him home and introduced him to his parents. Eunice Hickock, Richard's mother, quickly surmised that Smith would be trouble and refused to let him stay at the house. Instead, he roomed at the Hotel Olathe, which stood down the street from the Johnson County Courthouse. At the hotel, Hickock described his plan. He sketched a diagram of the Clutter home as described by Floyd Wells, and told Smith that they would leave Holcomb with lots of cash — but no living witnesses.

The deed, Hickock said, would be "a cinch."

At home, Hickock told his parents that he and Smith planned a weekend trip to Fort Scott, Kansas. Smith's sister lived there, Hickock said, and she was holding $1,500 for Smith. In truth, Perry Smith had no idea where his sister lived.

The two spent Friday evening at the home of the owner of the garage where Hickock worked. On Saturday morning, Hickock drove to Olathe, picked up Smith outside a café and drove his black 1949 Chevrolet to the garage to get it ready for a grueling overnight trip. The two cleaned up in the bathroom, got in the car and before noon on Saturday were headed west on two-lane highways across Kansas. They took along a hunting knife and a 12-gauge shotgun.

Half a day and 400 miles later, under a bright midnight moon, Hickock and Smith rolled up to the Clutter home, their headlights turned off. What happened next was recounted in detail in Capote's book and in several movies:

The two entered the Clutter house through an unlocked side door. It led directly to Herbert Clutter's office, where there was supposed to be the safe containing thousands of dollars. They found no safe. They did find Herbert Clutter in his bedroom, and forced him to lead them to his wife. Both denied that there was any safe. Hickock was convinced one existed, just as Floyd Wells had told him in prison. He decided to tie them up and search the home. They awakened Nancy Clutter and Kenyon, too, and eventually bound them all.

Perry Smith while in prison.

In the end, Smith cut Herbert Clutter's throat, and then finished the job with a blast from the 12-gauge shotgun. One by one, the murderers shot each of the Clutters to death, and then gathered the spent shells.

Soon the two were back in the Chevrolet, rolling east through the predawn hours back toward Johnson County.

In Holcomb the next morning, a Sunday, a friend of Nancy Clutter's arrived, as she did every Sunday. Because the friend's parents were not churchgoers, the Clutters gave her a ride into Garden City for church. When the family did not answer the door, she called on a schoolteacher who lived down the road. Together, they found Nancy's body in her bedroom. The bed and wall nearby were soaked with blood. A call to the sheriff brought a search of the house, and the discovery of the shocking, bloody results of Hickock's and Smith's work.

Within hours, word spread through Holcomb and on to Garden City.

About the same time, a fatigued Hickock was dropping Smith off at the Hotel Olathe and heading to his parents' home near Edgerton for Sunday dinner. Walter Hickock recalled his son's eating voraciously. Then he, Richard and Richard's brother sat down to watch a game on TV; two professional football games were broadcast that afternoon by Kansas City stations. Walter Hickock recalled his surprise that Richard, an avid sports fan, promptly fell asleep and stayed asleep for hours. Otherwise, Walter remembered, Richard acted no different from normal.

For the next week, Hickock and Smith stayed in the same place, leaving only to lunch at the Eagle Buffet on Main Street near downtown Kansas City, and finally going to downtown Kansas City, Kansas. Along Minnesota Avenue they went from store to store, Richard writing check after check for money he did not have — an easy task in the days before personalized, encoded checks. In one store, they bought a ring, which they promptly pawned for about $150. In another, they picked up a wristwatch. In Elko Camera, they bought a movie camera. At Sheperd's they bought clothing, and walked up to State Avenue, to Shopper's Paradise, where they bought more.

They wrote at least seven bad checks, typically for amounts larger the price of the items. They ended the day with cash and plenty of items to pawn.

In New York, Truman Capote was already preparing to use the events of the murder and the real characters surrounding it as the basis for his "non-fiction novel." The Clutter murders and the mystery surrounding them seemed to fit the bill. He headed for Kansas.

On Saturday night, November 21, one week after invading the Clutter home, Hickock and Smith left the Kansas City area and headed for Mexico. When midnight passed, they were out of Kansas.

That began a six-week journey into, around and back out of Mexico, then west, then back to the middle west and at one point in December back to Kansas City. The two were out of money and home territory was where

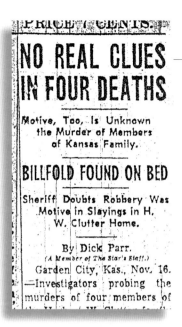

Hickock felt at ease with his bad-check routine — the Kansas City area was his "bank." Arriving in a car they stole in Iowa, they cleaned themselves in a lavatory at Kansas City Municipal airport and washed their clothes at a coin-operated laundry. While in town, Hickock returned to one of the auto companies that had once employed him and lifted a Kansas plate from a damaged car, using it to replace the Iowa plate on their stolen vehicle. This time, Hickock cashed bad checks at places where friends worked, among them his favorite lunch hangout, the Eagle Buffet.

By then, Floyd Wells had told authorities about his prison conversation with Hickock. He hoped to cash in on a reward offered by the *Hutchinson News* for the Clutter killers. As a result, Hickock and Smith were named as suspects in the Clutter murders. During their brief stay in Kansas City to raise cash, authorities got wind of their presence. Despite a broadcast pickup, the two made it out of town.

They headed to Florida, and then across the south and southwest to Las Vegas. There, on December 30, 1959, the two were arrested. Soon Hickock confessed. Then so did Smith.

A jury in Garden City, Kansas, convicted them in March 1960 and sentenced the two to death by hanging. For five years Hickock and Smith sat on death row at the Kansas State Penitentiary in Lansing, exhausting their appeals. Just after midnight April 14, 1965, they were marched to a gallows and hanged.

Hickock's father died of cancer not long after the trial. His mother, Eunice Hickock, moved first to Wyandotte County and then to Johnson County. The home near Edgerton has since been razed. Hickock's first wife remarried and brought up the sons in Johnson County, but under another name.

In 1967, six years after the murders, Truman

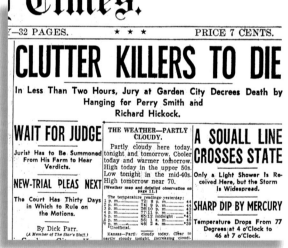

Capote published *In Cold Blood*, a massively successful book. It was turned into a movie that used Holcomb as the central setting for a story about the workings of the criminal mind — a mind shaped in the environs of Kansas City.

During the filming of "In Cold Blood", the story of the Clutter murders, Scott Wilson, the actor playing Dick Hickock, chatted with director Richard Brooks, center, in the yard of the former Hickock home in Edgerton.

La Pistolera

Stand in Sharon Kinne's way — for love or money, in the U.S. or Mexico — and you might wind up dead.

THE CRIME

- » **When:** 1960s
- » **What:** A woman was linked to the shooting deaths of her husband and a boyfriend's wife in Independence, and an acquaintance south of the border.
- » **Where:** Independence, Missouri, and Mexico
- » **Status:** Serving time in a Mexico City prison, she escaped and was never heard from again.

Sharon Kinne demanded excitement in her life. Her marriage did not provide it.

She despised the quiet ways of her husband, James Kinne, and she despised his reluctance to spend money. In turn, James resented her free spending, and also worried that Sharon was seeing other men. By March 1960 the couple, who lived on the outskirts of Independence, Missouri, had been married four years and were deep in debt. Sharon wanted to spend even more for new cars and expensive vacations. James did not.

Something had to give. The something was James Kinne's life.

Beginning that March and continuing at least the next nine years, Sharon Kinne would live through all the excitement she could have wanted. She would face four trials for murder, entangle herself in a jailhouse romance, go free on bond, and then travel to Mexico and wind up embroiled in another murder there. Convicted and imprisoned in that country, she would escape. Then — as far as the rest of the world knows — she would disappear from the face of the earth.

Sharon Elizabeth Hall and James Kinne met in 1956 at a Mormon church gathering in Independence. She was 16. He was a 22-year-old college student, home between semesters at Brigham Young University in Utah. After he returned to school, she wrote him that she was pregnant. In mid-semester, he traveled back to Independence to marry her. The couple went to Utah, but before the end of 1956, James dropped out of school, returned home with his bride and took a job at Bendix Aviation Corp. in south Kansas City. As for the pregnancy, Sharon later claimed that at some point she had miscarried.

The Kinnes moved into a home in a subdivision just outside the city limits of Independence. They had two children, but their marriage began to crumble.

They quarreled often, making enough noise sometimes for the neighbors to hear. As their disputes grew hotter, they talked frankly about divorce.

On March 19, 1960, Sharon Kinne called the police. Her 25-year-old husband, she reported, had been shot in the back of the head while he napped at their home. The weapon was a target pistol, one of the firearms James Kinne liked to collect and to clean. The killer? According to Sharon Kinne, it was the couple's 2½-year-old daughter, Danna

Sharon Kinne as she reluctantly left home under escort by sheriff's deputies.

Kinne. The little girl loved to play with her toy guns. That afternoon, according to Sharon Kinne, Danna had decided to play with a real one.

Sharon Kinne said she was in the bathroom dressing for a church supper when she overheard Danna ask: "How does this thing work, Daddy? How does it work?"

Then, her story went, the little girl accidentally fired the pistol at her own father.

Jackson County sheriff's officers, arriving at the Kinne home, found James Kinne in his bed, mortally wounded. The pistol, a .22-caliber Hi-Standard semi-automatic, lay on a pillow, its barrel pointed toward his head.

The offices had some reservations, but authorities eventually accepted Sharon Kinne's story that little Danna Kinne had shot her own father. The girl, they found, was capable of disengaging the safety on the pistol and of pulling the trigger. No fingerprints were taken from the oil-coated pistol, and no other chemical tests done.

After a few days, James Kinne's death was labeled an accidental homicide. No charges were filed.

Sharon Kinne spent only a brief time mourning her husband's loss. Within a week or so she collected the life-insurance proceeds and used them to buy her dream car, a blue Ford Thunderbird.

It wasn't long before she wished the car had air conditioning. She talked a salesman into replacing it with yet another new Thunderbird, this one with factory air. She also lured the 24-year-old salesman, Walter Jones, into an affair. That was in mid-April 1960, less than a month after the death of her husband.

In late May, Sharon Kinne came back from a trip to visit relatives in the Pacific Northwest. On May 25 she stunned Walter Jones by telling him she was pregnant by him. The news presented difficulty for Jones, who was married and the father of two children.

Would Walter Jones divorce his wife, Patricia Jones, and marry her? His answer was noncommittal.

Eager to take the matter into her own hands, Sharon Kinne called Patricia Jones and said the two needed to talk. The evening of May 26, friends dropped Patricia Jones off after work at an agreed-upon place, and saw her get into a car driven by Sharon Kinne.

The Ford Thunderbird Sharon Kinne purchased with her life insurance proceeds from her husband's death. Below, Patrica Jones.

Two days later, the body of Patricia Jones turned up in a wooded area outside Independence, a local lover's lane. A couple had driven to the place, planning to make love in their car, and the headlights had revealed the corpse. The man called police. His name was John Boldizs. The woman told him not to mention her name to police, but he did anyway. Her name was Sharon Kinne.

She and Boldizs had known each other since their days together at William Chrisman High School in Independence. They kept seeing each other right through Sharon's marriage to James Kinne. The night they found the body was not the first they had spent at the lover's lane.

Investigators found that Patricia Jones had been shot four times with a .22-caliber Hi-Standard brand target pistol, the same brand and model as the weapon that

John Boldizs

had killed Sharon Kinne's husband two months earlier. However, that earlier weapon — the one Sharon Kinne said was fired by her daughter — remained in police storage and could not have been used to kill Patricia Jones.

Then it was determined that, only weeks before Patricia Jones' shooting, a co-worker of Sharon Kinne's had bought a pistol for her secondhand at a sporting goods store in Mission, Kansas. Records showed it was a .22-caliber Hi-Standard. Detectives found the box for it in Sharon Kinne's home, but she said she could not remember what happened to the weapon itself.

Prosecutors charged Sharon Kinne with the murder of Patricia Jones. Reconsidering James Kinne's death, they charged her with that, too. A grand jury followed up with indictments in both slayings.

In fewer than three months, the name of Sharon Elizabeth Kinne was propelled from obscurity into day-after-day headlines. She had not yet turned 21.

She was also pregnant; she had not lied when she told that to Walter Jones. Her trials were delayed until 1961, after she delivered a daughter.

Six months after the birth, Sharon Kinne went on trial in the death of Patricia Jones. Prosecutors demanded the death penalty. They painted a portrait of Kinne as a strong-willed woman who demanded that she dominate any relationship. She was sexually aggressive, they said, and confident of her ability to make men do as she wished. Walter Jones, the car salesman, and other witnesses supported much of that in their testimony.

Kinne's lawyers, meanwhile, focused on uncertainty about the time of Patricia Jones' death and on the fact that the weapon used to kill Patricia Jones was missing. The previous owner of that pistol, an airline pilot, disclosed that he had once test-fired it a tree near the Olathe airport. Lawyers on both sides eagerly sent representatives to observe as the tree was cut down. Evidently used often for target practice by more than one shooter, the tree contained many slugs. As it turned out, none of the .22-caliber slugs embedded in the wood came from the kind of pistol Kinne owned.

Throughout her trial, she appeared poised and often unconcerned, no matter what was being said in the courtroom. Somehow, she brought spectators around to her side. She did the same with the jurors.

The all-male jury deliberated a little more than one and one-half hours before finding her not guilty. The courtroom erupted in applause. Before leaving the room, one juror got her autograph.

In January 1962, she was tried in the shooting death of her husband. This time, a jury of 11 men and one woman rejected her claim that the couple's daughter pulled the trigger, and found Sharon Kinne guilty. Again, the courtroom burst into applause. She was sentenced to life in prison.

Walter Jones

Kinne appealed the verdict and in March 1963 the Missouri Supreme Court overturned it, pointing to contradictory testimony given by John Boldizs. Before the grand jury, Boldizs had testified that Kinne had offered him $1,000 to do in her husband. At the trial, he modified that damning statement by testifying that she had only been joking when she said it. After her successful appeal, she was freed on $25,000 bond guaranteed by family and friends.

Promptly, prosecutors retried her. Promptly, the retrial ended after the prosecutor reported that one of the jurors had once been represented by the prosecutor's law partner.

In late June 1964, Sharon Kinne's third trial in her husband's death got underway. This time, the jury heard testimony from Margaret Hopkins, who in 1962 had become Sharon Kinne's lover while both were held in the women's section of the Jackson County jail. Kinne and Hopkins had signed a handwritten "marriage" contract to seal their devotion. That relationship ended when Sharon Kinne was transferred to the women's prison in Tipton, Missouri, and she took up with another woman.

Now, the spurned Hopkins told the court that Sharon Kinne had admitted shooting her husband. She also produced letters written to her by Kinne, asking her to remove a firearm that Kinne had hidden in a wall at her grandmother's house. Investigators followed up. Not realizing Kinne's grandmother had moved, however, they tore into the walls of the wrong house and found no weapon.

For the first time in any of her trials, Sharon Kinne testified. The result was a deadlocked jury, and a mistrial was declared.

Now, Sharon Kinne faced a fourth trial in her husband's death and her fifth since the slaying of Patricia Jones. Still free on the $25,000 bond, she was at a Missouri unemployment office one day in August 1964 when she happened upon an itinerant named Francis Samuel Puglise. Like her, he was in his 20s. The two hit it off.

The next month, Kinne and Puglise signed their own handwritten "marriage" contract. They headed to Mexico for a vacation. Nothing in her bond agreement kept her from doing that. Kinne told her lawyers that she and Puglise would stay in Mexico only a couple of weeks, and that she would return for her retrial in October.

Puglise and Kinne traveled from Kansas City to the Mexican border in an old car, and then rode a bus the 700 miles to Mexico City. Unaccustomed to the food and water, both fell ill. On September 18, as Puglise remained in their hotel, Kinne walked outside to look for a pharmacy. She was hoping to find something to rid them of their illness. On the way, she stopped in a bar.

There she met Francisco Parades Ordonez, a native

Sharon Kinne signed autographs after her acquittal in the trial for the murder of Patrica Jones.

 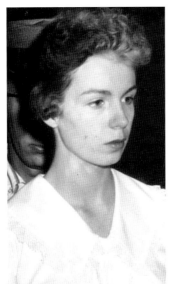  

Sharon Kinne, on trial and in prison.

Mexican reared in the United States. He had once been a radio announcer in Chicago. Offering her a ride back to her hotel, he took her not to her hotel but to his. According to one version of the story, she tried to rob him. According to Kinne's version, he began to grope her. When she struggled, he struck her in the face. She reached into her purse, grabbed a pistol that she and Puglise had bought in Mexico City and shot Ordonez dead.

The noise brought the night clerk to the room. Kinne shot him, too. Wounded, he grabbed the pistol. Police were notified. She was arrested.

Back at the couple's hotel authorities took Puglise into custody and collected his and Kinne's belongings. Among them they discovered a pistol, a .22 caliber Hi-Standard, the kind used to kill Patricia Jones.

Intrigued, Jackson County authorities sent a representative to Mexico City to test fire it and retrieve the slugs. Back in the states, ballistics tests showed that the marks on the test-fired slugs matched those on the bullets found in Patricia Jones.

Because of U.S. rules against double jeopardy, Sharon Kinne could not be tried again in Patricia Jones' slaying. Nevertheless, Patricia's murder case was considered closed.

In October 1964, Puglise was deported to the United States. After landing in San Antonio, he disappeared.

As for Kinne, Mexico refused to release her to American authorities for retrial in her husband's death. The Mexicans had the murder of Ordonez to address. Newspapers there adopted a headline name for her, La Pistolera.

In 1965, a three-judge panel found La Pistolera guilty in the slaying at the motel, and sentenced her to 10 years at a women's prison on the outskirts of Mexico City.

There Sharon Kinne stayed and there matters stood for the next four years.

Occasionally, reporters came to interview her. One of them heard her reveal how she felt trapped in her marriage to James Kinne:

> "Apparently, her solution to a problem was to kill somebody. It's hard to believe she's run out of problems."

Francis Samuel Puglise

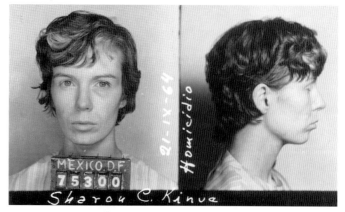

Sharon Kinne in her last known incarceration — in Mexico. She escaped from the Ixtapalapa prison and was never heard from again.

"I knew that out there, out of Kansas City and Independence, the world was going on its way someplace. And I wasn't going anywhere."

That was why she had begged her husband for exotic vacations. That was why she wanted a new Thunderbird.

Meanwhile, her mother and brother left Independence for Alaska. Her three children were adopted by James Kinne's parents. They moved away, too.

Then on December 7, 1969, a Sunday and visiting day at the prison, a bed-check discovered that Sharon Kinne was missing. The authorities in Mexico kept the news to themselves for two days. Once they learned of the escape, Jackson County authorities were astounded at Mexico's keeping it under wraps. Given a couple of days' lead, she was able to vanish.

More than three decades later, authorities in Jackson County still have heard nothing from her or about her. Because Sharon Kinne's retrial for James Kinne's death never was completed, the case remains open.

What happened to Sharon Kinne? Some speculated that she bribed the Mexican guards to help her escape. Perhaps someone brought her civilian clothes and she walked out with departing visitors that day. Perhaps someone helped her scale the prison wall. Perhaps she was helped to escape and then killed by friends of Ordonez. Perhaps she moved to central America.

In 1974, a *Kansas City Star* reporter spoke about Sharon Kinne with current and former prosecutors.

"Apparently," one of them said, "her solution to a problem was to kill somebody. It's hard to believe she's run out of problems."

Another investigator concurred, saying her nature would have made it difficult for her to live quietly. She demanded excitement, no matter the outcome.

In 2010, Sharon Kinne would have turned 71 years old.

To the rescue

An immigrant tries to aid his teacher, whose purse was stolen. He pays with his life and becomes a local hero.

THE CRIME

- **When:** 1967
- **What:** A West Side youth was killed trying to protect his English teacher.
- **Where:** Westport High School, Kansas City, Missouri.
- **Status:** Primitivo Garcia's killer was sentenced to 25 years in prison.

In his home state of Chihuahua in Mexico, Primitivo Garcia showed a taste for pugilism. Like two older brothers, he gladly climbed into the boxing ring for matches — until a head injury forced him to stop. Nevertheless, as a teenager he had once gone to the aid of a man who was being stabbed, pulled off the assailant and helped the victim to a hospital.

Eventually, Garcia soured on his homeland. The few jobs he could find paid poorly and offered no future. He followed his mother and eight siblings who had emigrated to a better life in the United States. They had come a few at a time since the early 1950s. All except one lived in Kansas City.

When Primitivo Garcia arrived with temporary papers in the middle 1960s, he was found after three months to be in violation of U.S. immigration laws and deported. Then rules changed and allowed Mexicans to remain if they had a legitimate reason. In early 1967, his mother grew gravely ill and Garcia had his reason. He landed a job as a shipping clerk and was allowed to stay with his mother and several siblings on Kansas City's West Side.

He got engaged, and made plans to build an addition to the family home at 27th and Holly streets for him and his bride.

In October 1967 Primitivo Garcia, now 23 years old, began taking night English classes with his brother Alfredo at Westport High School. The class, taught by Margaret Kindermann, prepared students to become U. S. citizens.

About 9 o'clock on the cold night of November 15, after class let out, Kindermann — who was 25 years old, married and five months pregnant — waited outside the Oak Street door of the high school for her brother to give her a ride home. The street was poorly lighted.

Suddenly she was approached by two teenage boys, one 14 and one 16. As Primitivo and Alfredo Garcia watched, one of the youths grabbed Kindermann's purse and ran across the street. She followed to retrieve it. She found that the two boys were part of a larger group of six teenagers. All lived within two blocks of each other near 36th Street and Benton Boulevard. They had driven to the school that night, evidently up to no good.

Winford Ray Durant, who had grabbed the purse and who at 14 was the youngest of the group, and the 16-year-old youth, Aaron Robinson, began looking through the purse. Kindermann arrived on their side of the street and asked for it back.

Well-wishers sent condolence messages to Primitivo's mother, who was surrounded by family members and a priest, above. Garcia's funeral, right. John Edward Rowden, below right, was convicted of manslaughter in the slaying of Garcia.

"I wasn't afraid because I saw two friends of mine," she said, referring to the Garcia brothers. "They didn't say anything. It was like they were there to say, 'We are here, Mrs. Kindermann, don't be afraid.'"

But in the milling crowd, the pregnant teacher was knocked to the sidewalk. As she got back to her feet, Robinson handed her the purse.

As he had that day years before in Mexico, Primitivo Garcia was infuriated by what he saw. He pushed one of the youths aside and began throwing punches. The blows landed on Winford Ray Durant and Robinson.

Another member of the group, 18-year-old John Edward Rowden, had a gun, which he kept tucked in his belt. Several of the youths demanded that he shoot Primitivo Garcia, but Rowden refused. Instead, the gun wound up in the hands of Winford Ray Durant, who did not hesitate to use the weapon.

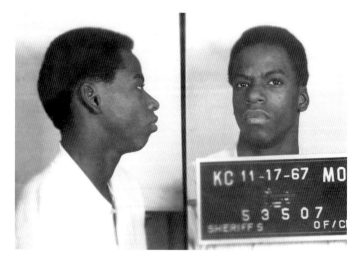

The 14-year-old ran toward Primitivo Garcia, who was running north toward 39th Street. Amid cries of "Shoot him!" Winford Ray Durant raised the pistol and fired twice, missing. Garcia whirled around, and the boy fired once more, striking him in the stomach. Garcia fell to the ground, wounded. He was taken to General Hospital.

Primitivo Garcia immediately became a hero in the eyes of Kansas Citians. Kindermann returned the next day to her daytime teaching position at Kensington Elementary.

As the days wound on in the hospital, Garcia's bullet wound led to blood poisoning. He was transferred to St. Mary's Hospital, but his condition reached critical. On November 28, during surgery, Primitivo Garcia's heart stopped.

"I just kept praying that he would live," Kindermann told reporters. "People have come to me to ask me, to beg me, how they could help."

Before he died, Kansas Citians contributed to a fund aimed at helping pay for his medical expenses. The fund reached $14,000 — worth more than $90,000 in 21st-century dollars. After his death, the money was set aside for victims of violent crimes in Kansas City. His story was retold in *Time* Magazine, and from around the country condolences poured in to the Garcia family.

Kansas City teachers and school personnel established a memorial fund of about $2,500. It was used to make several payments on the Garcias' West Side home.

Primitivo Garcia's funeral was held at Sacred Heart Church and he was buried in Calvary Cemetery dressed in a suit chosen by his fiancée.

Winford Ray Durant pleaded guilty to second-degree murder in Garcia's death and was sentenced to 25 years in prison. John Edward Rowden, whose pistol was used in the slaying, was found guilty of manslaughter and also imprisoned. The other youths with them were either acquitted or charges were dropped.

In the months after his death, Kindermann gave birth to a healthy baby girl.

"Primitivo was a good student," Kindermann recalled after Garcia's death. "The night he was shot, it seemed to me that the boys who attacked him were

A class under way at Primitivo Garcia Elementary School.

just fooling around. I just makes me sick that there are people who think they can get away with this."

In death, Primitivo Garcia was honored by the Carnegie Hero Fund, the Junior Chamber of Commerce, Kansas City Police Board and the Missouri House of Representatives. In the 1990s, the Kansas City school district named a new West Side school after him.

Left for dead

On the verge of a new life with a fun-loving fiance, a girl is found dead. The boyfriend, indicted, disappears.

THE CRIME

- **When:** 1970
- **What:** Recent high school graduate Jo Ellen Weigel was found dead in Lake Winnebago.
- **Where:** South of Lee's Summit, Missouri.
- **Status:** Jo Ellen's fiance, Mike Cline, was indicted but then disappeared and was never heard from again. The case remains open.

For teenagers everywhere, the summer after high school graduation marks an exciting and yet anxious time of transition. Summer 1970 promised to turn out that way for Jo Ellen Weigel and Mike Cline.

Each of them was 18. They had graduated together from Lee's Summit High School, and both were members of the National Honor Society. They had dated about a year, and now they were engaged to be married.

Jo Ellen Weigel lived with her parents in a working-class neighborhood less than a mile from old downtown Lee's Summit. She spent her days at a summer job at Sears and evenings on dates with Mike. She wore his ring.

Mike Cline spent his summer days palling around with friends and water skiing at Lake Winnebago, an exclusive community founded in the middle 1960s near the boundary of Jackson and Cass counties. Mike lived there with his father, a veterinarian, his mother and three siblings in a home with an expansive backyard lining the shore of the manmade lake. The family owned three boats.

On July 5, Mike planned to embark with about 200 other teenagers on a student trip to Europe and Israel. With the days dwindling before his scheduled departure, Mike and Jo Ellen made plans to go out together. About 6:45 p.m. the evening of July 2, a Thursday, Cline picked her up at her home.

Afterward, the plan was for Mike to drop off Jo Ellen at a girlfriend's house. She would spend the night there. The next morning, she was either to return home or to call home from the friend's house and then go straight to her summer job. She took along an overnight bag.

Mike Cline. Right: Jo Ellen Weigel.

That evening's date began rancorously. Outside her home, Mike and Jo Ellen got into an argument. They stood there exchanging words for 20 minutes. Then they drove away.

Jo Ellen and Mike Cline on the night of a high school prom.

It was the last time Jo Ellen's family saw her alive.

On Friday morning, July 3, she did not call. The Weigels tried to reach Mike but could not. Friday evening, Jo Ellen did not come home from work. Her mother called the friend with whom Jo Ellen had planned to spend the night. The friend's response, her mother said at the time, was muddled. The Weigels called Independence police, who said there was little to be done. No missing-person report was filed.

At 11 p.m. Friday, Mike finally returned the Weigels' call. What he told them was at least unusual, at worst preposterous:

He and Jo Ellen had gotten married, he said, and then he had promptly put his new bride on a bus to Columbia, Missouri, where a Weigel family member lived.

Jo Ellen's parents drove to Columbia, but the relative told them she had not heard from their daughter.

The Weigels returned home and spoke to Mike again. This time, he told them that he dropped her at a bus station but did not know whether she had actually boarded a bus.

Later, Mike went to the Weigel home and offered a third version of events. They had not married after all, he said. However, he had put her on a bus and sent a telegram to the Columbia family member. The family member knew nothing of that, either.

By now, the holiday weekend had wound on through Saturday, Independence Day, and into Sunday, July 5. With the question of Jo Ellen's whereabouts unanswered, Mike boarded a plane, as scheduled, for the student trip overseas.

About 3:30 that same afternoon, a water skier on Lake Winnebago dropped into the water in a heavily traveled area near the community's yacht club. When he came to the surface, he saw a body floating next to him. A boy driving the ski boat circled back to the scene. The body was that of a woman, clad in a girdle, panty hose and part of a dress. The upper part of her body was wrapped with fishing net and her legs with ski ropes. Two one-gallon plastic jugs filled with water and a concrete block also were attached to the body.

The body was taken to a funeral home. There, her mother identified it as that of Jo Ellen Weigel based on a piece of cloth, part of a dress her mother made and that Weigel was wearing the last time they saw her.

Investigators found that a yellow-and-white rope wrapped around the body was identical to rope on the Cline family speedboat. The concrete block came from the home of Cline's best friend. In Mike Cline's car, authorities found a white towel with hair from Joe Ellen Weigel's head. The hair had been removed by force.

Investigators wanted to talk to Mike Cline. By then, he was in Rome with the rest of the touring students. Mike received a message to call Alex Peebles, a Kansas City defense lawyer who had been hired by Cline's father. Arrangements were made for Mike to leave the tour,

Investigators removed the body of Jo Ellen Weigel from Lake Winnebago on July 5, 1970.

and on July 9, he arrived back home.

However, he was no help to investigators. A Metro Squad of police from various agencies, called together in the event of major crimes, established a post at the three-year-old Lake Winnebago Yacht Club. It searched the Clines' home and the area.

On advice from Peebles, neither Mike Cline nor his parents would give a statement. It was the first time since the Metro Squad's inception, which covered 33 crimes, that a suspect had refused to talk.

It was only the first rebuff the officers would face. Like the Clines, some other residents rebuffed the detectives' attempts to question them. Others made remarks about interrupting activities inside the yacht club, and a few residents acted openly hostile.

Mike, meanwhile, resumed partying and water skiing, the lifestyle he had pursued all summer. One day, he skied into a cove visible from the room where the Metro Squad was headquartered and, in plain view of the detectives, flashed them an obscene gesture.

Investigators considered Mike defiant and cocky. Nevertheless, they were closing in on him.

An autopsy revealed that Jo Ellen Weigel had been strangled. Strikingly, it also revealed that she was four months pregnant. She had told her best friend about the pregnancy. She and Mike would be married soon, she confided, and showed off her ring. Mike had declined to wear one.

Prosecutors now suspected that Mike wanted to go to college without the encumbrance of a wife.

The autopsy result, the hair found in Mike's car trunk, the rope from the speedboat and the concrete block for the friend's house were enough to take to a Cass County grand jury. The body was the first grand jury to sit in the mostly rural county in almost a quarter-century.

On July 24, nineteen days after Jo Ellen's body was found in Lake Winnebago, the grand jury indicted Mike for murder.

That evening, police went to the Cline home to arrest him. The home had been under watch.

However, he was gone. Mike had been spirited away — some guessed in the trunk of a car, others speculated by swimming to another shore and hopping into a waiting car. Family members told the investigators they had no idea where he was.

A federal charge of unlawful flight to avoid prosecution was lodged against Cline and the FBI opened its own investigation. Some investigators believed he left the country

In 1971, federal prosecutors subpoenaed eight relatives of Mike Cline for a grand jury investigation. At least some told them he was dead.

The FBI did not believe it. At Christmastime that year, Mike Cline telephoned an old pal and told him he was going to college. He asked the friend to tell his parents that he was well.

Today, four decades after Jo Ellen Weigel's murder, Mike Cline has not been found. His father died in 1988 and that year or the next his mother moved to Arizona.

In 1972, an FBI agent told *The Kansas City Star*, "We're not going to give up on this thing. I don't care if he's 50 years old and we catch him."

Mike Cline would have turned 58 in 2010.

Looking back at the homicide, an area policeman said: "Some day…some day. That old warrant's just sitting back there waiting."

> Today, four decades after Jo Ellen Weigel's murder, Mike Cline has not been found.

Ambushed

A mob-style hit takes the life of the most powerful civil rights leader in Kansas City

THE CRIME

- » **When:** 1970
- » **What:** Leon Jordan was gunned down on the street as he left his place of business.
- » **Where:** In front of his tavern at 26th and Prospect, Kansas City, Missouri.
- » **Status:** Jordan's killers remain unknown.

Civil rights activist, former police detective, businessman and politician — Leon Jordan led the emergence of black political power in Kansas City in the 1960s.

He conceived, co-founded and in 1962 became the first president of Freedom Inc. With that, the black community cast off decades of deference to various white ward bosses who had wrangled black votes through a combination of intimidation, favors and patronage jobs. Through Freedom Inc., the black community gained control of its own political destiny.

By the end of the 1960s, Leon Jordan had become the most powerful African-American in Kansas City and, some believed, in the state of Missouri. Along the way, he won elections and made friends. But one summer night in 1970, events proved that he had also developed enemies — ones who wanted him dead.

Jordan had always been a man to be reckoned with.

"I'm not a conformist," he once told a newspaper reporter. "I've been running in and out of lines for quite a while."

Leon Jordan was born in the segregated Kansas City of 1905, attended all-black Lincoln High School and earned a degree from Wilberforce University, a historically black institution in Ohio. In 1938, he joined the Kansas City Police Department and rose to the rank of detective sergeant. In 1947, he received a leave of absence to go to Liberia to organize and train a 450-member police force in that west African country. His wife, Orchid Jordan, went along.

Returning to Kansas City in 1952, Jordan received an assignment that he believed gave him little real authority, and he complained about it to the Police Board. Afterward, he was promoted to lieutenant. Nevertheless, Jordan resigned from the force and he and his wife went once more to Liberia. Again, Jordan oversaw the country's police force.

In 1955, after once again returning to Kansas City, Jordan bought the Green Duck Tavern at 26th Street and Prospect Avenue. Over time, he turned it into his political headquarters. A Freedom Inc. office was opened next door, and in 1962 the organization went to work.

Leon Jordan

The Green Duck Tavern, with Freedom Inc. headquarters next door. Below: Jordan's vehicle outside the tavern. Stains from his blood mark the street.

Two years later, in 1964, Freedom Inc. showed its new clout. Jordan's ally Bruce Watkins — one of two men who the year before became the first black people elected to the City Council — introduced an ordinance banning racial discrimination in Kansas City's public accommodations. The council approved it, but after protests from some tavern owners the issue was placed on the ballot. Under Jordan's leadership Freedom Inc. registered thousands of new, black voters and followed up by getting them to the polls. The public accommodations measure won huge majorities in the predominantly black wards where Freedom Inc. was strong. Even though it failed in 15 of the city's 24 wards, the overwhelming majorities in Freedom wards carried the ordinance to victory.

The same year, that electoral muscle elected Jordan to the Missouri General Assembly. Jordan worked quietly there, spending much time in his office and rarely participating in floor debate.

He continued to accomplish much of his local political work at the Green Duck on Kansas City's East Side, recruiting workers, getting out the vote on election days and negotiating with other factions in the city. Soon, even candidates for statewide office began calling at the tavern, seeking the blessing of Jordan and of Freedom Inc.

In the 1968 primary for U.S. Senate, three Democratic candidates sought Jordan's support. It went to Thomas Eagleton, helping him to victory in the August primary and in the general election that November. The same year, Jordan split openly with Governor Warren Hearnes at the Democratic state convention. In the general election, he endorsed Hearnes' Republican opponent. Jordan's ward supported the Republican 3-to-1, but in all other races on the ballot backed Democrats by a similar ratio.

By summer 1970 Jordan was running for his fourth term as a state representative. At age 65, he was challenged in the August primary by a 25-year-old activist.

The night of July 14 Jordan was, as usual, at the Green Duck, which also had a sign identifying it as "Leon's." Shortly after 1 a.m. on July 15 he walked out the front door of the tavern to his car, which was parked at the curb on Prospect. An employee remained inside to clean up and close up.

It was Jordan's habit to carry a .38-caliber revolver with him on the way to his car to protect the night's receipts. Most nights, he carried the pistol in his hand, ready for anything, and then placed it in his pocket as he reached his car. On this night, he carried little money. As Jordan rounded the front of his car and approached the door, another car drove up.

From it came a blast from a shotgun, and Jordan went down, struck in the chest by 00 buckshot, the kind used by police in riot guns and by big-game hunters. The car stopped. Someone got out and fired two more shots at close range, striking Jordan in the left knee and the right hip.

The gunman or gunmen got back into the car, and it sped away. Firemen from a firehouse nearby ran out and went to Jordan's side. They used a resuscitator on him, but without success. He was taken to General Hospital, where he was pronounced dead.

The ambush-style slaying, according to speculation at the time, was probably accomplished by someone who had precise knowledge of Jordan's habits. No money was stolen from him. Police found Jordan's pistol in his right trouser pocket, still fully loaded.

Witnesses said the ambush vehicle had two men in the front seat and one in the rear.

Bruce Watkins, the former city councilman and circuit clerk who was a close ally of Jordan's said he was "certain the killing had a political connection."

"It was some kind of plot," Watkins said. "Nobody was going to do that thing unless there was some outside money involved."

An emergency Metro Squad of police, sometimes numbering 60 or more, began investigating. Two days after the shooting, Jackson County prosecutors charged two men with Jordan's murder. The charges were based on an identification made by a 14-year-old boy who saw Jordan being killed.

On July 27, however, the charges against the two men were dropped after the boy failed a lie-detector test. The indication was that the teenager had named at least one of them because of a grudge.

Detectives in the Police Department's crimes against persons unit pursued leads through the rest of 1970 and through 1971 and 1972. Then in January 1973 prosecutors charged a 38-year-old Kansas City, Kansas, man in the slaying. Within two months, they had charged two other men, a 41-year-old inmate at a U.S. prison and a 38-year-old Kansas City, Missouri, man.

The shotgun used to kill Jordan.

Once again, however, the charges fell apart. At the trial of the first man in December 1973, a jury agreed with his claim that he was not in Kansas City when Jordan was killed. In the process, they rejected the prosecution's two main witnesses as unreliable. A few days later, charges against the other two men were dropped.

Years later, Jordan's widow, Orchid Jordan, speculated that the slaying resulted from her husband's opposition to drug peddling. A detective involved in the investigation speculated that somehow a debt "to some other organization" was involved.

Orchid Jordan took her husband's place as a candidate for the General Assembly. With the support of Freedom Inc., she won in 1970 and continued to win elections by large margins, serving 16 years as a state representative before stepping down. She died in 1995.

Orchid Jordan

The leadership of Freedom Inc. went to Bruce Watkins, who in 1979 lost a bid to become Kansas City's first black mayor. He died in 1980.

Four decades after he was slain, Leon Jordan's death remained unsolved.

Mob rule

How Kansas City's outfit extended its tentacles from the River Quay all the way to Las Vegas.

THE CRIME

- » **When:** 1970s
- » **What:** Continual violence by the local mob.
- » **Where:** Kansas City, Missouri.
- » **Status:** The influence of organized crime in Kansas City has diminished since the 1980s, but has not disappeared.

In the 1970s, things came to a head for organized crime in Kansas City. From time to time through the 20th century the local mob had come to public attention — Black Hand slayings in the early 1900s, the murders of John Lazia in 1934 and Charles Binaggio in 1950, Congressional investigations and occasional reports of vice crackdowns. Never until the 1970s, however, had Kansas City seen such continual and outlandish violence among mobsters as it witnessed in that decade and for a few years after.

Bodies stuffed in trunks, shotgun slayings in restaurants, buildings wiped out by explosions — criminals waged a shattering and seemingly endless war among themselves. The rest of Kansas City looked on in dismay. In the process, many died, some went to prison and the local outfit wobbled. The public recoiled, and federal agents moved in.

The violence stood out starkly in a decade that began with a burst of civic optimism. Within a few short years in the early 1970s, Kansas City opened a new airport with "international" in its title, a new sports arena, and new football and baseball stadiums. It opened a massive new convention center downtown. Business leaders rolled out a marketing campaign with the motto: "Kansas City: One of the few liveable cities left."

One of the liveable features was an entertainment district that sprang to life in 1972 in the oldest part of Kansas City, near the City Market. It was called the River Quay, evoking the 1850s when steamboats tied up at a rocky outcropping, a natural landing place or quay, along the Missouri River. The district featured restaurants, dinner theaters, craft

Above: A River Quay welcome sign marked its optimistic beginning. Right: the Quay's messy end.

In its heyday in the early '70s, the River Quay buzzed with shops and restaurants, above and below

shops and art studios centered on Delaware Street just north of the freeway loop. River Quay was the brainchild of Marion Trozzolo, a University of Chicago graduate who came to Kansas City in 1951 to teach economics and business administration at Rockhurst College. Trozzolo showed an entrepreneurial side by devising a method of applying Teflon to frying pans. His "Happy Pan" was the first nonstick cooking utensil in the United States, and it quickly became an American culinary and business sensation.

In 1972, Trozzolo sold the company and concentrated on urban development. An exponent of Kansas City's returning to its roots and a fan of refurbishing old buildings, he acquired more than a score of parcels near the City Market and transformed them into an entertainment and shopping mecca. Nineteenth-century structures were sandblasted and refurbished to

give the area an old-timey feel.

When his River Quay opened in 1972, Kansas Citians and tourists liked it. By 1973, more than a score of businesses operated in the area and visitors flocked in by the tens of thousands. On summer nights, people could stroll the sidewalks, buy an ice cream cone, window-shop among craft stores and art studios and, for the first time in years, relax in an outdoor urban setting.

That atmosphere, however, was soon to change. About the same time that River Quay began to boom, civic leaders were dealing with a longtime embarrassment about seven blocks to the south. It was the 12th Street strip, an infamous block or so of taverns and strip joints between Central and Wyandotte. The block represented the last bit of bawdy 12th Street night life that, in the 1930s, had stretched along many of the blocks east to Troost Avenue and had been the jumpingest part of Tom Pendergast's wide-open town.

Now in the early 1970s at new convention center, Bartle Hall, was about to open on the south side of 12th Street between Broadway and Central. Civic leaders believed that the 12th Street strip would blot Kansas City's "Liveable City" image. They aimed to build a new hotel to attract conventions to Bartle Hall, so what better place than 12th Street, between Central and Wyandotte? Out would go the strip joints, and in would come a fabulous new building.

Local mobsters had interests in many of the businesses along the block. Worried that they were being forced out of an important source of income, the owners searched around for a new place to set up shop. The River Quay already attracted sizable crowds, and it looked perfect.

An early arrival in the Quay was Uncle Joe's Tavern, a bar owned by Joe Cammisano. It opened in August 1975.

Quickly, the new mob-related operations came into conflict with Fred Bonadonna, owner of a popular River Quay nightspot, Poor Freddie's, and head of the merchants' association in the Quay. Bonadonna led opposition to the incursion of adult entertainment into the area.

Cammisano, with his brother William Cammisano Sr., tried to take over lucrative parking lots near the Quay, parking lots owned by Fred Bonadonna. Threats were made, first to Bonadonna and then to a City Council member. Bonadonna's teenage son was beaten up.

The old 12th Street scene was one of strip joints and bars.

Fred Bonadonna's father, David Bonadonna, was killed and left in a car trunk in July 1976. The elder Bonadonna had, in fact, been a longtime member of the Kansas City mob.

Faced with increasing threats, Bonadonna was forced to support the Cammisanos' inroads in the Quay.

Mob factions, meanwhile, chose sides. On the one hand were longtime organized crime powers who did things their way. On the other were criminals who wanted to break in on the riches of the old line. The Quay was the root of events that would spread far beyond its boundaries.

Other reasons figured in the Quay's demise. Amid

William Cammisano Sr., left, and Joe Cammisano, right. Joe ran Uncle Joe's Tavern in the River Quay.

the U.S. economic problems touched off by the oil crisis of 1973, Marion Trozzolo sold most of his River Quay interests to a New Orleans developer who promised to expand the Quay, making it into a "French Quarter without the grillwork." The developer annoyed existing Quay merchants by raising rents and asking the City Council for power to buy out property owners. Never did he deliver on his large promises.

The mob inroads, however, made the biggest difference — at least in the public perception. The number of taverns in the Quay grew while the number of other businesses diminished. An X-rated movie house opened for business.

Nervous business owners referred to the influx of "marginal" merchants and "the rough element." That meant organized crime.

The free-and-easy atmosphere of the River Quay evaporated. So did many of its once-thriving businesses, and so did its throngs of patrons.

Looking back, Marion Trozzolo was shocked by the changes in his River Quay.

"We became the hazardous-waste disposal area for

the city," he would recall.

In September 1976, fire broke out at Uncle Joe's Tavern, run by the Cammisanos of the old line. Two months later, an adherent of the insurgents was tortured, strangled and left in the trunk of his car at Kansas City International Airport. Then another tavern in the Quay area burned. The owner of Big John's saloon in the Quay was shot to death in February 1977 as he drove into the garage of his home. Within three days, a friend and bodyguard of Fred Bonadonna's was shot to death at a bar on Broadway near Armour Boulevard. The murder weapon was found the next day in Hyde Park, several blocks east.

Then came the biggest noises.

In March 1977, explosions destroyed two nightclubs at Fourth and Wyandotte streets, Pat O'Brien's and Judge Roy Bean's. That July, another explosion leveled Uncle Joe's tavern.

In August another man was killed by a car bomb. In September, a fire was set at the Godfather Lounge on Fourth Street.

By the end of the decade, the River Quay, once so promising, had become a ghost town.

Fred Bonadonna eventually testified against the Cammisanos and then went into the witness protection program. In 1978, one Cammisano pleaded guilty to extortion attempts on Fred Bonadonna.

The Quay symbolized the Kansas City mob's toxic, internecine battles in the 1970s, but the violence and its causes extended well beyond the short-lived popularity of the entertainment district. At the heart of things, as always, were organized crime's business interests. One group of criminals wanted a foothold in the action. The men in control weren't interested in sharing their power or their proceeds.

Chief among the mob hierarchy, as he had been for more then two decades, was Nick Civella. Civella was born 1912 in Kansas City's North End, then called "Little Italy." He began his criminal career doing small robberies and dealing in illicit goods. By the late 1930s, Civella had become a soldier for Charles Binaggio. In the years after Binaggio's murder in 1950, Civella rapidly rose to the top

A fire destroyed Uncle Joe's Tavern, above, in 1977. The body of John Brocato was found in the trunk of his car at Kansas City International Airport, below, in 1976.

of organized crime in Kansas City. He would stay on top for a quarter-century, an impressively long reign for a Kansas City underworld boss.

Civella accomplished the feat through a combination of superior intelligence, a steely willingness to eliminate anyone who challenged him and — for a much of the time — an ability to stay out of public view.

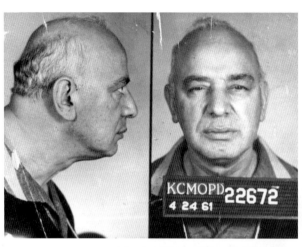

Nick Civella through the years: in 1960, above left; mugshot in 1961 above; in 1977, far right, and in a 1980 snowstorm, right.

In 1957, Civella came to national attention as one of only two Kansas City men who attended the notorious summit meeting near Apalachin, New York, of mob bosses from across the country. By 1966, *The Kansas City Star* was pointing to Civella as the chief figure in the Kansas City mob. In 1969, a U.S. Senate committee identified him as part of the principal family in the local underworld.

Then came challengers. By 1973, Nick Civella and his associates evidently believed their sternest test was coming from four brothers named Spero — Nick, Michael, Joseph and Carl. One by one over the years, the Spero brothers were thrust aside, each time with bloody, headline-making results.

In April 1973, Nick Spero's body was discovered inside the trunk of a 1966 Cadillac convertible parked along a secluded street in the Village of Oakwood in Clay County. The 37-year-old Spero — who appeared on the Kansas City Crime Commission's 1970s list of the organized crime family and whose occupation was listed as a truck driver — had been shot twice by a .38-caliber weapon.

The three surviving Spero brothers believed that Nick Spero's death was the work of the henchmen of Nick Civella and his brother and chief lieutenant, Carl Civella. The Civillas' motive, informants believed, was fear that Nick Spero was trying to gain power in the Teamsters Union local. The Civellas had made important inroads into that local.

In May 1978, Mike and Joseph Spero were sitting together in a booth at the Virginian Tavern on Admiral Boulevard, and Carl was standing at the bar. Men wearing masks entered the Virginian, walked up to the booth and opened fire.

Nick Spero   *Michael Spero*   *Joseph Spero*   *Carl Spero*

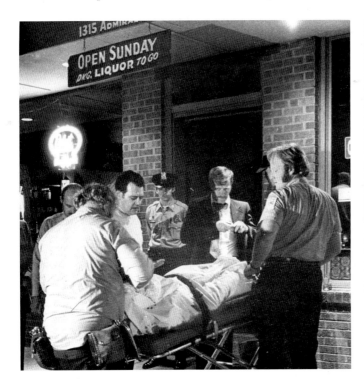

Violent ends: Michael Spero died in an attack by gunmen at the Virginian Tavern in 1978, above, and his brothers Joseph and Carl were wounded; Nick Spero's body was discovered inside the trunk of his 1966 Cadillac convertible, right center; Carl Spero, wheelchair-bound from the Virginian Tavern incident, died in an explosion at a cousin's used-car lot, lower right.

Michael Spero, 39, was killed. Joseph Spero was wounded. Carl Spero, who tried to escape, was shot as he crossed the street and wound up paralyzed from the waist down. Joseph Spero later wrote a letter to authorities identifying the gunmen as three Civella protégés.

In retaliation, Joseph Spero made a remote-controlled, dynamite bomb to place under the car of Civella's street boss, whom Spero believed was one of the gunmen at the Virginian Tavern. In May 1979, shortly before it was to have been used, the bomb was seized by Kansas City police and federal agents. Joseph Spero was convicted in the plot that October.

A year later, in June 1980, a bomb exploded at a Clay County storage shed, hurling Joseph Spero 50 yards through the wall of the shed, killing him instantly. At first, authorities believed that the 48-year-old Spero had accidentally set off the bomb himself. A decade later, an FBI agent quoted an informant as saying the dynamite had been booby-trapped on orders of the Civella organization.

The feud carried on until January 1984, when the last surviving Spero brother died in an explosion at a used-car lot owned by his cousin on East 12th Street. Carl Spero was 44 when the blast took place and wheelchair-bound from the wounds he suffered at the Virginian Tavern in 1978.

Through the cacophony of the 1970s, through the murders and fires and explosions and retributions, the Civella group maintained its grip on the local mob. What the Speros' best efforts had failed to do, however, was eventually accomplished by federal agents using the power of the wiretap and eavesdropping technology.

The Stardust Hotel and Casino in Las Vegas.

In 1978 the FBI's Kansas City office won court authority to plant listening devices in a restaurant where the Civella faction was known to hang out. The devices were installed by early June 1978, weeks after the shooting of the Speros at the Virginian Tavern. The agents hoped to get leads concerning that event.

Instead, they came upon even more intriguing matters.

The Kansas City mob, they learned through their listening devices, was pulling strings in a place more than 1,000 miles away — Las Vegas — and making nice money for the effort. The agents learned about interests held by Nick Civella, his brother and chief lieutenant, Carl Civella, and their allies in Kansas City, and also about cozy arrangements they had with the mob in Chicago, Cleveland and Milwaukee.

Las Vegas and its gamblers, the authorities knew, could be a crime family's golden goose. That was why the state of Nevada had rules against criminal ownership in or interference with the hotels and casinos.

In 1960, the Nevada Gaming Commission created its List of Excluded Persons, its so-called Black Book, which was to contain the names of those who were "notorious

> **The Kansas City mob was pulling strings in a place more than 1,000 miles away – Las Vegas – and making nice money for the effort.**

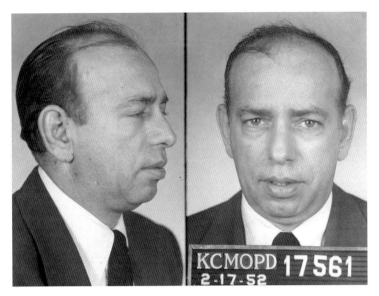  

Carl Civella through the years. Above, in a 1952 mugshot; above right and far right, in 1961, and in 1982, below right.

police figures" and also frequent visitors. Only 11 names appeared, and Nick and Carl Civella were two of them. That was supposed to mean that they were prohibited from visiting gambling establishments in Las Vegas, Reno, Lake Tahoe or anywhere else in Nevada. How, then, could these mobsters from Kansas City gain a share of control in the country's biggest entertainment and gambling mecca?

One method was money, quietly invested in big hotels with other people as fronts.

Big chunks came from the fabulously wealthy pension fund of one of the country's biggest and most controversial unions — the Teamsters. Through enticement and intimidation, mobsters had insinuated themselves into Teamster leadership. The Kansas City outfit controlled a local man, Roy Lee Williams, who was an agent of the pension fund and who would rise to the presidency of the union.

The Teamsters fund had given a $62 million loan to a San Diego businessman who used the money to purchase the Stardust and three other hotels under the umbrella of the Argent Corporation. Besides the Kansas City outfit, organized crime families in Milwaukee, Cleveland and Chicago got involved in the loan. Naturally, the underworld expected a reward for directing the money toward the purchase. Some of the proceeds from the gambling operations were removed from the casino before being recorded, and then delivered to mobsters in various cities. The technique was called "skimming." Because the proceeds were not recorded for the Internal Revenue Service, they were tax-free.

At the Tropicana Hotel, meanwhile, the Civella group found its way to power through an agent, Joseph Agosto, who had worked himself into top management. From there it was a simple process: A cashier stole money from the Tropicana's tables and handed it to Agosto, who in turn gave it to a courier who carried it to Kansas City.

Money from the various skimming operations, the Argent hotels and the Tropicana, was parceled out to the

Kansas City outfit and to its friends in Chicago, Cleveland and Milwaukee.

In Kansas City, FBI agents heard it all as they eavesdropped on the mobsters' conversations at the restaurant and through wiretaps at hotels, homes and business offices. Because Civella was in prison, the conversations overheard by the agents were among underlings. Eventually, pay telephones at various hotels were tapped, and Civella himself was overheard laying plans, asking questions and giving orders.

Roy Lee Williams

The agents code-named their investigation Strawman, for the San Diego businessman who had borrowed teamster money to invest in the Argent hotels, only to wind up a figurehead or "straw man," in the casino ownership.

In the end, the federal investigation ended the mobsters' hold on the operations.

In late 1981 Nick Civella, his brother, Carl Civella, and 10 other mob figures were indicted in the Tropicana skimming. To get the indictments, the government used a star witness — former Tropicana intermediary Joseph Agosto.

The same year, Roy Lee Williams of the Teamsters was indicted for trying to bribe a U.S. senator from Nevada. Despite the indictment, he was elected president of the powerful union. Eventually convicted of the bribery scheme, Williams, too, became a witness for the government.

He told how he and Civella had met in the early 1950s at a local political gathering, how they had become friends and done one another favors. Williams revealed that Civella had told him about the Apalachin summit, where he said Civella had been blessed as boss of Kansas City. Also at the summit, working relationships were worked out with mobs in other cities such as Chicago, Cleveland and New Orleans.

In September 1983 a federal grand jury in Kansas City indicted 15 defendants in the skimming from the Stardust and other hotels under the Argent umbrella. When the dust settled, multiple mobsters from Kansas City, Chicago, Milwaukee and Cleveland received prison terms, along with Chicago policemen and Las Vegas hotel employees.

Nick Civella was not among them. He died before he could go on trial in the Las Vegas cases. In 1981, he was imprisoned for trying to bribe a prison employee. In early 1983 he was paroled and two weeks later died at a Kansas City hospital at age 70.

Nick Civella's brother, Carl Civella, was convicted in the Tropicana skimming, and later pleaded guilty in the Argent operation. He went to prison in October 1983 and was still serving sentences when he died in October 1994.

With the death of Nick Civella, leadership of the Kansas City outfit weakened. No one has reached his status as a crime boss. Organized crime itself has diminished in influence in Kansas City, according to FBI agents who tracked it for years, but it has not disappeared.

Ruins in the River Quay, product of its mob troubles.

Family dysfunction

Her stepson annoyed her, so Sueanne Hobson set up her own son and a friend to do away with him.

THE CRIME

» **When:** 1980

» **What:** Sueanne Hobson persuaded her natural son and a friend to kill her stepson.

» **Where:** Johnson and Miami counties, Kansas.

» **Status:** Sueanne Hobson was convicted of murder in 1982 and sentenced to life in prison. In 2010 she was held in the Topeka Correctional Facility.

On December 2, 1978, in the chapel of the Country Club Christian Church — a gothic-style landmark on Kansas City's exclusive Ward Parkway — Sueanne Sallee Crumm married Ed Hobson.

Each was 36 years old. For each, it was a second marriage. Each brought children to the new union, and the family faced the task of blending everything together.

The result: catastrophe.

Within four years, one child would be cruelly murdered, another child would be behind bars for carrying it out, and one parent would be in prison for ordering it done.

But on this day in 1978, things were still happy. For the bride, the comfortable setting of her marriage ceremony fit nicely with her early life. Sueanne Sallee was the child of churchgoing parents, and grew up in affluent suburban Johnson County, Kansas. Outwardly, hers seemed an easy life.

Growing up, however, she argued often with her mother. She spent less than a semester at the University of Kansas, dropped out, met a construction worker named Crumm and got pregnant. The two eloped.

Their first child was a boy, their second a girl. By 1968, her first husband was drinking heavily and she had run up big bills. The couple filed for bankruptcy. Three years later, they divorced. She got custody of the children, but turned the boy over to her ex-husband's relatives. She kept the girl.

Now, on the first day of her second marriage, the newly minted Sueanne Hobson brought to the family herself and her daughter, Suzanne, who was by then 12.

The groom, a millwright, grew up in a farming family in rural northwest Missouri. In 1964, he married a woman 11 years older than he. Ed Hobson had met her on a visit to the Jewel Box, a legendary Kansas City bar featuring female impersonators. She was a waitress there, and the mother of a girl. The couple had a boy, Christen, or Chris, in 1967. He would be Ed Hobson's only natural child.

Sueanne Hobson, free on bond, sat with husband Ed in their Overland Park home in 1981.

Eventually, Ed's first marriage became as rocky as Sueanne's first. In 1973, his stepdaughter argued with her boyfriend, struck him with her car, and then, according to the police, committed suicide. In 1976, Hobson's first wife was diagnosed with cancer and suffered a lingering death. Afterward Chris developed emotional problems.

Now, on the first day of his second marriage, Ed Hobson brought to the family himself and Chris, who was 10. He also brought money. Through hard work on the farm, Ed Hobson's parents had accumulated enough for him to receive an inheritance of $160,000.

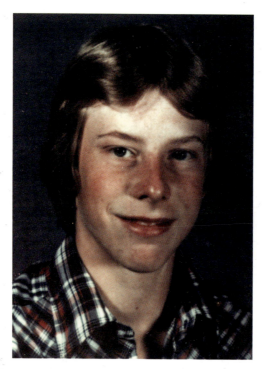

Christen Hobson

Beginning their new life together, Ed, Sueanne, Christen and Suzanne moved into a duplex near 103rd Street and Nall Avenue in Overland Park. A few months later, in May 1979, at the urging of Suzanne, the family took in her long-absent brother, James Crumm. He was the boy Sueanne had turned over to her first husband after their divorce. Now, he was back.

Right away, the newly formed family began to come apart. The parents found marijuana and cocaine in James Crumm's bedroom. They found that James was using stolen credit cards. They discovered goods he took from a department store where he worked.

Chris helped, revealing where James hid his drugs and telling about the credit cards. That angered Sueanne Hobson. Apparently in retaliation, she began telling James that Chris had hit her and also his sister, Suzanne. James learned quickly to dislike Chris Hobson.

Sueanne believed Chris had his own failings. He did not keep things in order around the house — at least orderly enough to suit his stepmother. Sueanne, a stickler for neatness, demanded cleanliness and obedience from Chris. Under her criticism, Chris ran to his father. Ed and Sueanne argued.

In early 1980, less than a year after James Crumm moved in with the now-dysfunctional family, he moved out and rented his own apartment. He was 17 and still attending Shawnee Mission South High School. There, he had fallen in with Paul Sorrentino, who had a reputation as a troublemaker. Sorrentino was 16 and had dropped out of school.

On April 17, 1980, Ed and Sueanne returned from dinner at a hamburger restaurant and discovered that Chris Hobson was gone. The 13-year-old had simply disappeared. Ed Hobson called the police.

Had he run away, as other teenagers sometimes did? As the days wore on, police began to have doubts. None of Chris' clothes were missing. His homework remained on a table, and his motorcycle and bicycle remained in the garage. Ominously, a 12-gauge shotgun owned by Ed Hobson had vanished from the home the same day as Chris.

Overland Park Police interviewed friends and relatives for a week. On April 23, a shopper at Metcalf South Shopping Center found the missing boy's billfold on the floor. It contained Chris' identification card from Indian Creek Junior High School, a Social Security card and a picture of his parents.

The next day, the police mounted an air and ground search. Accompanied by one of Chris' friends, they combed a four-mile stretch of Indian Creek from Mission Road to Metcalf. The area lay south of the Hobsons' home and was a place where Chris took walks. The search yielded nothing except some clothes that turned out not to belong to Chris.

Another week passed. Then on May 3, a Saturday, two boys went fishing near Bull Creek in Miami County, Kansas. It was a wooded, mostly rural area south of

Johnson County scheduled to be covered within a couple of years by water that would fill Hillsdale Reservoir.

Exploring the creek, the boys, 14 and 17, came upon newly overturned earth. Poking around in it, they saw part of a shirt. Poking around some more, they realized that had come upon a human body.

Dental records showed it was the body of Chris Hobson. He had been shot three times with a shotgun and buried in a shallow grave.

The news shocked his father.

"I knew he hadn't run away," Ed Hobson told reporters. "I was all he had and we were close."

More shocking news arrived. By the next morning, May 4, authorities from Miami and Johnson counties had arrested three suspects.

One was Chris' stepbrother, James Crumm. Another was Crumm's friend, Paul Sorrentino. They were accused of killing Chris.

The third was Sueanne Hobson. At 37 years old, she stood accused of conspiracy to commit murder — of putting her natural son and his pal up to the job of killing her stepson.

In the two weeks that Chris had been missing, James Crumm retreated noticeably into a shell, avoiding conversation, not eating and losing weight. Paul Sorrentino, on the other hand, began bragging. He and Crumm, he told friends, had lured Chris Hobson away from the home and killed him. One day, one of Sorrentino's friends went to police with the information.

The cruel story then was revealed.

On the night Chris Hobson disappeared, while Sueanne and Ed Hobson ate dinner out, James Crumm and Paul Sorrentino arrived at the family duplex. They told Chris that they were about to do a drug deal and invited the boy to come along. In the process, James Crumm grabbed his father's 12-gauge shotgun.

The three drove aimlessly south, past the developed part of Johnson County, into the countryside and eventually on to the country roads of Miami County. They parked on an unpaved road near Bull Creek and told Chris to get out of the car.

The two older boys handed Chris a shovel and told him to start digging. When the hole was big enough, they told him to lie in it. After counting to three, they blasted him three times, once in the head and twice in the chest. They tossed dirt over his body, collected the spent shells and drove away.

Drinking and smoking marijuana, they returned to James Crumm's apartment.

After their arrest, neither could recall the precise spot where they killed and buried Chris. They could,

James Crumm, above, and Paul Sorrentino, below.

Outside a courtroom, the Hobsons headed for an elevator during a recess in her preliminary hearing in July 1981.

however, recall what Sueanne Hobson had offered them to do the job. Her son, James Crumm, would get a new car. As for Paul Sorrentino, she would pay the $300 or $400 it would take to repair his motorcycle.

Over time, more evidence against Sueanne Hobson spilled out.

James Crumm said his mother had tried earlier to kill Chris by adding Quaaludes to his ice cream and forcing Chris to eat it all. Although staggered, Chris survived. On another occasion, she put cocaine on a piece of gum and gave it to the boy. When those efforts failed, she began badgering James Crumm to get rid of Chris.

A former friend told how Sueanne Hobson had frequently complained that Chris embarrassed her in public, and how he caused problems between her and Ed.

Once the boy disappeared, the friend said, Sueanne Hobson invited her over for a drink to toast the occasion. Even before Chris' body was found, she decided to redecorate Chris' room and gave away all the furniture in it.

Suzanne Hobson, Sueanne Hobson's natural daughter, told authorities she heard her mother plotting the murder with James Crumm.

Early on, Ed Hobson maintained that the family was happy and that Chris and his stepmother got along well. After Chris' body was discovered, he began to recant.

Were the two close? a reporter asked.

"No, they weren't," Hobson replied. "I think he wanted them to be but I don't think they were."

Crushed by the death of his son, Ed Hobson divorced Sueanne Hobson on grounds of incompatibility.

For her part, Sueanne Hobson steadfastly denied she had put her son and Sorrentino up to the crime. Evidently, she convinced her ex-husband. Before the year was out, Ed Hobson remarried her.

Meanwhile, the conspiracy charge against her was dismissed in July 1980 because of a lack of witnesses.

In 1981 the trials began. James Crumm's came first. It took place in Paola, Kansas, seat of Miami County, where Chris Hobson's body was found. Crumm's lawyer used insanity as a defense.

The defendant, by then 18 years old, was described as a "walking conflict" of emotions and ideas, product of a broken home and of a mother he thought was ashamed of him. He began drinking and using marijuana in elementary school.

A tape recording of Crumm's confession was played. On May 2, after deliberating an hour and 50 minutes, the jury convicted Crumm. He then agreed to testify against his mother.

Seven weeks later, after prosecutors cut a deal with him, Paul Sorrentino, now also 18, pleaded guilty to aiding in the murder of Chris Hobson. In return he, too, agreed to testify against Sueanne Hobson.

Three days afterward, on June 22, 1981, prosecutors charged Sueanne Hobson with first-degree murder.

Free on bond, she talked to reporters over the Independence Day weekend, blaming her son and Paul Sorrentino for the crime, saying they invented the idea of her involvement and accusing the prosecutor of being motivated by politics. Ed Hobson, sitting next to her, said that early on he doubted Sueanne's story, and that had led to their rapid divorce. As time went by he began to believe she was innocent. Since their remarriage in December, he said, he had been unshakably convinced of her innocence. Chris' murder, the couple maintained, resulted from sibling rivalry — James Crumm vs. Chris Hobson.

Crumm's version, told in court, was that Sueanne Hobson believed Chris was disrupting her marriage to Ed Hobson. First, he said, she asked him to find someone to do away with Chris. Then she asked him to do the job.

In April 1982, Sueanne Hobson went on trial. She was convicted in May. That summer, the 39-year-old was sentenced to life in prison. Her appeals were turned down.

In 1989, she came up for parole but was rejected. In the years afterward, she applied time and time again to

Ed Hobson: His mind changed about Sueanne

no avail. On many of those occasions, Ed Hobson came to her defense. Eventually, he stopped appearing on her behalf.

In early 1999, over the objections of Ed Hobson, James Crumm won his parole and promised to move to Texas. His sentence was discharged in 2003. In 2010, he would turn 48 years old, as would his accomplice, Paul Sorrentino, who was paroled to Florida in 2000 and discharged from his sentence in summer 2004.

As for Sueanne, prosecutors have steadfastly opposed her release. In recent years, they have said they would drop that opposition if she admitted to the crime. Never has she done so, and in 2010, the year she turned 68 years old, Sueanne Hobson remained in prison at the Topeka Correctional Facility.

Notorious

A Midtown man lures victims to his house, where they meet a gruesome end. Who would have guessed?

THE CRIME

- **When:** 1980s
- **What:** A series of grisly tortures and murders.
- **Where:** Midtown Kansas City, Missouri
- **Status:** Robert Berdella offered a confession in return for life in prison. He died of a heart attack in prison in 1992.

Robert Berdella raised nastiness to a new level in Kansas City. He confessed to killing six people after binding and torturing them for days or weeks. He blinded his victims with drain cleaner, injected caulk into their ears to make them deaf and administered electric shocks. He dismembered bodies, packed them in plastic bags and left them for streetside garbage pickup. For many victims, he kept copious notes about his acts.

The whole time he was committing those horrific things inside his frame home near Hyde Park in midtown, he was running a curio shop on Westport Road and getting along nicely with his neighbors.

Berdella's worst crimes — the serial tortures and killings that are known — began in the middle 1980s, when he was in his middle 30s. His secrets unraveled on Easter weekend of 1988, when his last victim escaped and told a gruesome story to Kansas City Police.

Until that day, Berdella had lived an outwardly unremarkable life. Inwardly, he had faced a series of troubles. As a child in Ohio, he had severe vision problems and wore glasses from the time he was 5. His father beat him with a leather strap. When Berdella was 16, he was homosexually raped by a co-worker at a restaurant. The same year, his father died of a heart attack and his mother quickly re-married, events that reportedly emotionally jarred the teenage Berdella.

Berdella's house on Charlotte Street.

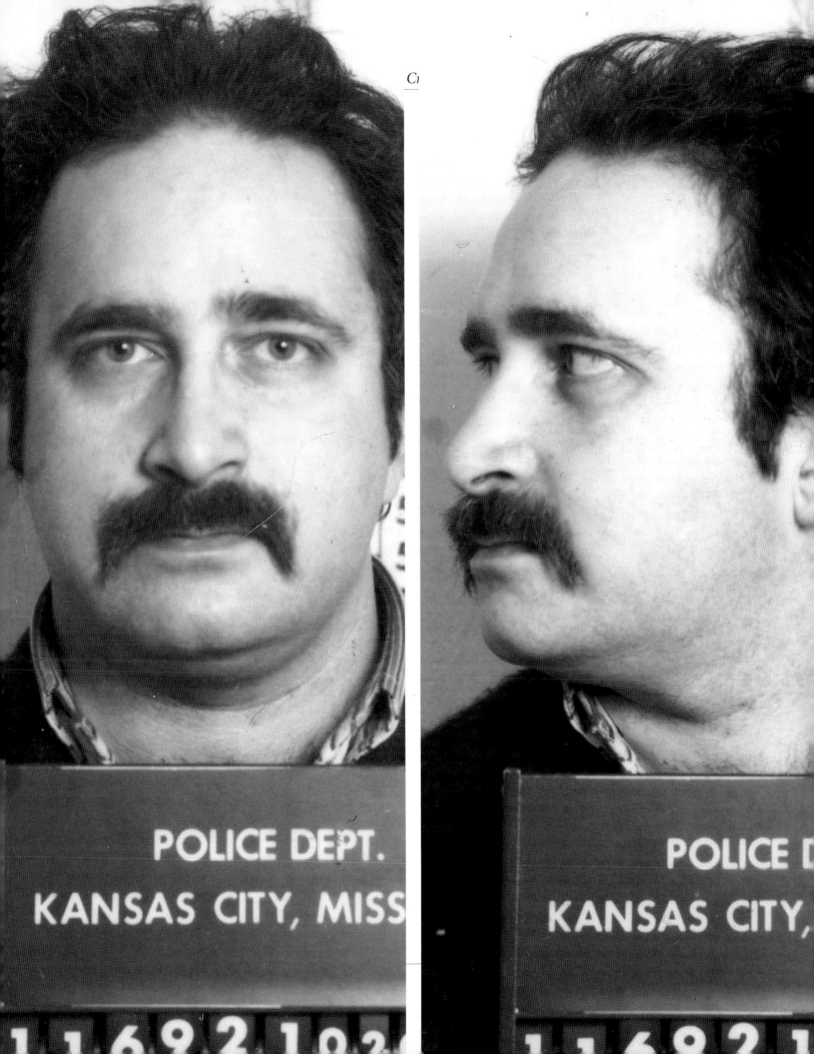

Community volunteer Berdella, right, appeared on a KCPT fundraiser in 1981. Pledge-takers dressed in medieval garb.

He also saw a movie that he would later say affected him deeply, "The Collector," about an introverted British bank clerk who kidnaps an art student and keeps her captive in his basement.

In 1967, Berdella enrolled in the Kansas City Art Institute. Over the next two years, he took classes, worked as a short-order cook, and bought a house at 4315 Charlotte Street east of Hyde Park. Also, he began abusing and selling drugs. At the end of 1969, he dropped out of the Art Institute.

Through the 1970s, Berdella worked his way up in the ranks of chefs at Kansas City-area restaurants. He helped organize classes for would-be chefs and participated in his neighborhood watch group. He also began selling oddities at a Westport Road flea market.

By the early 1980s, he left professional cooking and devoted all his working efforts to the shop, which he named Bob's Bazaar Bizarre — a marketplace, or bazaar, selling odd, eccentric — bizarre — merchandise.

He also began seeing male prostitutes, befriending some and offering them a place to stay. At first, Berdella's motive seemed to be to help them straighten out their lives.

In 1984, however, darker motives took over. Berdella struck up a friendship with Jerry Howell, 19. That summer, he drugged Howell, bound him to a bed, sodomized him and eventually asphyxiated him. He cut apart Howell's body, dumped it in a plastic bag and placed it out for the garbage crews.

Over the next four years, Berdella would continue that pattern. Each new victim was lured into the house at 4315 Charlotte, drugged, abused, killed and disposed of — unbeknownst even to neighbors. Meanwhile, Berdella kept notebooks carefully recording his methods. He also documented his efforts with snapshots.

In spring 1985, the victim was Robert Sheldon. Sheldon was the first whom Berdella blinded with drain cleaner. Berdella put his body out with the garbage, but buried his head in his back yard. That summer, the victim was Mark Wallace. That autumn, it was James Ferris.

In summer 1986 Berdella's mark was Todd Stoops, a 23-year-old male prostitute whom he tortured for weeks until Stoops died of blood loss. As with the others, Stoops' body went into the garbage.

Summer 1987 brought Larry Pearson to the house on Charlotte. Pearson's torture lasted six weeks before Berdella suffocated him with a plastic bag, disposed of the body and buried his head in the yard. In doing so, he retrieved Sheldon's skull and displayed it in his home.

His final victim, 22-year-old Chris Bryson, was a male prostitute whom Berdella took into his house on March 29, 1988. Escorting Bryson upstairs on a pretext, Berdella struck him on the head, drugged him, bound him and tortured him for days. The morning of April 2, a

In a search for evidence of his victims, police dug several times in Berdella's backyard in April 1988.

Saturday, Berdella left Bryson at home while he opened his shop on Westport Road. Bryson found a match, burned through his ropes and jumped from the second-story window of the house. Naked except for a dog collar around his neck, Bryson was spotted by a meter man, who went to a neighbor.

The neighbor called police, and the Berdella saga began to unfold. First, the police searched the house, uncovering his torture notebooks, photographs, syringes and other devices, along with two skulls and human teeth and vertebrae. With that evidence, he was charged with sodomy, unlawful restraint and assault, and was put in jail. After it was determined that one of the men in the photographs was dead, the authorities dug up Berdella's backyard. There they found Pearson's skull.

In late July 1988, Berdella was indicted in Pearson's murder. Within two weeks, he pleaded guilty in hopes of avoiding the death penalty.

But more trouble arrived for Berdella in early September, when he was indicted in Sheldon's death. This time Berdella offered a full confession — in return for a life sentence. To the dismay of the families of several victims, who thought the death penalty was in order, Jackson County Prosecutor Albert Riederer agreed to the deal.

Over three days in mid-December 1988, Berdella told prosecutors the intricate tale of each of his victims. Then he was delivered to the state penitentiary in Jefferson City to spend the rest of his life.

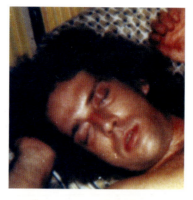
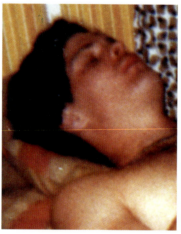
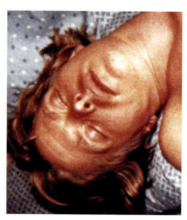

The victims: Berdella documented his deeds on film.

He remained nevertheless in the limelight. Berdella told a Kansas City television reporter that police and the news media had distorted his actions. He said he had established a $50,000 fund to help the families of his victims. Yet he faced lawsuits from those same families. The mother of Todd Stopps won a $5 billion judgment against him for her son's wrongful death. The amount exceeded anything Berdella could pay, but made it possible to prevent him from keeping any money he might make from his story, such as from writing a book.

Even in prison, Berdella continued to prove difficult.

He filed lawsuit after lawsuit that Jackson County paid tens of thousands of dollars to defend. At least five times he sued lawyers who had represented him. He taunted other inmates and turned against anyone who tried to help him. When he wasn't manipulating other people, he complained about them.

"He boasted about his crimes, he boasted about his lawsuits and he teased other inmates by playing head games with them," said a fellow inmate.

As a result, Berdella had to be kept in protective custody.

His nastiness would not continue long, however. In late summer or early autumn 1992, he wrote his mother in Ohio that he was feeling "yucky."

On October 8, 1992, Berdella began complaining of chest pains. He was taken by ambulance to a Jefferson City hospital, and died at 3:55 p.m. that day. A little more than four years after going to prison, the city's most notorious serial killer was dead of a heart attack. He was 43, only four years past the age when his father had died, also of a heart attack.

"There was no grief at his death," a fellow inmate

Convict Berdella in his first television news interview, complaining about his treatment.

said. "There wasn't a frown in the house."

Riederer, the Jackson County prosecutor who made the deal in exchange for Berdella's confessions, commented, "What was it the poet said about going not with a bang but a whimper?"

The wife of one of his victims had this view: "The guy didn't suffer long enough. We didn't get (Berdella) executed, but God did."

Most of Berdella's possessions were bought at auction by local millionaire Del Dunmire. Among them were artworks created by Berdella. A reporter piecing through some of the items found the art alternately juvenile and abstract. One portfolio, however, was violently erotic.

Dunmire bought Berdella's house, too. After a running battle with neighbors, he had the infamous yellow-and-brown structure on Charlotte Street torn down.

As the work got under way in late 1993, a reporter asked one of the demolition workers what he thought would turn up.

"It's a strange feeling," the worker said. "You kind of wonder what you might find when you take a wall panel out. As far as it goes, whether we find any body parts or not, we're going to take that as it comes."

They found nothing.

> "He boasted about his crimes, he boasted about his lawsuits and he teased other inmates by playing head games with them," said a fellow inmate.

Gone in an instant

Six firefighters lose their lives in an explosion that rocks the metro area. Who is responsible?

THE CRIME

- » **When:** 1988
- » **What:** Six firefighters died in a mysterious explosion.
- » **Where:** Near U.S. 71, southern Kansas City, Missouri.
- » **Status:** Five people were sentenced to life in prison for setting the fires to cover up a bungled burglary. The fires drew the firefighters to the scene and led to the explosions.

At 3:40 a.m. in the windy predawn darkness of the Tuesday after Thanksgiving 1988, a security guard at a highway construction site called the Kansas City Fire Department. A pickup truck, the guard reported, was on fire.

The dispatcher sent two pumper trucks to the scene, a pit near U.S. 71 and 87th Street, where the new Bruce R. Watkins Memorial Drive was being built. The area was used to house explosives for blasting away limestone. Two trailers loaded with a mixture of ammonium nitrate, fuel oil and aluminum pellets stood there, too. Between them they carried 50,000 pounds of the explosive, along with fuel oil. The trailers' markings probably were covered, which federal regulations then allowed to deter theft and vandalism. Other containers with blasting caps were marked.

The security guard updated the dispatcher: Not only was a pickup truck on fire, but also flames were visible in the area where explosives were stored. The dispatcher cautioned the firefighters about the presence of explosives.

At 3:47 a.m. Pumper 41 from the Bannister Road fire station arrived at the truck, noticed the second fire and radioed for more help. About five minutes later Pumper 30 reached the area from its station on Prospect Avenue, drove up a gravel access road and parked near the trailer. Then 41 asked the dispatcher to urge Pumper 30 not to get too close to the trailers. After that, 41 extinguished the fire in the pickup and drove up to the second fire to help Pumper 30.

At 4:04 a.m., one of the firefighters radioed his battalion chief:

"Apparently, this thing's already blowed up. He's got magnesium or somethin' burnin' up there."

Four minutes later, a chief pulled up a quarter-mile away, and sensed trouble.

He reached for his radio to tell his men to pull back. He was too late. At that instant, the contents of one trailer blew with astounding force and noise. A boom rolled

Firefighters carried the remains of one of their colleagues from the site of the explosion.

PUMPER 41

James H. Kilventon

Michael R. Oldham

Robert D. McKarnin

PUMPER 30

Gerald C. Halloran

Luther Eugene Hurd

Thomas Fry

Kansas City Crime Central

across the construction site, breaking windows, rattling doors and shaking walls across south Kansas City, and sweeping outward. Tens of thousands of sleepers across the metropolitan area awoke, wondering what happened. People heard it 50 miles away.

"Pumper 30," a fire dispatcher called. "Pumper 41."

There was no response.

In an instant, all six firefighters had died, obliterated before they could know what hit them.

More fire trucks arrived, but chiefs kept them back. Flames spread to a second trailer and 40 minutes after the first blast, a second explosion tore through the night. It was bigger even than the first.

Each explosion created a crater 80 to 100 feet in diameter and eight feet deep.

The events of that dark morning, November 29, 1988, began as a simple case of arson — a small fire set as a prank, or a provocation, or a distraction. It ended with a city wide awake and wondering, and with six firefighters dead.

From Pumper 41:

* 54-year-old James H. Kilventon Jr., married with two children. He had served more than 27 years on the force.

* Michael R. Oldham, 32, married with two children, at 11-year veteran of the department. His father had been a firefighter.

* Robert D. McKarnin, 41, who had spent almost 20 years with the Fire Department. He served all that time at Station 41. He was married with two children.

From Pumper 30:

* Gerald C. Halloran, 57, married with three children and six grandchildren. Halloran had served more than 37 years and was considering retirement at the end of 1988.

* Luther Eugene Hurd, 41, married with three children. Ordinarily, he worked at Station 23 on the East Side but volunteered to fill in at Station 30 that night. He was a 10-year veteran of the department.

* Thomas Fry, 41, was divorced with one child, and had been a firefighter more than 15 years.

A security guard's burned pick-up near the explosion site.

The material that killed the six was the same explosive used only the year before at the federal office building in Oklahoma City — only the Kansas City amount was five times as large.

Soon it became clear that no one had intended to touch off such an Armageddon, nor to kill the firefighters. But just as clearly someone had set the fires, and investigators turned to finding out who.

Because concrete was delivered to the site by a non-union company, one theory was that the fires resulted from union vandalism. That theory never reached the stage of charging anyone.

Another theory: Someone set fire to the pickup as an insurance scam, and the fire got out of hand.

The third theory: Petty thieves aimed to loot the site, and set a fire either as a distraction, a warning, or simply a demonstration of prowess.

For more than seven years, witnesses were questioned and leads followed. Investigators paid close attention to the account of the security guards, a brother and sister who said they had seen trespassers and left the site to try to follow them, leaving the sister's truck behind. They went to a convenience store a mile north, where they were told by the manager that he had seen no prowlers. The guards bought food and drinks and sat in the parking lot, until a passerby pulled in and reported seeing the fires.

Finally in June 1996, authorities acted on the third theory. They charged five police characters — thieves, rowdies, drug users and high school dropouts — who

Frank Sheppard *Earl "Skip" Sheppard* *Bryan Sheppard* *Darlene Edwards* *Richard Brown*

lived in the nearby Marlborough neighborhood.

Using more than 50 witnesses who said they had heard the defendants brag about being at the scene before the blast, or otherwise indicate they were responsible, prosecutors said the five aimed to steal tools, dynamite and two-way radios. Failing in attempts to break into the trailers filled with explosives, they set one on fire — either from frustration or to cover up their crime.

In July 1997 a jury convicted the five:

* Frank Sheppard.
* Earl "Skip" Sheppard.
* Bryan Sheppard, a nephew of Frank and Earl.
* Darlene Edwards, Frank's girlfriend.
* Richard Brown, Bryan's friend.

All five were sentenced to life in prison, yet the convictions did not put the matter to rest. Ever since, evidence has popped up hinting that the five were not guilty after all. Among other things, three passed polygraph tests, and none would testify against the others, even in return for shorter sentences.

Of the 50-plus witnesses against the five, 24 were felons with 76 convictions among them, and 14 were serving time in jail.

Earl Sheppard died in July 2009, maintaining to the end his innocence of the firefighter explosion. The others, too, have continued to claim innocence. Meanwhile, several of the witnesses said they were pressured by investigators to snitch, either with inducements such as money and promises of shorter prison terms, or by threats to prosecute.

The firefighters, meanwhile, have been remembered in several lasting ways. At the site of their deaths, six stone crosses and a flagpole were built, and about 5000 feet of 87th Street renamed 30/41 Memorial Drive.

On 31st Street just east of Broadway, a Firefighters Fountain was dedicated in 1991 as a memorial to the six who died.

Perhaps most lasting, Kansas Citians enacted a sales tax to support a Hazardous Materials team to aid firefighters at emergencies. Also, Kansas City undertook a labeling program for structures, which paved the way for the now-ubiquitous diamond-shaped placards on buildings and containers, indicating hazardous materials used or stored inside.

Memorial to the dead firefighters along U.S. 71.

Senseless death

Six people die when their home is firebombed in a neighborhood retribution that got out of hand.

THE CRIME

- **When:** 1989
- **What:** Six family members died in a house fire.
- **Where:** Kansas City, Missouri.
- **Status:** Aaron Frazier was sentenced to life in prison for his part in hiring associates to set the house ablaze.

In the wee hours of a January morning in 1989, thirteen people lay asleep in a house in one of Kansas City's poorest and most troubled neighborhoods. All were part of the same family, four generations of it. The oldest was Velma Coleman, in her 70s and bedfast. The youngest was a 6-month old baby.

In this neighborhood drug use and dealing were commonplace; one dealer lived no more than a block away. Things there were little different from other, similar parts of America in the late 1980s, when crack cocaine mixed with gangs and turned neighborhoods into virtual tinderboxes.

At 2:45 a.m. on January 20, the house at 3032 Olive Street — where 13 people slept — became a real tinderbox.

As the clock neared 3 a.m. a bottle filled with gasoline and topped with a lighted wick crashed through a first-floor window. Flames shot through the house so fast no smoke detector could have awakened the sleepers.

Fire trucks arrived within two minutes after the first call was made to 911. Firefighters saw flames shoot from the front windows, heard the sound of small explosions and then, as they reached the front porch, halted briefly as an explosion blew out a corner window. Knocking back the fire with high-pressure hoses, the firemen climbed the stairs and began searching for the occupants. They found six of them, all dead, on the second floor.

The body of the 6-month-old, Mark Sanders Jr., lay in the arms of his 19-year-old mother, Tricia Phillips, who had retreated from the smoke and flames to the closet of a front bedroom. Both died there. Firefighters found the baby's grandmother, Nola Phillips, 59, in a rear bedroom. Velma Coleman, the baby's great-grandmother, was found in a bed two bedrooms away. The bodies of two 3-year-olds, Jason and Courtney Addison, were found on the floor in the middle of the house.

One man was rescued alive from the second floor, burned over a quarter of his body.

The body of one of the family members — a three-year old toddler — is carried from the house.

The dead: Top left, Courtney Addison; top center, Nola Phillips; middle left, Velma Coleman; above, Tricia Phillips; below left, Jason Addison. Shaun Hill, right, escaped from the fire by jumping from the second floor of the house.

Another man had jumped from a second-floor window, injuring his knee in the fall. Yet another man jumped without hurting himself.

Four more people from 2 years old to 29 escaped unharmed in the freezing temperatures.

Nearly as stunning as the crime itself was the identity of the person who set the awful event in motion.

Aaron O. Frazier was not an adult, at least not under the law. He was 17 years old, he lived not far from the house where the fire took place, and he made substantial money hiring others to distribute cocaine for him in inner-city housing projects. Since the age of 15, he had been not only a drug dealer but also an informant, slipping police the names of other drug dealers.

The day after the fire he turned himself into police.

Young Frazier had fallen far in a few short years. At one time, he played drums for his church, shoveled walks for pocket change and unloaded trucks at the City Market. In 1986, he and some teenage friends came on an 11-year-old girl who was being attacked by a man at a housing project. Frazier and his pals tackled the man, and then cornered him until police arrived. For that he was commended by the police.

Then he dropped out of the church, began having behavior problems at school and soon started building a record of traffic, weapons and disorderly conduct charges. He took to wearing fine jewelry and carrying a firearm, neighbors said.

"There are countless Aaron Fraziers out there," Alvin Brooks said at the time. Brooks founded the Ad Hoc Group Against Crime and later became a Kansas City Council member.

Frazier did not, however, set the fire. That was done by another man, one whom Frazier hired to avenge an insult. Among the people asleep at 3032 Olive that morning was a man who had punched Frazier in the eye. A friend taunted Frazier about the blow, and Frazier decided to get back at his assailant. He offered an accomplice $150 to set a fire in the house where his rival lived — but only enough of a fire to kill his rival.

Early on the morning of January 20, 1989, the man reported to Frazier that the job was done, and collected his money. He shared it with two other men who helped

Aaron Frazier, who encouraged the arson, pleaded guilty to six charges of first-degree murder.

with the firebombing.

The day after the fire, Frazier told police he had hired the assailant to do his dirty work, but first said he only wanted the man to rough up his intended victim. Not long afterward, Frazier changed his story. Now he told his interviewers that he had authorized a firebombing, but only after two of the perpetrators convinced him that only his intended victim would die.

"They wasn't supposed to burn the whole house down, you know," Frazier said. "The kids or adults, nobody was supposed to be involved (except the man who punched him)."

The man who was the target of the firebomb, in fact, lived. He acknowledged later that he had hit Frazier, thus triggering the fiery retribution, but had done so because a pal of Frazier's had hit the man's aunt in the back of the head.

In spring 1990, Frazier pleaded guilty to six charges of first-degree murder in exchange for testifying against the three men he identified as the ones who set the fire. One of those was acquitted when a jury failed to believe Frazier's testimony. By early autumn, charges against the second man were dropped. The third man fingered by Frazier pleaded guilty in January 1991 in exchange for authorities' dropping the threat of a death penalty.

Frazier, who was imprisoned for life, symbolized the gritty urban existence of the late 1980s.

"I don't like it," Alvin Brooks said, "but I guess I can understand the Aaron Fraziers. You have to look at a kid who grew up in the projects and sees (drug dealing) going on all around him, the fast cars, the money. What's he going to do, go to a restaurant and make $3.35 an hour?

"We have to reduce as best we can the reason these kids go wrong."

Youngsters prayed during a candlelight vigil in memory of those who died in the fire on Olive Street.

Gone missing

A handsome bodybuilder charmed young women into handing over their money, their cars — and their lives.

THE CRIME

» **When:** 1989

» **What:** Three women vanished.

» **Where:** Johnson County, Kansas, and Jackson County, Missouri.

» **Status:** Richard Grissom was convicted of first-degree murder in the deaths of the three women, although their bodies were never found.

In the space of a week in June 1989 three Johnson County women, all in their early 20s, disappeared without a trace.

At first the disappearances were incomprehensible. Then authorities named a suspect, an elusive one who at least once slipped just through the grasp of police. Fear suffused the metropolitan area, and it would subside only with his capture.

First of the women to vanish was 24-year-old Joan Butler, a media buyer for a Kansas City advertising agency. After a Saturday night of dancing, she spent time at a friend's apartment on the County Club Plaza. About 4 a.m. the next morning, June 18, she drove her rented maroon Chevrolet — her own car had been in an accident — to the Overland Park apartment where she lived alone. There she hung up the black dress she had worn the night before.

June 18 was Father's Day, and Butler had promised to call her father in Wichita. That call never happened.

On Monday morning, June 19, Butler did not show up for work. Family members reported her missing. Joan Butler's colleagues at the ad agency printed and distributed thousands of handbills about the disappearance. They arranged for space on billboards, begging the public for help.

Investigators found that $900 had been withdrawn from Butler's bank account at Capitol Federal over three days, June 18, 19 and 20. The withdrawals emptied her account.

A week later, on Sunday, June 25, a man tipped off police that he had seen Butler's maroon rental car in an apartment parking lot in Lawrence, Kansas. When a policeman arrived to look at it, he found a man opening the trunk, and approached him to ask for

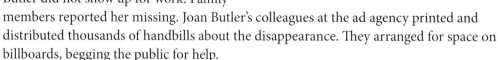

Billboards showing the missing Joan Marie Butler appeared in Kansas City after she disappeared. Richard Grissom, right.

  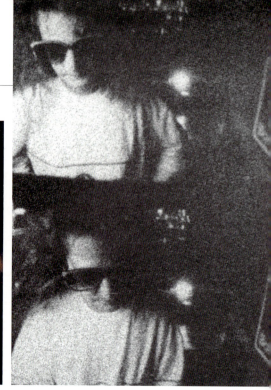

The missing: Joan Marie Butler, left; Theresa Brown, left with roommate Christine Rusch; Rusch at an ATM, right.

identification. The man shut the trunk, told the officer his identification was in an apartment and led him toward an apartment door. Before the officer could react, the man slammed the door shut and fled through a window. In the rental car, police found a wallet and checkbook.

Just after midnight the next morning, Monday, June 26, Christine Rusch said goodbye to friends at an Overland Park nightclub. Rusch was 22 years old, a graduate of Shawnee Mission South High School who worked in her father's contact lens manufacturing company in North Kansas City.

A few hours later, Theresa Brown, Rusch's roommate at an apartment in Lenexa, left her boyfriend's house. Brown, also 22, had been a prom queen in Camdenton, Missouri, near the Lake of the Ozarks and now worked as a dental assistant in Kansas City.

About 8:45 a.m. that Monday, Rusch called her place of work and said she was sick and could not make it. Then she called Brown's dental office and said she, too, was ill.

Within an hour, four checks totaling $2,400 were cashed on Rusch's account at different branches of Metcalf State Bank. That evening, Rusch was photographed by a security camera at a bank automatic teller machine in Belton, Missouri, withdrawing $300 from her roommate's bank account. Rusch wore sunglasses, and there appeared to be a bruise on her forehead.

Like Joan Butler and Theresa Brown, Christine Rusch was never seen by friends or family again.

On June 29, a Thursday, authorities searched a car at an apartment complex in Grandview, Missouri. In it, they found bank cards belonging to Rusch and Brown, three rings belonging to Rusch and keys to the apartments of not only Rusch and Brown but also of Joan Butler.

The owner of the car was the same man whose identification had been found in Joan Butler's car in Lawrence. Now, several pieces of evidence pointed at him, and authorities released to the public the name of a suspect:

Richard Grissom.

For Kansas Citians, those words instantly became synonymous with "predator." The man being sought had a method: lure young, attractive women on dates, persuade them to give him money, kill them and steal their cars. Was that what happened to the three young, attractive and missing women?

Thus began a tense string of days when neither authorities nor the public knew where Grissom was — or whether he might strike again.

The man they sought was 28 years old, an avid bodybuilder, handsome and popular with women. He had a painting and maintenance company that handled apartment complexes, which gave him access to keys to hundreds of apartments. He had a master key to most of the apartments in the complex where Rusch and Brown lived.

The suspect had been orphaned as an infant, and then adopted at age 3 by an American serviceman and his wife. By 1989, he already had an extensive criminal record for burglary and auto theft — and worse. At 16 he used a railroad spike to bludgeon to death a 72-year-old woman in Lansing, Kansas. Convicted as a juvenile, he served only two years in prison. Over time, he had used various aliases. Now, all of Kansas City knew him as Richard Grissom.

Across the metropolitan area, authorities searched woods and fields, lakes and ponds for signs of the missing women. The searches turned up nothing.

June turned into July. The Independence Day weekend passed with no sign of the suspect. Grissom's name dominated local television news broadcasts. The manhunt went nationwide, and the FBI joined the case.

Word reached authorities that Grissom had driven to Dallas in a stolen car. Finally, on July 7, an FBI agent saw the suspect at the Dallas-Fort Worth airport and arrested him.

With that, Kansas City breathed a sigh of relief.

Eight hours of interrogation in Dallas yielded more clues that Grissom had killed Butler, Rusch and Brown. At one point, he told authorities, "You'll dig them up," evidently referring to the bodies of his

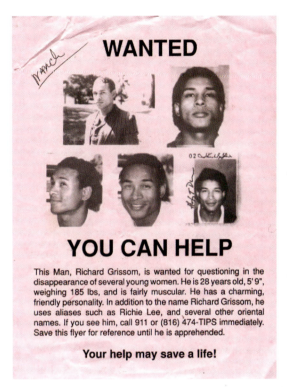

victims. He did not say where the remains could be found.

In early November 1989, Grissom was extradited to Kansas. He appeared in Johnson County District Court to face three charges of first-degree murder plus charges of kidnapping, burglary, theft and robbery.

In October 1990 Grissom went on trial. The proceedings marked the first time Johnson County had prosecuted a murder case without a victim's body. The 600 people summoned for jury duty were a record for the county, and the jurors who were chosen were sequestered more than two weeks. Spectators waited in line for a seat in the courtroom.

Testimony began October 19 and evidence spilled out,

DNA from blood found inside the trunk of Joan Butler's rental car, the car where Grissom's ID was found, showed the blood stain probably came from her. A Lawrence woman whom Grissom had dated said she had seen him driving a car that looked like Butler's.

He had given the same Lawrence woman a piece

Grissom as bodybuilder with piercing look, and as an amusing raconteur.

of jewelry taken from a burglary at the Overland Park apartment complex where Butler lived. Another piece of jewelry taken in the same burglary wound up on the floor of Butler's apartment.

A co-worker testified that Grissom had introduced him to Theresa Brown and Christine Rusch at a pool party at their Lenexa apartment complex in May 1989. He also said Grissom had once snooped through drawers in the women's apartment.

Not long after Rusch cashed the four checks totaling $2,400 on the morning of June 26, Brown and Grissom rented a storage locker in Raytown, Missouri.

Closing arguments were presented on November 4. The next day, a Sunday, the jury returned its verdict:

Guilty in the three murders and in all but one of the other counts.

Grissom received consecutive prison sentences, making him ineligible for parole until 2093. In 2010, now 49 years old, he was serving time at a Kansas prison in El Dorado.

Grissom after his arrest in Texas, far left; under guard in Olathe, left, and at his trial, below.

Search parties scoured a field near Lawrence, looking for remains of Grissom victims. They found none.

Grissom continued to maintain his innocence in the deaths of the three women. Despite repeated questioning by authorities over the years, Grissom never revealed what became of the bodies — evidently waiting for someone to offer him a deal.

No deal has been made.

A family affair

Oncologist Debora Green descended into depression, drugs and jealousy that ended in death for two children.

THE CRIME

- **When:** 1995
- **What:** Physician Debora Green set fire to her home, killing two of her three children and tried to poison her husband.
- **Where:** Prairie Village, Kansas.
- **Status:** Green is serving a life sentence at a Topeka prison.

If brains alone could have saved their marriage, then Debora Green and Michael Farrar would have succeeded. Both scored genius or near-genius IQ's, and both had impressed teachers and professors throughout their school and college careers. Both were physicians — he a cardiologist with a lucrative practice, she an oncologist who was not practicing. Their son and two daughters were attractive, athletic and smart to boot.

However, IQ wasn't enough.

Debora Jones Green and Michael Farrar were wed in 1979, and as the marriage wore on, Farrar watched his wife fly into rages — often over minor problems. She suffered debilitating headaches. More than once she descended into drugs, some of which she had prescribed for patients, and alcohol.

Meanwhile, Green discovered that her husband was having an affair.

Off and on, they tried to make their union work but mostly they simply endured, remaining husband and wife for a decade and a half. There was the idea of commitment, which had mattered to each, and also the well-being of the three children. By the early 1990s the marriage of Debora Green and Michael Farrar clearly was failing.

Breakups traditionally cause heartache, but this would end in sickness, destruction and shocking death.

The beginning of the end came in January 1994. With his wife descending into bouts in which she hit things or herself, the situation became unbearable for Farrar. For her part, Green told friends that Farrar was cheating on her.

He asked for a divorce. He moved out of the family's home, which stood on West 61st Terrace just off Kansas City's Ward Parkway, and into an apartment near the Country Club Plaza.

Green fought the breakup. For a while, she calmed down and the two discussed reconciliation.

In court, Debora Green watched the videotaped statement she made the day of the fire. In it she sometimes referred to her children in the past tense.

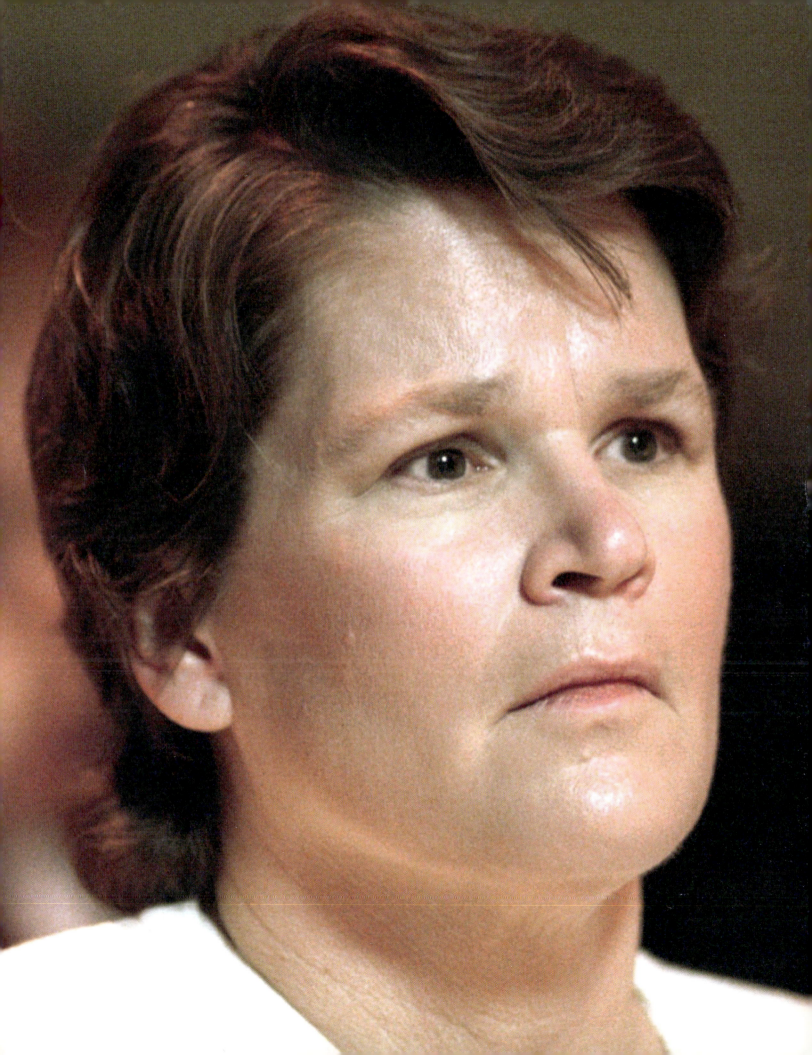

One day in May 1994, a fire broke out at the house. None of the family was home. Their son was playing soccer; Green and the two girls were in the car together. The cause was an electrical wire wrapped around a pipe. The wire shorted out, igniting wood paneling nearby.

Unable to live in their burned home, Green and the three children moved briefly into Farrar's apartment. Then, Mom and Dad decided to reconcile. As part of their attempt to start things anew, they bought a big new house on Canterbury Court in Prairie Village across the state line. The house featured six bedrooms and a four-car garage. In June 1994 they moved in.

By early 1995, however, Green's and Farrar's old difficulties bubbled back up, and their arguing and fighting resumed. Still, they stayed together. That year, she turned 44 and he turned 40.

In summer 1995 Pembroke Hill, a private school attended by their son and older daughter, organized a two-week trip to Peru for students and their parents. Farrar and Green signed up, along with their 13-year-old son, Tim. Also signed up was another Pembroke Hill parent, a married nurse, who accompanied her own offspring.

On the voyage, a romance kindled between Farrar and the nurse. After the parents and students returned to the United States, the romance turned into a full-fledged affair.

Again, Farrar again asked for a divorce from Green. Again, Green fought it. She also turned to heavy drinking and increasingly acted erratic. She cursed him in front of the children, telling Tim and his sisters about their father's dalliance and lacing the stories with crude language.

In August 1995, Green left a sandwich for her husband in the refrigerator of the home on Canterbury Court. Farrar ate it, although he thought it tasted bitter. Within hours, he felt sick. Within days, the illness became violent, his fever topped 104 degrees, and he entered the hospital. His doctors were puzzled. Was it a late-arising result of the trip to South America?

In late August, Farrar was discharged and came home. One night, Green brought him a spaghetti dinner. Again, he grew violently sick and again he went into the hospital.

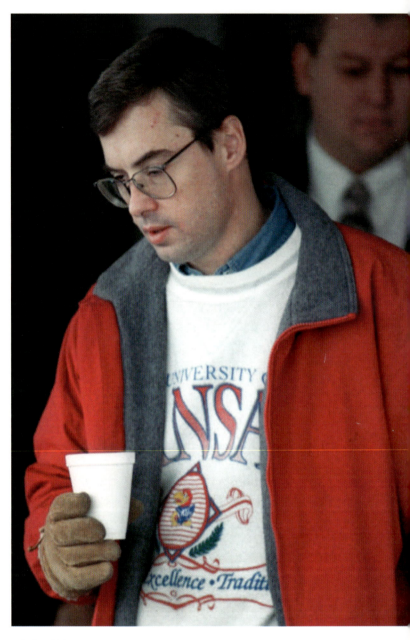

Michael Farrar in 1995

Home by the Labor Day weekend, Green once more brought him a meal and once more Farrar got sick. Doctors wondered whether his ailment had something to do with his diet.

It did.

In late September, Farrar searched his wife's purse and found packets of seed labeled "Castor beans," along

Tim Farrar *Kelly Farrar*

with a receipt from a garden store in Olathe. Green told him she intended to plant them. He had never seen her plant anything; Debora Green was no gardener.

Quick research told Farrar that the seeds contained a poisonous substance, ricin. Ground up, the substance could be mixed into any dish.

Already bedeviled by his wife's behavior and frightened about what she meant to do, he called the police to have her committed to a mental hospital. When they arrived, he turned the seed packets over to them.

Green spent four days at the Menninger Clinic in Topeka, having agreed to the commitment. Because she entered voluntarily, Green could check out when she wanted. After four days she did, and returned to Prairie Village. Farrar moved out, taking an apartment in Merriam.

Farrar's affair with the nurse continued, and so did his battles with Green. On the night of October 23, 1995, he drove Tim to his hockey game and took along daughter Kelly. After he returned the two children to the house on Canterbury Court, he got into a late-night shouting match with his estranged wife on the telephone. They talked about whether Green was taking care of the children, trading loud accusations back and forth.

Farrar told her she was crazy, and that he would try to take the children from her.

A half-hour after midnight on October 24, Farrar received another call. It was from a neighbor on Canterbury Court: The house was burning, and two of his children were inside.

When Farrar arrived, he found police and firemen on the scene. All were too late. The fire had raced through the house with breathtaking speed, blowing out windows and doors. The middle child, 10-year-old Kate Farrar, had escaped through her second-floor bedroom window to the garage roof, and then jumped to safety. Green fled the fire through her bedroom door, which opened to a patio.

That left Tim and his 6-year-old sister, Kelly, unaccounted for. Firemen plunged into the burning wreckage, hoping to find them. The blaze drove the firemen back.

Police noted that the surviving daughter acted frantic.

Her mother, they said, remained calm.

Afterward, investigators discovered on Green's bed a singed copy of *Necessary Lives* by Janice Daugharty, a book about several children burning to death in an arson fire. In the book, the female protagonist is accused, falsely, of the crime. According to library records, Green had checked out several books about people killed by family members.

Green and Farrar went to the Prairie Village police station for interviews, which were conducted separately. In her interview, videotaped hours after the fire yet before the children's bodies were found, Green sometimes referred to her children in the past tense.

> The perpetrator, they said, had poured fuel in four places in the house, particularly on the stairway, where the blaze would block any exit from the upstairs bedrooms.

The day after the fire on Canterbury Court investigators studied the shell of the Greens' house. It has since been razed.

Of Tim, she said, "He used to be my 13-year-old son."

Tim Farrar's body was found on a first-floor rafter, having fallen through from his bedroom upstairs. Death was caused by smoke inhalation and burns. Kelly Farrar's body was found in her bed, still curled up.

The day after the fire, Michael Farrar filed for divorce. He cited incompatibility.

On Oct. 27, investigators declared the fire arson. The perpetrator, they said, had poured fuel in four places in the house, particularly on the stairway, where the blaze would block any exit from the upstairs bedrooms.

On Nov. 22, 1995, police arrested Green in downtown Kansas City, where she had just dropped off her daughter for ballet practice. The girl had a starring role in the State Ballet of Missouri's production of "The Nutcracker." Her younger sister — had she lived — was to have played an angel.

Green was charged with two counts of capital murder in the deaths of her children. She was also charged with trying to kill the third child, with setting the fire and with poisoning her estranged husband. Prosecutors said her motive in each act was to hurt Farrar because of his threats to divorce her.

That same day, Farrar was at a hospital, receiving treatment for an infection that authorities believed was related to the poisoning.

At her court hearings, Green maintained that she was innocent. At those same hearings, observers noticed a surgical scar on Farrar's head, the result of operations aimed at overcoming the effects of the poison.

On April 17, 1996, Green abruptly switched her plea from not guilty to no contest to all the charges. In return, she would receive a life sentence. Prosecutors, she said, had "substantial evidence that I set the fire that caused the death of my children."

In September 2004, Green smiled at friends at a hearing to set aside her no-contest plea.

Green claimed she was not in control of herself the night of the fire. She never meant to harm the children, she said. The judge then declared her guilty on all counts.

On May 30, 1996, Debora Green received a sentence of life in prison. She would have to serve 40 years before being considered for parole. In a statement, she said:

"Alcohol, psychiatric illness and even more basic communication failures within our family set the stage for this tragedy. I do not seek to use that fact to escape my personal responsibility."

At her sentencing, a psychologist engaged by Green's lawyers said that Green saw herself as abandoned and betrayed by her husband. When she was hospitalized a month before the fire, she was diagnosed as having depression with suicidal tendencies. Green's binge drinking increased and she lost control of her impulses. Emotionally, Green was a like a child but her intelligence enabled her to mask the weakness.

The divorce of Farrar from Green was made final on July 26, 1996. Eventually, Farrar regained his health, and in 1997, he married a lawyer. The nurse he was seeing the year of the fire moved to the West Coast.

About a decade later, after the Kansas Supreme Court ruled the death penalty unconstitutional, Green tried to withdraw her plea. She also filed challenges based on new methods of arson investigation. In 2007, however, the state Supreme Court turned her down.

In 2010, she was serving her sentence at the Topeka Correctional Facility.

Persuasion

A family man and ex-Scoutmaster leads a double life of swindling, deception and murder.

THE CRIME

- **When:** 1980s-2000
- **What:** John E. Robinson Sr. promised women money, fame and sex -- and ended up torturing and killing eight of them.
- **Where:** The Kansas City metro area
- **Status:** Robinson was sentenced to death and in 2010 was sitting on death row in Kansas while he appealed.

For most of the four decades he lived in the Kansas City area, John E. Robinson Sr. proved a master persuader.

As a young man seeking work, Robinson convinced hospitals and even Harry S. Truman's personal physician that he was a certified X-ray technician and persuaded them to hire him. As he grew older and settled into regular community activities, he impressed others, and they named him to lead fund-raising efforts. From at least the mid-1980s on, he lured investors into putting money into somewhat exotic agricultural schemes. At the same time, he told other people that he could help them find jobs, and a better life. They believed him.

Time after time, the people he had persuaded wound up disappointed. A hospital fired him after finding he barely knew how to operate X-ray machines. A doctor lost tens of thousands of dollars in embezzled funds. Charity groups found his leadership simply self-serving. Investors saw their money waste away.

Then there were the people — all women — who hoped he would escort them to a better life. They ended up dead.

The bodies of three were discovered stuffed into 85-gallon barrels and left on Robinson's property in rural Linn County, Kansas. Barrels containing the bodies of two more turned up in a rental storage unit in Raymore, Missouri. The bodies of three more victims were never found.

Robinson lured most of them into his clutches with promises of a job, or job training, or a better life with him. As it happened, several of his victims also shared his interest in exotic sex acts — bondage, discipline and sado-masochism. After a few years or a few months with him, for one reason or another, he put them to death, usually by striking them on the head. One by one, each was disposed of and John E. Robinson Sr. went on to his next victim.

At home evenings with his family in Olathe, Kansas, Robinson played father and grandfather, filling his walls with pictures of his offspring. He was married to the same woman for 41 years.

At least four times in the 1970s Robinson served as a Scoutmaster or Cubmaster.

Robinson's multiple lives included Scoutmaster, church elder and manufactured home representative.

As a boy, he had attained Eagle rank. He taught Sunday school and volunteered as an elder at a small church in the Johnson County community of Stanley. At one point, he and his family lived in a comfortable house there, and Robinson was head of the homes association. In his free time he refereed volleyball games, rose in the refereeing field and wound up assigning referees to games.

But he spent his days in darker activities, creating a false world in which he was a CIA agent who traveled around the world under constant secrecy, or a wealthy man about to depart on his yacht for faraway ports of call.

In the words of a prosecutor, John E. Robinson Sr. was a liar "of galactic proportions." He lied about everything imaginable, and he was good at it.

When he started was unclear. Robinson grew up in Cicero, Illinois, and attended a junior college there but did not get a degree.

By the middle 1960s, when he was in his 20s, Robinson was working in Kansas City as an X-ray technician at General Hospital and Children's Mercy. He covered the walls of his office with degrees, certificates and citations. Despite that appearance of technical skill, his co-workers found they had to help him with the equipment. His bumbling and poor results got him fired. His successor was impressed by the framed accolades he left behind — until she found a box of blank certificates he also left behind, all waiting for another bogus achievement or honor to be filled in.

He persuaded Wallace Graham, Harry S. Truman's personal physician, to hire him as an X-ray technician. That job ended when Robinson was convicted of embezzling $33,000 from the office accounts by falsifying Graham's signature on checks. The doctor's son believed that was only about a third of what Robinson actually stole.

In the middle 1970s, Robinson formed a medical management consultant business, swindled investors and pleaded no contest to fraud. The investors lost only money on the proposition. Then he went to work for Guy's Foods in Liberty, where he was charged with stealing money from the company. He pleaded guilty.

In the 1980s, Robinson started a company called Hydro-Gro, which supposedly would make its shareholders money by selling water-based home gardening systems. He also ran an Overland Park corporation called Equi-II. At times, he described himself as a consultant in medical, agricultural and even charitable ventures.

Along the way, Robinson joined the board of directors of a sheltered workshop, showing lots of energy and pledging to raise lots of money. His main achievement was maneuvering himself into being named a sheltered workshop "Man of the Year." Then he stepped down.

But the worst of his series of swindles involved the women he lured into his web and then killed.

Robinson's earliest known victim was 19-year-old Paula Godfrey, a graduate of Olathe North High School, whom he persuaded to go to work for him. In 1984, he picked her up at her Overland Park home, telling her father he would drive her to Kansas City International for a flight to San Antonio. There, supposedly, she would take a clerical skills course. Instead, he argued with her over a debt, took her to a motel in Belton and clubbed her over the head with a lamp. Authorities believe an accomplice disposed of Godfrey's body, which was never found.

Early the next year, another 19-year-old, Lisa Stasi of Kansas City, disappeared. She met Robinson after he told a social worker at Truman Medical Center in Kansas City that he was a businessman trying to help young, unwed mothers. The social worker told him about Stasi and about her baby, Tiffany, who had been born months earlier. Robinson was questioned about the disappearance of Stasi at the time, but no charges were filed — until 15 years later, when it was discovered that he killed her with a blow to the skull. Like Godfrey, her body was never found. After forging adoption papers, Robinson turned Tiffany over to his brother and sister-in-law, who lived in the Chicago area and believed Robinson's story that the child's mother had committed suicide. Tiffany grew up with her adoptive family. Neither the brother nor his wife nor the child learned the truth for a decade and a half.

In 1987, a one-time drug abuser seeking to rehabilitate herself answered a Robinson come-on and moved from Wichita Falls, Texas, to Overland Park. Like Godfrey, 27-year-old Catherine Clampitt went to work for Robinson. Also like Godfrey, Clampitt and Robinson got into an argument over money. Robinson clubbed her

over the head, too, at an apartment in Belton. He told an accomplice how to dispose of the body. Like the two victims who preceded her, Clampitt's body was never found.

Robinson met his third and fourth victims in 1994, when he lured Sheila Faith and her teenage daughter, Debbie Faith, from their home in Pueblo, Colorado, with promises of world travel, and a private school for Debbie, who was disabled and in a wheelchair. He rented a mailbox in Olathe, where he had the Faiths' Social Security checks sent. In autumn 1996, Robinson used a pipe to kill Debbie and Sheila, who was then 45. The Social Security checks kept arriving for four years. Meanwhile, the Faiths' relatives in Texas received letters saying mother and daughter were heading to Australia with a wonderful man. Instead, their bodies were found in barrels at a storage unit in Raymore, Missouri.

In the early 1990s, when Robinson was serving one of his prison terms for white-collar crime in Cameron, Missouri, he became acquainted with the prison librarian, Beverly Bonner. Her husband, who was treating Robinson for high blood pressure, divorced her in 1994 after she took up with Robinson. Then, saying she was taking a job that required overseas travel, she disappeared. Meanwhile, her husband regularly mailed $1,000 checks intended for Bonner to an Olathe post office box. The box was rented by Robinson. In January 1997, Robinson killed the 49-year-old Bonner, another murder done by a blow

> In the words of a prosecutor, John E. Robinson Sr. was a liar "of galactic proportions." He lied about everything imaginable, and he was good at it.

Paula Godfrey

Lisa Stasi

Sheila Faith

Debbie Faith

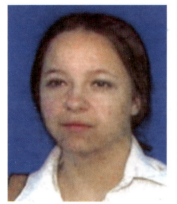
Izabela Lewicka

Catherine Clampitt

Beverly Bonner

to the head in Belton, Missouri. Hers was the third body found in a barrel at the Raymore storage facility.

In June 1997, Izabela Lewicka, a Purdue University student whose scientist parents had moved to West Lafayette, Indiana, from Poland when she was 11, left home and headed west. She said she had lined up an internship in Kansas. Friends in Indiana described Lewicka as an artist, a dreamer and a rebel — with interests in paganism, goth, bondage and discipline sex. In fact, Robinson had lured her west by telling her he was an international book agent who could give her a chance to illustrate books. He rented an apartment in Olathe for her, and she helped him publish a magazine for the mobile home industry. She was last seen in fall 1999. Her body was found in a barrel on Robinson's farm property in Linn County, Kansas.

Robinson's eighth known murder victim was the one who unraveled his activities and brought him to the attention of authorities. In February 2000, 27-year-old Suzette Trouten of Newport in southeast Michigan met Robinson on the internet. Friends said she had an interest in some of the same exotic sex acts as Robinson pursued, and moved to Kansas to pursue a business and personal relationship with him. He killed her, stuffed her body in a barrel and left it at the Linn County farm next to Lewicka's. Then he began to send letters to her family, signed and addressed by Suzette Trouten before he killed her. The letters told them all was well.

In spring 2000, Suzette Trouten's sister, Dawn Trouten, called authorities in Johnson County to report her sister missing. She told them she had moved to the Kansas City area to work for John E. Robinson Sr.

Police from Lenexa and Overland Park began watching Robinson's home and tracking his movements.

The bodies of two victims were found in barrels on Robinson-owned land in Linn County, Kansas.

Barrels containing three more Robinson victims turned up in a storage facility in Raymore, Missouri.

Flanked by his attorneys, John Robinson made a court appearance in November 2001.

They followed his bank and credit-card statements and his telephone records. They found a payment made on March 1, 2000, to an animal clinic in Olathe. It was for boarding two dogs, both of which belonged to Suzette Trouten. Relatives said she was never apart from them.

In late April and mid-May police tracked encounters between Robinson and two new acquaintances, both of whom reported bad experiences with him to police. Then Robinson went to work on an out-of-town woman, trying to persuade her to move to Kansas City with her child. He tried to manipulate a homeless teenager to become his mistress and move into a trailer on his Linn County property.

The authorities had seen enough. On June 2, 2000, they arrested him at his mobile home in Olathe and began searching his house and storage locker. The next day, at his property in Linn County, the investigators found two yellow metal barrels containing the bodies of Suzette Trouten and Izabela Lewicka. In Raymore, they found the other three bodies in barrels.

In fall 2002 Robinson was tried by a Johnson County court, and a jury convicted him in the murders of Trouten, Lewicka and Stasi. For two of the murders, he was sentenced to death.

The next year, he pleaded guilty in Cass County, Missouri, to killing Godfrey, Clampitt, Bonner and the two Faiths. In 2007, the girl he had turned over as an adoptee to his brother and sister-in-law, now 15 years old, won a $5 billion judgment for the strain he had caused her. The amount was set extraordinarily high to ensure that Robinson would never profit from a book or movie about his exploits.

His wife of more than four decades, meanwhile, filed for divorce in 2005.

In 2010, at age 66, Robinson remained in the Kansas prison system, at the El Dorado Correctional Facility, awaiting execution while undertaking various appeals.

Who is she?

Police come upon a brutally murdered child.
A community rallies to find her name and her killer.

THE CRIME

» **When:** 2001

» **What:** The headless body of a 3-year-old girl was found in brush along a dirt road. Later her head was found nearby in a plastic sack.

» **Where:** Eastern Kansas City, Missouri.

» **Status:** The girl's father was sentenced to life in prison for the murder of his daughter. The mother got 25 years.

On the night of April 28, 2001, a man called Kansas City police to report that an elderly friend had wandered away from home and into a wooded area near 59th Street and Kensington Avenue. The woods lay less than a mile north of Swope Park, between Swope Parkway and I-435.

Two policemen arrived and walked down a winding dirt road that disappeared into bushes and trees. Within minutes, word reached them that the elderly man had been found. They ended the search and began walking back to their car.

Along the way, they noticed something just off the dirt road. It was the body of a child. The body had no clothes. It also had no head.

The policemen summoned the murder squad.

So began a search that would stretch four long, frustrating years into the future. The questions were many:

Who was the little girl? Who killed her? Was she from Kansas City or somewhere else? Had anyone anywhere reported her missing? Finally, did anyone care?

The last question was the first answered. Innumerable people cared.

Among the first was a 51-year-old man who said he had been trained in searching by the Army. The morning of May 1, after he heard news of the girl's discovery, he walked down the same dirt road where the child's body was found and headed into the brush, sometimes walking and sometimes on hands and knees. About noon, four hours after he began, he paused to rest. As he glanced at the sky he heard insects buzzing nearby. He looked down. Three feet away lay a doubled-up plastic trash bad, knotted and wedged

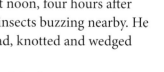

Likenesses of Precious Doe such as the one above were circulated for four years until she was identified as Erica Michelle Marie Green, facing page.

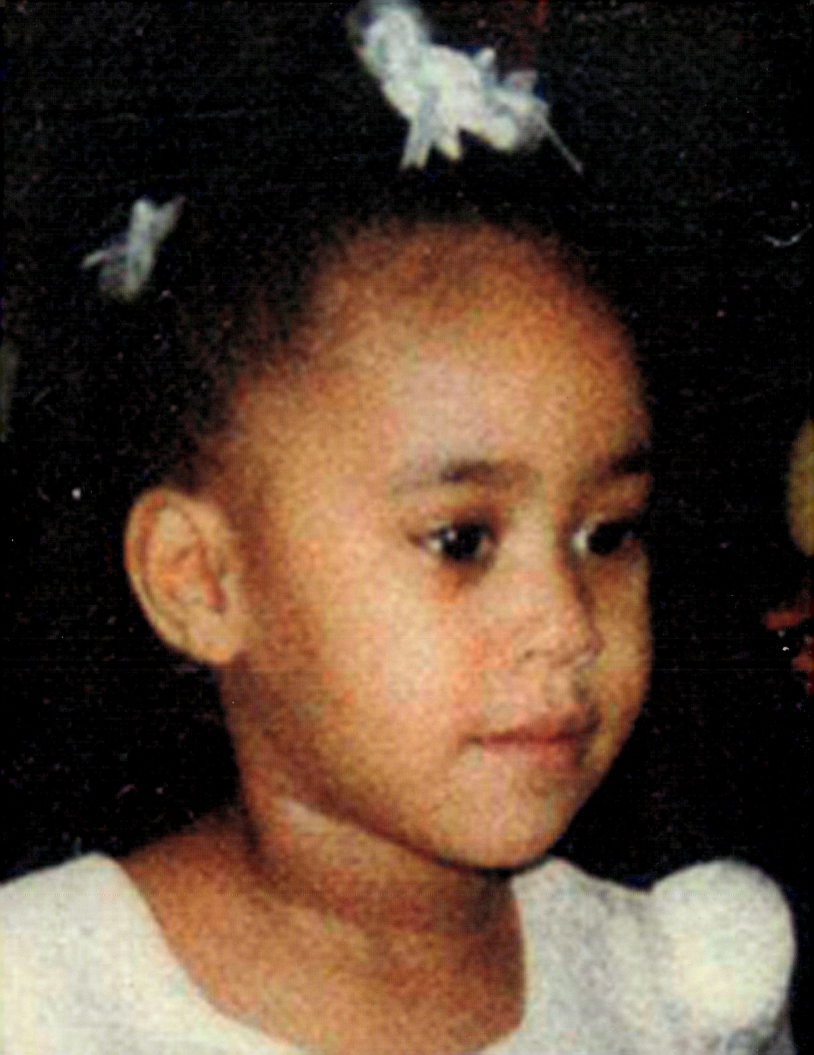

Community activists kept up the search for Precious Doe's identity.

between an old tire and a rock. He traced it with his cane, and thought the contents felt like a face.

Police were summoned again. Inside the trash bag they found the deteriorated head of a child. Snapshots of it were sent to the local branch of the National Center for Missing and Exploited Children, and forwarded to reconstruction experts in the organization's national office in Washington. Soon, a computer image was e-mailed back to Kansas City. It showed a girl with large bright eyes and her hair in cornrows.

Now, there was a face to show the public. Then came a name.

Move UP — an organization based in the black community that merged efforts of earlier groups formed to battle crime and drug abuse — named the child "Precious Doe." Volunteers raised reward money, handed out fliers with the computer image across the city and pressed police to find leads. Rallies were held. A reward fund grew to $5,500 and later to $33,000.

"I've never seen so many people want to get involved as in this case," said a leader of the effort. "Somehow this case has struck a chord. It transcends racial lines, social lines, economic lines. I've seen all types of people very involved and touched by the story."

Scores of leads arrived at the Police Department, but all fizzled out. No one recognized her and no one identified her.

"It's sad to me," said a policeman, "to think that in this girl's life, that no one would miss her if she disappeared."

Months passed. In late August 2001, a three-dimensional bust of the girl — created by a Philadelphia artist from photographs of the child's remains — was unveiled.

Precious Doe was thought to have been from 3 to 4 years old when she died, and her body was believed to have been in the woods only a few days.

In December 2001, the Jackson County medical examiner released the girl's body for burial, and funeral services were held.

The "America's Most Wanted" television show featured the case of Precious Doe multiple times. Authorities performed DNA tests on 10 missing girls from across the country; none of them turned out to be Precious Doe.

Through all of 2002 and into 2003 the investigation continued. In May 2003, police unveiled a third likeness of the girl, this one done by a sketch artist. That summer, police and cemetery workers exhumed Precious Doe's remains and delivered them to Louisiana State University, where experts tried once more to create a realistic bust of the girl.

In September 2003 the result, a soft-clay bust, was revealed to the public. Still, the child remained unidentified.

Finally, in spring 2005 police received a useful lead. A man called from Oklahoma, saying he was related to Precious Doe, knew her identity, the identity of her mother and the name of her killer. Two Kansas City detectives drove to Oklahoma to check out his story. It checked out.

On May 5, 2005, Precious Doe was identified as Erica Michelle Marie Green. She was 3 years old and from Muskogee in eastern Oklahoma.

All at once, after four years, information about the

Two busts of Precious Doe: One created by a Philadelphia artist in 2001, top, and another created at Louisiana State University in 2003.

dead child came spilling out. Erica's mother was Michelle Johnson, 30, a prostitute who by then had seven other children. Erica was born while her mother was serving time in prison. Michelle Johnson had fallen in with a customer, 25-year-old Harrell Johnson, who also had a prison record.

Because of their past, both Michelle and Harrell Johnson had no luck finding jobs in Muskogee. In spring 2001, they drove to Kansas City to look for work. They took Erica with them, and stayed with relatives.

One night Erica refused to lie down to go to bed. Harrell Johnson, drunk and drugged with PCP, kicked her in the head, and Erica collapsed. The parents, worried that they would be arrested on outstanding warrants, did not call for help. After at least two days breathing but unconscious, Erica died. Trying to hide her identity, Harrell Johnson decapitated her with hedge trimmers.

When the Johnsons returned to Muskogee, neighbors asked what had happened to Erica. They replied variously that the child was being cared for in Chicago, or was living with someone in Kansas City. Less than eight months after Erica was killed, Michelle Johnson gave birth to another child.

In 2002, Michelle and Harrell Johnson were married. From prison, Harrell Johnson wrote letters to Michelle Johnson, expressing regret for some undefined act. Later, Michelle Johnson let the man who eventually tipped off Kansas City police read the letters. He heard her threaten Harrell Johnson with life in prison.

Eventually, the tipster's identity was made known. He was 81-year-old Thurmon McIntosh of Muskogee, Harrell Johnson's grandfather.

McIntosh had come to Kansas City to attend a funeral in 2004. He called police about Erica's case, but the detective did not believe his story. Then McIntosh saw an ad in *The Kansas City Call*, to which he had a mail subscription because of family members in Kansas City. It showed two of the depictions of Precious Doe. McIntosh thought he recognized her.

As it turned out, McIntosh called Kansas City police 50 times in the months to come, but only three calls were logged and none of the calls was believed — until the last one. In that conversation, McIntosh reported that he had confronted his grandson about the murder. The details McIntosh relayed along to police were those only the killer would have known.

Under interrogation, Harrell Johnson confessed to the crime. In October 2008 he was convicted of first-degree murder and sentenced to life in prison. A judge told him: "Your actions were ghoulish, vile and by any measure revolting."

Michelle Johnson pleaded guilty to second-degree murder in September 2007 and received a 25-year sentence. She testified against Harrell Johnson.

The body of Erica Green, which had remained in the Jackson County morgue since her exhumation, was reburied in August 2005.

In 2009 the area where her body was found was dedicated as a memorial to her and to more than two dozen Kansas City-children who had been murdered.

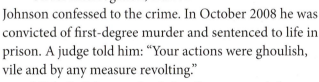
The house in Kansas City where Erica Green was killed.

Michelle Johnson

Harrell Johnson

Thurmon McIntosh

Diluted

Robert Courtney: An upstanding pharmacist — or so it seems — until his drugs prove to have been weakened.

THE CRIME

- **When:** Early 1990s - 2001
- **What:** Pharmacist Robert Courtney diluted tens of thousands of prescriptions and pocketed the money he saved.
- **Where:** Kansas City, Missouri.
- **Status:** Courtney was sentenced to no more than 30 years in prison in exchange for revealing the extent of his crime.

Growing up the son of an itinerant revivalist minister, Robert Courtney learned what it was like to scratch for a living.

From Palco, Kansas, to Wynne, Arkansas, to Pickens, Alabama, to Kimball and Beaver City, Nebraska, to the Texas Panhandle, Courtney's father took his family along a trail of rural congregations, none of which could afford to pay a preacher much.

In the late 1960s, when Robert Courtney reached high school age, his family had reached Wichita. Robert's father preached a few years at Trinity Assembly of God in an industrial area of town. Young Robert graduated from Wichita South High School and entered Wichita State University, where he spent two years.

In 1972, he transferred to the University of Missouri-Kansas City and in 1975 he graduated from its School of Pharmacy.

Courtney appeared to be a fine fit in a profession typified by probity. Patients and doctors, after all, depend on pharmacists to do their work carefully and reliably. Acquaintances regarded him as introverted and disciplined and, true to his upbringing in a minister's family, deeply religious.

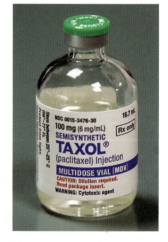

Taxol, a cancer drug, was one of many that Robert Courtney diluted in his pharmaceutical career.

As the years passed Courtney made a success of himself. In the middle 1980s he bought Research Medical Tower Pharmacy near the Research Medical Center and later another pharmacy in Johnson County near Shawnee Mission Medical Center. He won the respect of his peers for pioneering efforts in the field and made the kind of money he could only have dreamed of in his early years.

By 2001, when he turned 48 years old, Courtney lived in a large home in the Northland with his third wife and children. The family traveled often to ski resorts in

Robert Courtney, clockwise from above: as a child with his parents and sisters, as a Wichita high school student, as a UMKC pharmacy student, videotaped giving his deposition in 2002. Below: Courtney's Northland home.

Colorado and to the Caribbean, but rarely socialized with others in the neighborhood.

Courtney owned millions in stock, and almost a million in property plus the two pharmacies. He gave $600,000 to his church. He moved his father, the one-time traveling minister, into another house in the Northland.

Then Courtney's success came crashing down. With it went his reputation. Shocking information came to light — first in a trickle and then in a torrent — that he was diluting the drugs he sold.

His prescriptions, it turned out, gave too little or no help to unsuspecting, seriously ill patients. People suffering lung cancer, breast cancer, ovarian cancer and scores of other grievous and life-threatening ailments got only a fraction of what their doctors prescribed.

Conversely, those same medications cost far more than they were worth.

One sample of an order for 1,900 milligrams of

Gemzar, a chemotherapy drug, showed it contained only 24 percent of the amount prescribed. Courtney's charge for the full amount was $1,021, but he delivered only

Courtney's pharmacy near Research Medical Center. Below: an array of drugs Courtney diluted over the years.

$242 worth. The difference of $780, compounded with hundreds of similar shortages in other prescriptions, was enough to make him rich.

Courtney began diluting drugs in 1992. Eventually more than 1,000 recipients of his bad dosages were identified. Authorities estimated as many as 4,200 patients might have been affected.

The scheme unraveled because of a sharp-eyed pharmaceutical representative and a concerned doctor. In mid-May 2001, a salesman for the Eli Lilly pharmaceutical company told a Kansas City oncologist that Courtney's pharmacy had bought from Lilly only one-third of the amount of the drug Gemzar that he purportedly provided to the oncologist and that he billed to her office.

The oncologist had a sample from Courtney's office tested. It contained only one-third the amount prescribed. The oncologist stopped doing business with Courtney and went to her lawyer. Her lawyer went to agents of the FBI.

The agents tested more of the Courtney pharmacy's products and found they contained only 17 percent to 39 percent of the prescribed amount. They asked the oncologist to order more, and tested that prescription. It, too, contained only a fraction of the required medication.

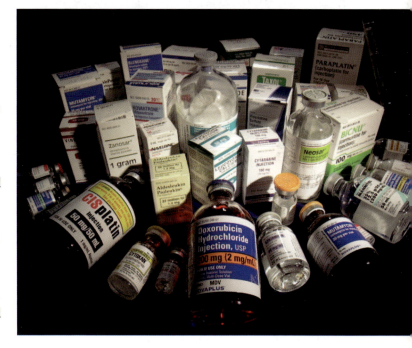

The more the agents looked, the more diluted examples they found. One sample contained less than 1 percent of the prescribed amount.

Some victims of Courtney's tampering: S.C. Coates lost his wife to cancer, top left; Shirley Thompson lost a relative to cancer, top right; cancer patient Delia Chelston with her husband, above left; cancer victim Adelia Atwood and her husband, above center; cancer victim Georgia Hayes, above right.

In mid-August 2001, Courtney was charged with one felony count of misbranding and adulterating a drug. He turned himself in. Barely a week later, the number of suspected dilutions and victims was growing.

By late August about 80 agents and employees of the FBI and the Food and Drug Administration were working on what was developing into a massive case of pharmaceutical fraud.

Along the way, they learned how Courtney maintained his customers' confidence while cheating them. They interviewed a victim who had gone to Courtney's pharmacy near Research Medical Center to pick up her medicine, which was contained in syringes. The patient found the syringes were only half full, and returned to the pharmacy for replacements. There, she met Courtney.

"He smiled at me," the patient recalled, "touched my arm and said, 'We'll take care of you.'"

The FBI tested one of those replacements. It was diluted.

The daughter of another cancer victim called Courtney "a real-life monster in a white coat who smiles and pretends to help you." The woman's mother had received diluted Taxol from Courtney before she died.

Courtney was charged with diluting the drugs of 34 cancer victims. At first, he confessed to agents, but in court pleaded not guilty.

He changed his plea to guilty in late February 2002. In exchange for a promise to serve no more than 30 years in prison, he admitted tampering with prescriptions of eight cancer patients, and also to 12 counts of adulterating chemotherapy medications.

In addition, he agreed that he diluted 50 additional doses of chemotherapy drugs prescribed for the eight patients in whose cases he was charged, and 102 doses to 26 additional cancer patients. He pledged to work with investigators to reveal the true scope of his dilutions.

Meanwhile, 17 of the 34 cancer patients died.

As agents interviewed Courtney further, the list grew. He admitted diluting 72 different medications over nearly a decade. Most of the drugs were cancer treatments, but others could have been used to treat AIDS, multiple sclerosis, arthritis and other diseases.

The authorities estimated his scheme could have touched 400 doctors, 4,200 patients and as many as 98,000 prescriptions.

At his sentencing in December 2002, the judge was direct.

"Your crimes are a shock to the conscience of a nation," U.S. District Judge Ortrie Smith told Courtney. "You alone have changed the way a nation thinks, the way a nation thinks about pharmacists, the way the nation thinks about prescription medication, the way a nation thinks about those institutions we trusted blindly."

His insurance company agreed to pay $35 million to settle cases brought by his victims, and two pharmaceutical makers paid $71 million in settlements.

His millions of dollars in assets were sold to create a fund for restitution. About 1,000 victims were identified and received more than $10,000 each.

Courtney's church returned his $600,000 donation through restitution funds.

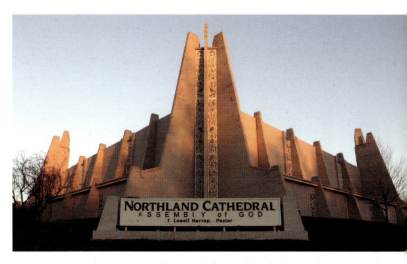

Courtney's former church returned his $600,000 donation by way of funds distributed to his victims.

Out of the blue

On the job one summer at a neighborhood pool, a 19-year-old dies at the hands of someone she has never met.

THE CRIME

» **When:** 2002
» **What:** Ali Kemp, 19, was murdered in the pump room of a surburban pool.
» **Where:** 123rd Street and State Line Road, Leawood, Kansas
» **Status:** Benjamin Appleby was convicted of the murder in 2006 and sentenced to life in prison without possibility of parole for 50 years.

The man who murdered Ali Kemp struck like a lightning bolt from a clear blue sky.

Until those horrific few minutes at the swimming pool where she worked — minutes when he strangled her, beat her and left her for dead in the pump room — he had never seen or heard of Ali Kemp. Likewise, she had never seen or heard of him.

Unlike stalkers, jilted lovers, robbers or revenge-seekers — unlike the majority of murderers — Benjamin Appleby did not intend to kill anyone when on June 18, 2002, he drove up to the Foxborough Community Pool in Leawood. He meant simply to sell his pool-cleaning services to the management, or at least to leave his name with any employee he could find.

Lugging a plastic bucket, the 26-year-old Appleby walked from his pickup truck to the gate and into the pool area. Cars were buzzing past along State Line Road to the east. Across 123rd Street to the north, people came and went at a shopping center. No one was swimming or lounging by the pool; the day had begun with discouraging clouds.

The only employee on duty that June afternoon, Alexandra "Ali" Kemp, had gone inside the pump room, where pool supplies, chairs and pool toys were stored in addition to housing the pumps. A 19-year-old student at Kansas State University, she signed on for the pool job in the summer between her freshman and sophomore years.

According to *Ali Was Here* by James Kirkpatrick Davis, at college Ali was her

Host John Walsh filmed a scene showing the pool and pump room for a segment of "America's Most Wanted."

Ali Kemp flanked by boyfriend Phil Howes and her father, above. Posing with friends, upper right. Ali was at center.

sorority's representative to the Panhellenic council, and an honors student who finished her first year in the top 10 percent of her class. She played intramural soccer and basketball. At Blue Valley North High School, she had posted a similar record. She was a member of the National Honor Society and of the Sweetheart court, and she lettered on the soccer team.

Benjamin Appleby — who dropped out of high school and had never been to college — surveyed the pool and its surroundings. Seeing no one, he peeked inside the pump house. There, he saw Ali Kemp, dressed casually in a T-shirt and shorts.

Immediately, he was filled with an aggressive, overwhelming lust. He began making advances, first with words and then physically. Ali Kemp resisted, and tried to get around Appleby in the doorway.

When she did, he reached for her. She struck him. He flew into a rage. He hit her several times and tossed her to the floor, and the two struggled. Over and over he tried to strangle her until she fell unconscious. Then he tried and failed to rape her.

Covering her with a tarpaulin, Appleby walked out of the pump house and through the pool complex gate, got in his pickup truck and drove away. The entire event, a battle between two people who had never seen or heard of one another, took about a quarter of an hour. Now, Ali Kemp lay dying.

Ali's younger brother, Tyler Kemp, was scheduled to work the next shift at the pool. When he showed up he did not see his sister, became worried and called home. Home was also in Leawood about a mile from the pool. Ali's father, Roger Kemp, had just arrived from work and took Tyler's call. Immediately, he drove to the pool.

There, in the pump room, he found his daughter, covered with bruises and her hair matted with blood. An ambulance took her to a hospital, where she was pronounced dead at 6:13 p.m.

Police investigators flocked to the pool and began looking for clues in the disarray of the pump room. Chief among them was a tube of antibiotic ointment that showed signs of blood stains. It was undoubtedly the blood of Ali's murderer, and a DNA test would show it was that of a particular Caucasian male. But of all the Caucasian males in the world, whose blood was it?

Tips came flooding in. Leawood Police detectives

spent days checking out sex criminals recently released from prison, with no results.

The "America's Most Wanted" television program broadcast a report about Ali's murder, and hundreds more tips poured into the show's telephone banks in Washington, D.C. Still, nothing clicked.

One person had seen Appleby at the Foxborough pool. A friend of Ali's drove up right after the murder, just as Appleby was leaving. He waved at her as he walked to his pickup. Knowing nothing about what had just happened, Ali's friend paid little attention to him. Not seeing Ali, she drove away.

Based on her memory, however, a composite illustration of the suspect was produced.

Roger Kemp, her father, worked through his grief by pitching in to help find the killer. He rounded up volunteers and put wanted posters displaying the composite illustration in stores and malls in Leawood and other suburbs of Kansas City. He put up a $5,000 reward and later increased it to $24,000. With help from the city of Leawood and the Kansas City Crime Commission, the reward grew to $50,000.

When none of those efforts produced a suspect, Roger Kemp hit upon the idea of putting the composite

Sketch artist Lee Hammond produced an illustration of the killer based on a sighting made as he left the murder scene. With her is retired policeman Craig Hill. Below: Roger Kemp created "wanted" billboards that were placed throughout metropolitan Kansas City.

illustration and a "wanted" message on billboards throughout the Kansas City metropolitan area. A new flood of leads came in to Leawood police.

Despite all those efforts, Benjamin Appleby stayed a step ahead of the law.

He was accustomed to it. Throughout the 1990s, Appleby had been in and out of trouble around Kansas City — fights, robberies and incidents of indecent exposure. He spent time in prison for the robberies and time in jail for exposing himself to young women. At one point in his incarceration, a therapist described him as extremely immature, deeply troubled and failing to understand the severity of his sexual misconduct.

In 1997, with a warrant out for his arrest on yet another case of indecent exposure, Appleby decided to leave town and to take on an alias. He chose the name of a dead childhood friend. Teddy Hoover had been killed in an accident when he was 13 years old.

Winding up in Connecticut, Appleby met a woman. The next year, he returned with her to the Kansas City area and got a job with a pool maintenance company. In 2001 he started Hoover Pool Services, the name of the company he represented on the day in June 2002 when he killed Ali Kemp.

The year 2002 ended with no progress toward finding Ali Kemp's killer, and the year 2003 unfolded with an equal lack of results.

Then came the first hint of Appleby's involvement. In mid-February, after the billboard campaign began, a caller to the Kansas City Crime Commission's hotline said a man named "Ben Hoover" looked like the composite and fit the verbal description of the suspect. Like the other tips, many of which also claimed to identify a person who looked like the suspect, the one about "Ben Hoover" was placed in a police database.

On June 18, 2003, the first anniversary of Ali Kemp's murder, a caller told Leawood police to look for "Teddy L. Hoover," and gave an address for him in Kansas City, Kansas. The tip was put in line for follow-up with the scores of others about people that detectives wanted to interview.

The follow-up came in early September. A Leawood detective visited the house mentioned by the tipster and spoke with the man using the name Teddy Hoover. Appleby began to feel the heat and in early October again left town.

In November, a third tip connected "Ben Hoover" to the crime. In the mixup over the first name by the tipsters, and amid a sea of other tips, this one seemed of no greater significance than many others.

By then, Benjamin Appleby was back in Connecticut with his girlfriend. There he opened a new pool-maintenance company and made no secret of the fact that he hailed from Kansas City. This time, he gave his name as Benjamin Appleby. Through September 2004 — two years and three months after he murdered Ali Kemp — he remained a free man.

In October, a Leawood detective, Joe Langer, was narrowing the field of suspects when he noticed a link. The man interviewed in Kansas City, Kansas, in

Benjamin Appleby as a teenager.

September 2003 — the man who called himself Teddy Hoover — was known to have lived with a woman named Lara Barr. That man had left town for parts unknown. Perhaps Lara Barr was with him and could be tracked down.

Langer contacted the U.S. Postal Service, which reported that a Lara Barr lived on Bantam Road in Bantam, Connecticut. A man received mail at that address, too, a man named Benjamin Appleby. Langer called the Connecticut State Police and asked them to check on that name and also on a Teddy Hoover. Their investigation revealed that a Teddy Hoover was wanted for two incidents of indecent exposure — these in Connecticut — in the late 1990s.

The Leawood police sensed they were on to something, but still there remained the confusion of names: Ben Hoover, Teddy Hoover, Benjamin Appleby.

A telephone number created the final link. As it happened, on June 18, 2002, only hours after he killed Ali Kemp, Benjamin Appleby had driven back to the Foxborough pool just before police cordoned off the parking lot. As the officers directed cars out of the area, they took the drivers' names. Appleby gave his as Teddy Hoover with a cellphone number of 913-488-1190.

None of the three telephone tipsters in 2003 had given that number when reporting on the suspect named Hoover.

Now it was October 2004. Eager to try anything, a detective began poring through automobile accident reports from the area near the pool. One was dated December 2001 — six months before Ali Kemp's murder. It listed a Teddy Hoover with a cell number of 913-488-1190. Now the name Hoover and the cellphone number were linked in the Kansas City area, along with the history

In jail clothes and handcuffs, Benjamin Appleby walked to court in Olathe in January 2005. Months later, he dressed up for his preliminary hearing.

of sex crimes by a Teddy Hoover in Connecticut. Various clues from the telephone tips in 2003 had indicated that Hoover — "Ben" or "Teddy" — had a violent temper, that he had displayed a cast on one hand the week after Ali Kemp's brutal death, that he had once lived in Connecticut and that at one point had gone by the first name, "Ben."

After that, Leawood detectives made quick work of the matter. They traveled to Connecticut and, with help of the state police, arrested Appleby. Within hours, he confessed twice to the slaying of Ali Kemp, once to detectives alone and then before a video camera. A sample of his DNA matched the sample that investigators had found on the ointment bottle at the pool.

In mid-November 2004, the authorities brought Benjamin Appleby back to Kansas, where he was charged in the murder of Ali Kemp. Two years later, after a series of legal motions had run its course, his trial got under way in Johnson County District Court in Olathe.

In early December 2006, a jury found him guilty of capital murder and attempted rape of Ali Kemp.

At Appleby's sentencing later that month, a specialist called by defense lawyers described the convict's miserable upbringing. As a child, Appleby was abused and mentally and beaten often in a home where cocaine was used and prostitution took place. After his parents divorced, the young Appleby bounced from one to the other. At age 16 he went out on his own. One traumatic event damaged his ability to be close to other people, the specialist said. It was the death of his boyhood friend and later namesake, Teddy Hoover.

Often, Appleby showed "a strong outpouring of rage"

out of proportion to any provocation. That appeared to match what happened on the day he killed Ali Kemp.

At 31 years of age, Benjamin Appleby was sentenced to life in prison without the possibility of parole for 50 years.

For the family of Ali Kemp, the most traumatic event of their lives was tempered somewhat by the good that came of the aftermath.

Believing his daughter might have survived the assault with proper training, Roger Kemp and his wife established a fund to teach young women self-defense. TAKE — The Ali Kemp Educational Foundation — has presented hundreds of classes to thousands of girls and women from coast to coast. Roger Kemp often accompanies the instructors, telling the students the story of his daughter's death.

Meanwhile, his idea for a billboard showing the composite of a crime suspect has been adopted in cities around the country, particularly with the advent of up-to-the-minute electronic billboards.

Ali Kemp, the family hopes, did not die in vain.

Courtroom spectators reviewed Benjamin Appleby's confession, videotaped in Connecticut the day he was arrested.

Below: Across the United States, thousands of women have taken self-defense classes provided by The Ali Kemp Educational Foundation — TAKE.

Roger Kemp at the site of Ali's grave and memorial in Kansas City.

BIBLIOGRAPHY/SUGGESTED READINGS

The Kansas City Star, Kansas City Times and *Kansas City Journal* covered many of the crimes in this book in great detail and much of the information comes from the work of their reporters, editors, artists and photographers. Several of these crimes and criminals have received book-length treatments, which were of course quite useful, and some of those are listed here. Still others have been treated in historical reviews or popular magazines.

The earliest chapter, covering the murder of the Rev. Thomas Johnson was drawn mostly from articles that appeared in century-old histories such as William G. Cutler's *History of the State of Kansas,* William E. Connelley's *A Standard History of Kansas and Kansans* and A. T. Andreas' *History of the State of Kansas.* Only one newspaper existed in Kansas City in January 1865, the *Journal*, and its articles about Johnson's death were rather spare.

Jesse James is, not unexpectedly, our most-discussed criminal. The list of books and articles about him and his gang is nearly voluminous enough to fill a book by itself. I found three books that were extensive, detailed and careful with facts. *Jesse James: Last Rebel of the Civil War* by T. J. Stiles and published in 2002 is thoroughly researched and has an interesting thesis about James' life. For several decades, the basic text on the outlaw's life has been *Jesse James Was His Name; or, Fact and Fiction concerning the Careers of the Notorious James Brothers of Missouri* by William A. Settle Jr. Ted Yeatman's *Frank & Jesse James: The Story Behind the Legend* is packed with information.

The shooting death of policeman Patrick Jones and the lynching of Levi Harrington have only been touched upon in histories of Kansas City. Contemporary newspaper accounts of the events, of the coroner's inquest afterward and of various court proceedings against the accused provided most of the information about this case. It deserves a closer look by future historians.

The murder of Belle Carr, which goes mostly unremembered these days, got extensive coverage in the Kansas City newspapers of the time. The same is true of James Sharp, a/k/a "Adam God," and his well-armed band of evangelists, young and old.

As for Thomas Swope and members of his clan who died or fell ill so mysteriously in that great mansion in Independence, much has been written in newspapers and magazines. In 2009, a gripping and extensively documented book about the matter appeared. It is Giles Fowler's *Deaths on Pleasant Street: The Ghastly Enigma of Colonel Swope and Doctor Hyde.*

The three kidnappings of the early 1930s, those of Michael Katz, Nell Donnelly and Mary McElroy, were detailed in newspapers of the day. The Donnelly matter is also covered in Terence O'Malley's book, *Nelly Don: A Stitch in Time.*

A must-read for anyone interested in the Kansas City of the Pendergast era is William Rettig's *Tom's Town.* It covers the three famous kidnappings plus the Union Station Massacre, the gangland hit on Ferris Anthon, the election-day violence of 1934, the slaying of John Lazia and the bloody death of Leila Welsh.

The Kansas City investigation : Pendergast's Downfall, 1938-1939 by Treasury agent Rudolph H. Hartmann gives a fascinating inside look at many of the characters who move in and out of these chapters.

For the shootout that tops them all, Robert Unger's *The Union Station Massacre: The Original Sin of J. Edgar Hoover's FBI* makes excellent use of FBI documents, and yet turns parts of the FBI's version of events on their head.

The literature about Clyde Barrow, Bonnie Parker and the gang is plentiful, and several books mention their visit to Platte County. Among those volumes are E. R. Milner's *The Lives and Times of Bonnie and Clyde* and Blanche Caldwell Barrow's and John Neal Phillips' *My Life with Bonnie & Clyde.*

As of this writing there's a possibility that a book will be in the works on the slaying of Leila Welsh, one of Kansas City's most intriguing events, not only for the crime itself but for the political spiderweb that entangled the investigation and prosecution.

The kidnapping and murder of Bobby Greenlease has inspired several books, chief among them *A Grave for Bobby: The Greenlease Slaying* by James Deakin. The latest is *Zero at the Bone: The Playboy, the Prostitute, and the Murder of Bobby Greenlease* by John Heidenry. Newspaper coverage, both text and photographic, was exhaustive and makes a fine resource.

Bibliography/Suggested Readings

Lowell Lee Andrews' bad deed might have been the subject of Truman Capote's great non-fiction novel, according to the author's own statement, but its mention toward the end of *In Cold Blood* is chilling enough.

As for that wildly failed moneymaking scheme of native son Richard Eugene Hickock, which was hatched in the environs of Kansas City and carried out by him and Perry Smith with the murders of the Clutter family in southwest Kansas, Capote's *In Cold Blood* remains the basic text. The author was stingy, however, with some Kansas City-area facts concerning Hickock. Newspaper accounts of the time and decades later in *The Daily News of Johnson County* and *The Kansas City Star* and *Times* were used in this book to fill in details. An interview with Ray Braun of Edgerton, Kansas, who remembered Hickock and his father, shed interesting light on the criminal's character.

The deeds and misdeeds of Sharon Kinne are definitely enough to fill a book, and that book is *I'm Just an Ordinary Girl : The Sharon Kinne Story* by James C. Hays. *The Kansas City Star* and *Times* also gave close attention to her bold criminal career.

Primitivo Garcia is considered a hero for trying to help his English-language teacher and getting mortally wounded in the process. No book has been written about him, but in his honor an elementary school on Kansas City's West Side bears his name.

Jo Ellen Weigel's death flashed briefly across the pages of newspapers in 1970. Occasional anniversary articles have mentioned how the man accused of killing her remains at large decades later.

The murder of Leon Jordan, who established Freedom Inc. and fought to wrest control of the black community from white politicians, has been dealt with in research papers and other material available at the LaBudde Special Collections at the University of Missouri-Kansas City's Miller Nichols Library. The library has an extensive collection of papers and images related to him. *The Star* and *Times* covered his slaying and the subsequent investigations and trials. Recently it has raised questions about the handling of evidence in the case.

Many books and websites about organized crime in the United States give information about the River Quay, mob wars and local organized crime's infiltration of Las Vegas casinos. Newspaper accounts and images of the 1970s and 1980s provide a wealth of information.

Sueanne Hobson is the subject of two books, both published in 1992 and both of which were used for this chapter along with newspaper files. The books: *Family Affairs* by Andy Hoffman and *Crazymaker* by Thomas J. O'Donnell.

Robert Berdella's grisly criminal career was covered closely by *The Star* and *Times* and also in *Rites of Burial* by former *Times* reporter Tom Jackman and policeman Troy Cole.

Richard Grissom's activities unfolded in *The Star* and *Times*, and were covered later in a book, *Suddenly Gone: The Kansas Murders of Serial Killer Richard Grissom* by Dan Mitrione.

The explosion that killed six firefighters and roused tens of thousands of Kansas Citians from their sleep has been covered extensively at the time and in years since by *The Star* and *Times*. The newspapers also provided information on Aaron Frazier's awful handiwork.

Debora Green's descent from physician to inmate was chronicled in Ann Rule's *Bitter Harvest: A Woman's Fury, a Mother's Sacrifice*, and in extensive newspaper coverage.

John E. Robinson's double life was covered in *The Star*, as were Robert Courtney's diluted prescriptions.

The brutal slaying of Ali Kemp has been detailed in *Ali Was Here: A Promising Life, a Brutal Murder, Justice and a Legacy of Hope* by James Kirkpatrick Davis.

ACKNOWLEDGMENTS

I am immensely grateful to the directors and staff members who work at the multitude of archives and libraries with which the Kansas City area is blessed. They have the keys to elusive facts and rare images that help create a book like this.

First, thanks to Derek Donovan and his staff in the research department of *The Kansas City Star* for allowing me to browse the newspaper's extensive library of clips, microfilm, books and images. Technological help came from *The Star*'s Rob Perschau. I thank him and also Les Weatherford, who was copy editor of this book.

Special thanks also go to Stuart Hinds and his staff of the LaBudde Special Collections at the Miller Nichols Library, University of Missouri-Kansas City. Among other things they alerted me to the existence of a late-19th-century crime that otherwise would not have appeared here. David Jackson of the Jackson County Historical Society provided not only images but also valuable information and contacts.

Mary Beveridge and her staff at the Missouri Valley Special Collections department of the Kansas City Public Library were their customary friendly and helpful selves, as were Mindi Love at the Johnson County Museum and Christine Montgomery at the State Historical Society of Missouri in Columbia, who aided me greatly with last-minute requests.

People in Edgerton, Kansas, aided my search for information about Richard Eugene Hickock. Ray Braun, a former businessman, sheriff's deputy and mayor, remembered Hickock and his father. The staff at Edgerton Elementary School helped me find Hickock's high school graduation photo.

Tony Sands of the Kansas City Police Department went out of his way to provide a rare image of Patrick Jones, the second Kansas City policeman to die in the line of duty.

As ever, I'm unendingly grateful to the book designer, Jean Donaldson Dodd, who is also my wife. She organizes books beautifully, creates a superb look for them, and inevitably offers valuable criticism of the text.

— *Monroe Dodd*

ILLUSTRATION CREDITS

Photographs and illustrations are from the files of *The Kansas City Star*, except as noted here.

2. Right: Kansas State Historical Society.

9. The State Historical Society of Missouri.

17. Library of Congress Prints and Photographs Division Washington, D.C.

18-19. Art © T. H. Benton and R. P. Benton Testamentary Trusts/UMB Bank Trustee/Licensed by VAGA, New York, NY.

20. Top: Library of Congress Prints and Photographs Division Washington, D.C. Middle: The State Historical Society of Missouri.

21. The State Historical Society of Missouri.

24. Kansas City Police Historical Society.

25. Missouri Valley Special Collections, Kansas City Public Library, Kansas City, Missouri.

27. Missouri Valley Special Collections, Kansas City Public Library, Kansas City, Missouri.

31. *Kansas City Journal*

32. *Kansas City Journal*

33. *Kansas City Journal*

34. *Kansas City Journal*

35. Top: Used by permission of the University of Missouri-Kansas City Libraries, Dr. Kenneth J. LaBudde Department of Special Collections. Bottom: *Kansas City Journal*.

43. Library of Congress Prints and Photographs Division Washington, D.C.

44. Library of Congress Prints and Photographs Division Washington, D.C.

45. Jackson County Historical Society Archives.

46. Upper: Reeves Library, Westminster College, Fulton, Missouri. Lower: Jackson County Historical Society Archives.

47. Left: Jackson County Historical Society Archives. Center and right:

48: Upper: Missouri Valley Special Collections, Kansas City Public Library, Kansas City, Missouri. Lower: Library of Congress Prints and Photographs Division Washington, D.C.

63: Upper: Missouri Valley Special Collections, Kansas City Public Library, Kansas City, Missouri.

74. Jim Spawn and Howard Breen.

75. Jim Spawn.

76. Jim Spawn.

77. Howard Breen.

80. Missouri Valley Special Collections, Kansas City Public Library, Kansas City, Missouri.

82. Missouri Valley Special Collections, Kansas City Public Library, Kansas City, Missouri.

84. Missouri Valley Special Collections, Kansas City Public Library, Kansas City, Missouri.

127. Right: Kansas State Historical Society.

128: Edgerton Elementary School, Edgerton, Kansas.

129: Kansas State Historical Society.

150: Left: Used by permission of the University of Missouri-Kansas City Libraries, Dr. Kenneth J. LaBudde Department of Special Collections.

219. Roger and Kathy Kemp.

220. Roger and Kathy Kemp.

INDEX

A

Adam God 36-41
Adam God cult 36-41
Addison, Courtney 184, 186
Addison, Jason 184, 186
Ad Hoc Group Against Crime.
.... 187
"America's Most Wanted" ....
.... 210, 218, 221
Andrews, Jennie Marie ....
.... 122, 124
Andrews, Lowell Lee ... 122-125
Andrews, Opal 122, 124
Andrews, William Lowell ....
.... 122, 124
Anthon, Ferris 80-87, 111
Anton, Evelyn 85
Appleby, Benjamin 218-224
Argent Corporation 163
Armour Boulevard 82

B

Barker, John T. 106
Barrow, Blanche 74-79
Barrow, Buck 74-79
Barrow, Clyde 74-79
Barrow gang 74-79
Bartle Hall 157
Bash, Jennie 80-84
Bash, Sheriff Tom 80-87, 99
Baxter, William 76
Berdella, Robert 172-177
Big John's saloon 159
Binaggio, Cecilia 110
Binaggio, Charles ....
.... 99, 108-113, 154, 159
Blair, George 54-58
Blue Valley North High School
.... 220
Bob's Bazaar Bizarre 174
Boldizs, John 136-138
Bonadonna, David 157
Bonadonna, Fred 157
Bonner, Beverly 205-206
Bonner Springs, Kansas 57
Border Wars 20
Bowersock, Justin 90
Brannon, Chief Bernard 116
Brooks, Alvin 187
Brown, Richard 182
Brown, Theresa 192
Bruce R. Watkins Memorial
Drive 178
Bureau of Investigation (see
Federal Bureau of Investigation)
bushwhackers 12, 14
Butler, Joan 190-194

C

Caffrey, Ray 68, 69, 70, 72
Calvary Cemetery 145
Cammisano, Joe 157-159
Cammisano, William Sr. ....
.... 157-159
Capote, Truman ....
.... 125, 126, 131, 132
Carr, Belle 30-35
Carr, Bettie Stephens 30-35
Carr, William 30-35
Carrollo, Charles 96-99, 110
Chesterfield Club 85
Citizens-Fusion 88
City Market 27, 94, 154
Civella, Carl 160, 162-164
Civella, Nick 113, 159, 160, 162-164
Civil War 9, 11, 14
Claiborne, Leonard 87
Clampitt, Catherine 205-206
Click, Clarence 62, 64, 65
Cline, Mike 146-149
Clutter, Bonnie 126, 130-131
Clutter, Herbert W. ....
.... 126, 130-131
Clutter, Kenyon ... 126, 130-131
Clutter, Nancy 126, 130-131
Coffey, Sheriff Holt 76-79
Cohn, Robert 113
Coleman, Velma 184, 186
Concourse, the 53
Co-Operative Club 80
Country Club Christian
Church 166
Courtney, Robert 212-217
crime suspect billboards 224
Crumm, James 168-171
Cuban Gardens 96

D

Depew, Martin 58-59
Doe, Precious (see Green, Erica
Michelle Marie)
Donnelly Garment Company ..
.... 54
Donnelly, Nell 54-59
Donnelly, Paul 54, 58
Durant, Winford Ray .. 142, 144

E

Edgerton Rural High School ....
.... 128
Edwards, Darlene 182
Edwards, John 20

F

Faith, Debbie 205-206
Faith, Sheila 205-206
Farrar, Michael 196-201
Federal Bureau of Investigation
(FBI) 69, 70, 72, 73, 162, 164,
193, 215, 216
Finley, William 90
firefighters' explosion .. 178-183
Firefighters Fountain 182
Flacy, Lee 90
Floyd, Charles "Pretty Boy" ......
.... 72-73
Ford, Robert 22
Foxborough Community Pool.
.... 218
Frazier, Aaron O. 187-188
Freedom Inc. 150, 152, 153
French Institute of Notre Dame
de Sion 114
Fry, Thomas 180-181

G

Garcia, Primitivo 142-145
Gargotta, Charles 85-87, 111-113
Godfather Lounge 159
Godfrey, Paula 205-206
Grant, George 29
Graves, W.W. 87
Green, Debora 196-201
Green Duck Tavern 150, 152
Green, Erica Michelle Marie
(Precious Doe) 208-211
Greenlease, Bobby 114-121
Greenlease Cadillac 114
Greenlease, Robert 114, 117-118, 120-121
Greenlease, Virginia ... 114, 116, 121
Griffen, Jack (alias Jack
Gregory) 98-99
Grissom, Richard 190-195
Grooms, William J. "Red" 68, 69, 70, 72
guerrillas 9, 14

H

Hall, Carl Austin 119-121
Halloran, Gerald C. 180, 181
Harrington, Levi 24-29
Heady, Bonnie Brown ....
119-121
Hermanson, Frank 68, 69, 70
Hickock, Richard Eugene ....
126-133
Hobson, Christen 166-171
Hobson, Ed 166-171
Hobson, Sueanne 166-171
Holt, George M. 36, 37
Hoover, J. Edgar ... 66, 72, 73, 99
Hoover Pool Services 221
Hunton, Moss 44-48
Hurd, Luther Eugene ... 180, 181
Hyde, Bennett Clark 44-49
Hyde, Frances Swope 45-48
Hymer, Sheriff Jacob H. ..33-35

J

James A. Reed Wildlife Area ....
.... 59
James, Frank 17, 23
James, Jesse 14-23
James, Zee 21
Jewel Box 166
Johnson, Harrell 211
Johnson, Michelle 211
Johnson, Rev. Thomas 8-13
Johnson, Sarah 8-13
Jones, "Buffalo Pat" 29
Jones, Mary 26
Jones, Patricia 136
Jones, Patrick 24
Jones, Walter 136
Jones, W.D. 74, 76, 79
Jordan, Leon 150-153
Jordan, Orchid 150, 153
Judge Roy Bean's 159

K

Kansas City Fire Department ..
.... 178-183, 184
Kansas City Industrial
Exposition 19
Kansas City Police Department

Index

24-29, 37, 69, 94-96, 150, 153
Kansas City Police Board.......... 108, 113
Kansas Redlegs...................... 12
Kansas State Penitentiary 125, 132
Kansas Territory 8
Katz drugstores 50
Katz, Isaac............................50-53
Katz, Michael....................50-53
Kearney, Missouri................. 19
Kefauver Commission 113, 154
Kefauver, Sen. Estes............. 113
Kemp, Ali..................... 218-225
Kemp, Roger.......................... 220-221, 224-225
Kemp, Tyler 220
Kilventon, James H...... 180, 181
Kindermann, Margaret............ 142, 145
kinetoscope 35
Kinne, James 134, 136, 137, 140
Kinne, Sharon 134-141

L

LaCapra, James Michael . 98, 99
Lackey, Joe 68, 69, 70, 72
Lake Lotawana 96
Lake Winnebago.......... 146, 147
Langer, Joe 222
Last Chance tavern.............. 113
Las Vegas............................ 162
Lazia, John... 58, 65, 69, 85, 91, 94-99, 108, 110, 154
Lazia, Marie..................... 96, 97
Lee's Summit High School........ 146
Lewicka, Izabela.................. 205
Lincoln High School 150
Little Italy.............................. 94

M

McElroy, Henry F.... 60, 63, 65, 94
McElroy, Mary 60-65
McGee, Walter 62-65
McIntosh, Thurmon 211
McKarnin, Robert D. ...180, 181
Mele, Charles.................. 58, 59
Menninger Clinic 125, 199
Metcalf South Shopping Center 168
Milburn Golf and Country
Club................................... 64
Miller, Verne..........69, 70, 72, 73
Move UP 210
Municipal Auditorium.......... 62

N

Nash, Frank ... 66, 68, 69, 70, 72
National Youth Movement ... 88
Nevada Gaming Commission.. 162

O

Oldham, Michael R. 180, 181
Oldham, P. W.......................... 90
Order No. 11 12

P

Parker, Bonnie...................74-79
Park, Governor Guy 90
Pat O'Brien's 159
Pembroke Hill 198
Pendergast, James 24
Pendergast machine ....
52, 58, 60, 65, 80, 88, 105, 110
Pendergast, Thomas J. ....
52, 60, 69, 92, 94, 97
Phillips, Nola 184, 186
Phillips, Tricia 184, 186
Platte City, Missouri 76
Platte County, Missouri 74
Poor Freddie's...................... 157
Portman, Bennie........50, 52, 53
Pratt, Della.................37, 39, 40
Primitivo Garcia Elementary School.................................... 145
Puglise, Francis Samuel 138, 139, 140

Q

Quantrill, William Clark 14

R

Red Crown............74, 76, 77, 79
Reed, James A. ....
47, 48, 57, 58, 59
Reed, Otto.............68, 69, 70, 72
Research Medical Center.... 212
Richart, Sheriff Granville.......... 105
Richetti, Adam 72-73
Rimann, Wolf C. 111
River Quay.................... 154-165
Robinson, Aaron........... 142, 144
Robinson, John E. 202-207
Rockhurst College 121
Rowden, John Edward 144
Rusch, Christine ..192, 193, 194

S

Sacred Heart Church............ 145
Sanders, Mark Jr 184, 186
Scheidt, Paul.....................58-59
Scola, Sam......................85, 86
Sexton Hotel..................52, 53
Sharp, James 37-41
Sharp, Melissa 36-41
Shawnee Indian Mission... 8, 11
Shawnee Indians 8
Shawnee Mission South High School.................................... 168
Sheppard, Bryan 182
Sheppard, Earl "Skip" 182
Sheppard, Frank................... 182
slaughterhouses.................... 24
Smith, Forrest.......108, 110, 111
Smith, Perry 129, 130, 132
Sorrentino, Paul 168-171
Spero, Carl 160-162
Spero, Joseph 16 160-162
Spero, Michael............... 160-162
Spero, Nick 160-162
Stasi, Lisa 205-207
Steuben Club 85
Stevens, Clarence.............62-64
St. Mary's Hospital............... 145
Swope, Chrisman..............45-48
Swope, Margaret "Maggie" .. 42, 46, 49
Swope, Margaret 45, 47
Swope Park 49
Swope, Thomas 42-49

T

Taylor, Melva 80, 82, 84, 86
Teamsters.............................. 163
The Ali Kemp Educational Foundation (TAKE) 224
Topeka Correctional Facility.... 171, 201
Tropicana Hotel 163
Trouten, Suzette 206, 207
Trozzolo, Marion 156, 158
Truman, Harry S................. 108
Twelfth Street 52, 157

U

Uncle Joe's Tavern................ 157
Union Depot 26
Union Station 66-73
University of Kansas City ... 102

V

Van Horn, Robert 11, 12
Vetterli, Reed.............68, 69, 70
Virginian Tavern.......... 160-162

W

Walsh, Frank 48
Ward Parkway 52
Watkins, Bruce............. 152, 153
Weigel, Jo Ellen 146-149
Welch, Casimir..... 85, 91-92, 96
Wells, Floyd 130-132
Welsh, George Winston Jr. 100-107
Welsh, Leila 100-107
Werner, Walter 58
West Bottoms 24
Westport High School......... 142
William Chrisman High School 136
Williams, Roy Lee........ 163, 164
Wolcott, Kansas ...122, 124, 125

Y

Young, Brigham 40
Younger, Cole 17